T0099273

Politics
AND THE AMERICAN LANGUAGE

Also by William O'Rourke

Fiction:

The Meekness of Isaac (1974)
Idle Hands (1981)
Criminal Tendencies (1987)
Notts (1996)

Nonfiction:

The Harrisburg 7 and the New Catholic Left (1972)
Signs of the Literary Times: Essays, Reviews, Profiles 1970–1992 (1993)
Campaign America '96: The View from the Couch (1997)
Campaign America 2000: The View from the Couch (2001)
On Having a Heart Attack (2006)
The Harrisburg 7 and the New Catholic Left (fortieth anniversary edition, 2012)
Confessions of a Guilty Freelancer (2012)

Edited works:

On the Job: Fiction about Work by Contemporary American Writers (editor, 1977)
Notre Dame Review: The First Ten Years (co-editor, 2009)

Politics AND THE AMERICAN LANGUAGE

Reviews, Rants, and Commentary, 2011–2018

William O'Rourke

Welcome Rain Publishers
NEW YORK

Politics and the American Language

Copyright © 2020 by William O'Rourke

All rights reserved, including the right of reproduction in whole or in part or in any form, electronic or mechanical, without written permission from the publisher.

The Acknowledgments on page 245 contains information that serves as an extension of this copyright page.

Cover photo of William O'Rourke by Jaimy Gordon (taken at a state park in the Florida Keys).

Designed by Laura Smyth

10 9 8 7 6 5 4 3 2 1

Library of Congress Cataloging in Publication Data is available from the publisher. Direct any inquiries to Welcome Rain LLC.

Printed in the USA

ISBN: 978-1-56649-403-8

For Joe and Emily

Contents

Preface 9

PART I. Reviews

Instructs and Entertains 14
Up Against the Workshop 26
The Media Burglary and the Media 31
Days of Rage 46
Patty Prevails 50
Richard and Roger 54
The Miracle of Dan Berrigan 65
O'Connor/Giroux 69

PART II. Rants

The Great Refudiator 73
Reality-Based Shooter 75
Mourning Becomes Them 77
Mommie Baddest 79
Class Warfare 81
Keyes to the Caindom 83
Saving Social Security, Not 85
Not Saving Social Security, Again (an Update) 87
The Superfluity of Iowa 88
The First Lady's Lack of Firsts 90
Dr. Gingrich and Mr. Chucky 92
Our Postsatirical Primaries 94
A Primary History Primer 96
Halftime in Pink America 98
Contraception Wars and Woes 100
Barney Rosset U. 103
Oh, Rush, Poor Rush 105
The Oak Ridge Three 107
Torture? What Torture? 111
To Kill a "Second" Novel 113
My Hillary Problem—and Yours 115
Accidental Presidencies 117
Revenge of the Sixties 119

The Haunting of Hillary 121
Ted's Excellent Mansplaining 123
Transforming The Donald 126
Clinton Exhaustion 128
Bye Bye Bernie 130
The Birther Business 132
Pensive Pence 135
Hillary's Voice 137
It's the Voter Suppression, Stupid! 139
Similarities 141
Trump, Trumped, Trumpery 143
Trump Monkeys 145
Trump Rising 148
Richie Rich, Baby Boomers, and, Look Out, 2018 Looming 150
"What a Dump!" the Presidency, That Is 153
Ken Burns, Boy Capitalist, and *The Vietnam War* (Part I) 156
Ken Burns, Boy Capitalist, and *The Vietnam War* (Part II) 159
Cuba and Carnage 162
Brett Kavanaugh, a Suit, and the Bro Culture 165

PART III. Commentary

Whither the New Catholic Left? 170
Profile: R. D. Skillings, Resolute Character 192
Profile: Judith Shahn, Greenwich Village, circa 1973 195
Irish Times Times Two: On Michael Collins 198
Making Poverty More Bearable 207
Edward Dahlberg: Letters to a Young Would-Be Writer 218

Acknowledgments 245
Index 247

Preface

Politics and the American Language is the third installment of what I term my incidental nonfiction. The first two (*Signs of the Literary Times* [1993], *Confessions of a Guilty Freelancer* [2012]), were published by university presses, the State University of New York Press and Indiana University Press, respectively. I suppose this condition continues to be a sign of the literary times, insofar as volumes such as mine, pieces of various lengths and different forms of nonfiction (reviews, columns, profiles, so-called long-form nonfiction, commentaries on divergent subjects, etc.) are not usually catnip to large commercial publishers. Homogeneity is their preferred calling card.

But there is something homogenous about this collection, not something that shows up so starkly in my earlier volumes. More overtly political, the present volume is informed by the politics of my first book, also nonfiction, *The Harrisburg 7 and the New Catholic Left*. Put together, many pieces herein concern conscientious, often religious, resistance to the status quo. And some of the same personnel who turned up way back when (in 1972), those whom I also treated in my Harrisburg book, resurface here.

Some of this continuity has to do with the longest piece I include here, what began as the afterword to the fortieth anniversary edition of the Harrisburg book. And the fact that a number of the long reviews concentrate on the radicals of the same generation who participated in the protests of the 1960s, '70s, and less so in the '80s. I never abandoned the politics of my generation, though I became ensconced in academia beginning in 1974, a young assistant professor in the English Department of Rutgers University–Newark, constructed of relatively new buildings, its cement fortresslike campus influenced by the riots of the sixties.

From there I went to the decidedly different bucolic campus of Mount Holyoke College for an idyllic three years and then on to the University of Notre Dame for more than three decades. In the 1990s, my second long work of nonfiction was on the 1996 presidential campaign, and subsequently I became a weekly columnist for the *Chicago Sun-Times*, writing on national politics. That ended in 2005.

There always has been a rich seam of memoir that runs through both my fiction and nonfiction and that continues in these pieces, published between 2011 and 2018. Here, though, that tendency is somewhat exaggerated, more so than in my earlier nonfiction collections. Growing older has something to do with that.

Having only one life, a bit of repetition intrudes, most of which I have attempted to lessen in this publication. This volume has gone through some editing and I have removed the most obvious sort of duplication. Nonetheless, I write about some of the same people more than once.

I have arranged the pieces chronologically in the main. And I have put the longer review essays at the beginning, since, by their nature, they are more complete and provide their own context. Second come what I call "Rants," given they are, mostly, columns, written about momentary events, appearing often soon after the subjects, the incidents, happened. It was Matthew Arnold, I believe, who said journalism is literature in a hurry. And these events prompted a rush to comment and, in their way, chart the rise of the current president, since they cover, by coincidence, the Obama years and the subsequent campaign for the 2016 election.

Again, I wrote a long book on the 1996 election, and what eventually occurred in 2016 was not an entire surprise to me, given the trajectory I described in my earlier book. That covered the second-term election of Bill Clinton, running against Bob Dole. All the ingredients of the 2016 race were simmering back then in 1996 and came to a head, a boil, by November 2016.

These short articles do, nonetheless, provide a context for the longer pieces that surround them. I do consider them literature, though of a hurried sort.

The volume's last piece publishes the letters of Edward Dahlberg, unpublished until they appeared in the *Notre Dame Review*, written to me. One can find separate volumes of Dahlberg's letters to Herbert Read and others. I have written about Dahlberg all my life. An essay I did about him as a teenager was my first "legitimate" national publication, appearing in *TriQuarterly* in 1970. So, it seems appropriate that his letters conclude this volume. That it fell largely to me to keep Dahlberg's name in print is a sour turn of events, since he remains one of America's best neglected twentieth-century writers. Many can claim this title "neglected," alas, but Dahlberg had the additional misfortune never to be filmed, and without becoming a walking and talking ghost image he has little life available in our current digitized visual age.

About the title: *Politics and the American Language*. Upon reflection, and in tribute to the majority of the work herein, I decided this title was the most appropriate, obviously a nod to George Orwell, who, one way or another, has shown up in all the books I have published. Once selected, I looked around to see if the formulation has appeared as a title elsewhere. The only example I discovered was an essay by Arthur Schlesinger Jr., of all people, published in 1974 by *The American Scholar*. Schlesinger points out that Orwell's famous essay ("Politics and the English Language") appeared "a generation ago." Depending on how you count, it's been more than two generations since Schlesinger used his variation. Of course, the historic battery of language has only gotten worse. As he writes in 1974, "We owe to Vietnam and Watergate a belated recognition of the fact that we are in linguistic as well as political crisis and that the two may be organically connected. As Emerson said, 'We infer the spirit of the nation in great measure from the language.'"

Certainly, I am not as genteel a writer as either Emerson or Schlesinger, but many of the pieces found here deal with the crimes committed against our language and indicate the many factors that are at play. They are structural as well as personal.

I had been tempted to use for a title "A Fatal Lack of Talent," but my better angels prevailed. That phrase appears in a tribute I did for a former student that ran in the *Irish Times*. Coincidentally, he, the novelist Michael Collins, was the closest simulacrum of myself vis-a-vis Dahlberg, meaning a young writer whom I tried to aid and humbly advance his career. But, it must be said, I did less for Collins than Dahlberg did for me. The horde of Irish crime writers (who knew how many there were?) I unwittingly offended merrily attacked me for slurring their trade by my remark, an aside, I made while lauding Michael. Ironically, it pointed out what a lively literary culture Ireland still has. Doubtless that has something to do with the size of the country. But it is a rebuking contrast to our own literary culture, which is actually, like the larger nation as a whole, a celebrity culture, first and foremost.

"A Fatal Lack of Talent," my discarded title, is perhaps, not so clearly, a variation on the trope of *stooping to conquer*, not something that is easily, or ever, expertly done. Everyone, I discovered after a half century of reading, writing, and teaching, writes as well as he, she, or they possibly can. One cannot limit one's abilities to please the masses. It is a question of sincerity; readers can spot insincerity, when an author attempts to dial down his or her style. Commercial writers, commercial successes, are writing at the top of their form. In other words, everyone is stuck with the talent one has—as the novelist Irini Spanidou once said to me, "Genius is a gift and talent is a curse." And, long ago, the novelist Jaimy Gordon quoted me, saying, "Trade publishing, overall, to borrow a trope from William O'Rourke, reacts to the complete spectrum of prose style no better than a dog's eye to the color spectrum. They see only the middle range, which has sufficient clarity or, more correctly, openness about it. Openness means access: they are concerned with how many readers will troop into the clearing." It's always rather sad to see a writer like Thomas Pynchon attempt to tamp down his prose, hungry to find a larger audience for what he might hope to pass off as a crime novel (see his *Inherent Vice* or even *Vineland*).

I did get to see, throughout the second half of the twentieth century to the present day, the journey from a literary age to a oral-visual one, a golden age of reading to a golden age of viewing, a subject that is one of the preoccupations of this volume. Another friend, the novelist Craig Nova, spoke to this transformation thusly: "We really did live in the last golden age of literature, and we did have a time there of 15 years or so, when the literary world wasn't dead yet. We didn't know it, at the time that we were living in such a grand state, but I don't think anyone ever does." Craig was speaking of, roughly, the late 1960s to the early '80s.

Yes, I, too, think it was a grand state, though I have no certain predictions of what will come next, but what understanding I do have will be found in a number of the pieces in this collection.

With the Trump Ascendency one hopes that we have finally reached a nadir and the only possibility left to us all is to rise upward. But, as with President Clinton leaving us with George W. Bush, whose contribution to the world was the immolations of so much of the Middle East, the igniting of permanent war, carrying out Orwell's gloomy prediction, President Obama, in a similar way, has left us with The Donald, an equal humiliation both former presidents should acknowledge and be ashamed of. How could either of Clinton's and Obama's presidencies be considered successful if they both resulted in their disastrous successors? Perhaps it is true, or even truer now, that, as is remarked in my 1996 campaign book, the presidency is now merely middle management and that is why the best people no longer run for the job.

All writing is hopeful, no matter how grim, since ink on a page sits there silent and invisible until someone reads it. The presumption is that it will be read, all evidence to the contrary. President Trump, by a variety of reports, hasn't read a book in years, if ever. He, given his current status as president, seems to be confirmation enough of the direst predictions I have wantonly made in this collection that we are at the end of an Age, the closing of a book, on books themselves. But, as this current volume is proof of, I'd be happy to be wrong.

March 18, 2019
Notre Dame, Indiana

PART I

■

REVIEWS

The following are, in the main, what are called review essays, or essay reviews. Most all were published in the Notre Dame Review (NDR)*, and often were extended versions of shorter reviews, with two exceptions ("Days of Rage" and "O'Connor/Giroux"), which I published only at the* National Catholic Reporter. *I have been reviewing books ever since I was a graduate student at the end of the 1960s, first starting at* The Nation. *In that way I started at the top, insofar as* The Nation *was, is, a national publication, housed in New York City, one with a long history. I have done this sort of reviewing over the years for publications from sea to shining sea, from the* New York Times Book Review *to the* Los Angeles Times *and many papers in between. Now most of the newspapers of America have dropped book reviewing altogether, which is one reason that these appeared in the* NDR. *As of 2018, there is only one publication that actually pays me for book reviews: the aforementioned* National Catholic Reporter. *There are many ironies buried here, but one payer is better than none.*

Instructs and Entertains

■ Charles J. Shields. *And So It Goes: Kurt Vonnegut: A Life.* Henry Holt, 2011.

I

Orwell's famous remark about every man at age fifty having the face he deserves may also apply to biographers. Every author has the biographer he deserves and, since Vonnegut gave Charles J. Shields permission to proceed, it holds true in this case. As an author, Vonnegut was always Kurt Vonnegut Jr., and to have kept the junior all his life is more a rarity in the father-son sweepstakes: most juniors try to escape the designation as they become adults, but Vonnegut wore it more or less proudly and even was miffed when it first got left off one of the covers of his books. Nonetheless, the "Jr." is left off the title of the book at hand.

Vonnegut turned Shields down at first ("demurring"), but Shields eventually sold himself to the elderly author by demonstrating traits that Vonnegut had or admired: the midwestern persistence on Shields's part. He wrote to Vonnegut, "I'd like the chance to make another pitch. A do-over. This time, I want to begin by telling you about myself." And he described any number of similarities he shared with Vonnegut, the fact that he had been raised in Indianapolis, the town of the Vonneguts, and his father had been a PR man at a large corporation, as Vonnegut himself had been.

So, the biography was on at last and Shields met with him three times and, on the third occasion, shortly after their meeting, Kurt Vonnegut Jr. died, or, rather, fell down the front steps of his Manhattan townhouse, injured his head badly, lapsed into coma, and was dead a month later.

After Vonnegut's death in 2007, cooperation with the executors of the Vonnegut estate, more or less, ceased for Shields. Vonnegut's wife at the time, his second, Jill Krementz, the photographer, wouldn't deal with him. But there is a downside to not dealing with a biographer; it is likely you will forfeit any sense of charity he or she might have been able to summon while portraying you for posterity.

And biographies, eventually, become virtual tombstones, of the modern sort; they speak to those who come after. Perhaps technology may make that happen in the not so distant future. Press a button on a tombstone and a hologram will appear and articulate the life of the deceased year by year.

I suppose some science fiction writer has already thought of that, since science fiction was Vonnegut's first mode of fiction. Eventually the literary world caught up with him and converted his practice of that lowly genre to metafiction.

Vonnegut is a significant literary figure in any number of ways. It can be claimed that he is the last of the species of literary culture hero, a type that is no longer being recognized, since literature now plays a decidedly different role in the culture than it did in the era of Vonnegut's heyday: the sixties and seventies, the culminating era of the writers born into the so-called Greatest Generation, writers who came of age during World War II. Here is an image: Robert Lowell, Norman Mailer, Kurt Vonnegut, all appearing at various Vietnam War–era protests, or other do-good events populated by the energized young. The three writers covered all the genres—poetry, nonfiction, fiction—literary giants all in the eyes of their many supporters, but known to larger audiences, too, thanks to what passed for mass media back then.

As I have written elsewhere, at the close of 1960, according to the U.S. Office of Education, there were 3,215,455 Americans enrolled in institutions of higher learning; by 1971 there were 8,948,000. That unprecedented increase (the number had not even doubled from 1919 till 1960, much less tripled within a decade) had a profound impact, especially on the literary world. It was the golden age of reading and made everlasting stars of numerous writers of that World War II generation. They, of course, are now dying off, Mailer, Lowell, now Vonnegut, as well as various others, including Joseph Heller, another veteran, Saul Bellow, and so forth, and the necropolis continues to be filled with the veterans of the golden age, those who caught the tail end, such as John Updike. These writers were launched into a celebrity orbit so high they couldn't fall from it once reached. Now, even when a writer might approach orbit, usually with a first book (those bloated advances of the 1990s and early 2000s), they often tumble back into the atmosphere like so much space junk.

It is a golden age no longer. But that time did accelerate the notion that personality was as important as the prose. The old saw of the post–World War II generation—that everyone had one book in them—has been turned into everyone has one publishing company in them, as so many "writers" take to self-publishing, coterie publishing, and small presses, resulting in publishers everywhere.

Vonnegut did see it coming: his science fiction-y mind did make him an amateur futurist and in the 1950s he did predict "the decline of slick magazines as venues for fiction" and that "'playing short story pinball for a living [was] obsolete'" (130). Look at the back of the latest *Best American Short Stories* volume and see the pages and pages of outlets, 95 percent of the literary magazines found there are based at universities, who pay little or nothing for short fiction and then look at a volume from the 1940s and 1950s, only a page long, but nearly three-quarters being the high paying slicks.

And the science fiction, futurist side of Vonnegut has him representing another split, much discussed in the 1950s: the "two cultures," Science vs. the Humanities, a British division via C. P. Snow, between the privileged world of the humanities and the more meritocratic world of the upwardly mobile geeks, nerds, elbowing their way through the British class system. In America, it was more plain science versus the humanities, the simplistic split between those with literary knowledge and those with scientific knowledge. Vonnegut, in his youthful sporadic forays in higher education, was a science major.

This accounts for some of his unhappiness at the literary establishment for relegating him to the world of science fiction genre writers, not according him the literary status he thought he deserved. Why did he think he deserved it, especially early in his career? Shields doesn't actually answer that in his long biography, though I would lean toward the fact, well-drawn by Shields, of Vonnegut's upper-class background, his entitlement endowed by membership in the much-accomplished Vonnegut clan of Indianapolis, even though when Vonnegut was experiencing it, the endowments of both his father's and his mother's families were diminishing. And, he was never short of a large ego, though one annoyed by insecurities, some of the profound sort brought about by his mother's suicide on Mother's Day in 1944, when the young enlistee Vonnegut was home on leave.

He was at Cornell in 1940 and in the ROTC, eventually writing for the *Cornell Daily Sun* and being a general campus cut-up, but dropped out from both; not finishing any higher education was, paradoxically, helpful, insofar as it gave him a bit of empathy with the dolts and do-nothings, the uncredentialed. Not enough, surely, but it did give him a taste of being a "self-made" man, a type of nineteenth-century figure like so many of his successful forebears. There were plenty of paradoxes to go around in Vonnegut's life, but unlike a number of contemporaries, he was able to profit from them, until the end.

Vonnegut also represents a transitional figure in the world of creative writing programs. He embodied the "visiting writer" model of the 1960s, where writers of some reputation were invited to teach in the handful of programs that existed then. Vonnegut was a replacement pick for the University of Iowa's Writers' Workshop of 1965–66, substituting for Robert Lowell. The switch of genres from poetry to fiction doesn't seem odd to Shields, in his account, but Vonnegut's most recent novel at the time, *God Bless You, Mr. Rosewater*, had received a good amount of attention, and more of America's youth had begun to take notice in the mid-1960s.

Including me. I had spent the summer of 1965 in West Barnstable, Massachusetts, home of Kurt Vonnegut Jr. His big house on Scudder's Lane was just a stone's throw from the smaller saltbox house, the front painted pink, of Alexandra Crane, who worked with me at Captain Gray's Swedish Smorgasbord, one of the odder summer tourist restaurants in the town of Barnstable. Lexa taught me how to sail that summer and the Vonneguts came up in conversation now and then.

West Barnstable was more a literary place than Shields makes it out to be in *So It Goes*. The Crane family owned Crane Duplicating, further down route 6A near a public school, a printing concern that made many of the bound galleys for the New York publishing world. A lot of fiction was lying around Lexa's home, and I was introduced there to Vonnegut's work.

At Captain Gray's there were six fetching, in all senses of the word, waitresses and one busboy, me. At nineteen, I thought the arrangement wonderful. Lexa's husband-to-be was off on a graduate school fellowship, doing something anthropological in a foreign land. I was doing more immediate anthropology, another midwesterner, like KV, encountering the natives of Cape Cod.

So, I heard tales about the Vonneguts, long before they were chronicled in the pages of any biography. Kurt didn't seem to be around that summer; his family had doubled its size in the late 1950s when his beloved sister Alice and her husband died within a week of each other, the former of natural causes, and the latter in a train accident. It was a riotous household that resulted and the local rumors floating around during that period and later included one that Kurt had a vasectomy and was headed for Esalen, the free love zone in California's Big Sur region, which had begun to acquire some notoriety. Rumors of this sort are what writers who are on the cusp of success put up with and, as preposterous as they might be, the vasectomy one had the currency of possible truth, because of the tragic explosion, given the circumstances, of kids in the Vonnegut household.

Shields doesn't traffic in any of these rumors (no mention of Esalen), or even discuss their existence. They are, after all, just the small town talk that amuses bored residents while abusing the targets of the tales. But Shields does detail a number of affairs Kurt began in this period and, eventually, there were no more biological Vonnegut offspring.

Nonetheless, my introduction to Vonnegut was that summer sailing around Barnstable bay. Vonnegut is the exception that proves the rule in any number of ways. His background in American business, the world of PR for GE, provided him with ample material, as well as service in the army during World War II, the good luck of surviving the firebombing of Dresden. He, like Norman Mailer, knew he wanted to be a writer when he went off to war. Mailer, who also had a nonliterary education (he studied engineering at Harvard) just as Vonnegut had had, but still saw literature as a viable career. To baby boomers today such an aspiration only seems funny.

Vonnegut's generation was the last that saw the wholesale abnegation of wives to their husbands' careers, and Jane Vonnegut was no exception. She thought her husband was a genius and even though she was a college graduate (Swarthmore), unlike her husband, she did all the domestic chores and child-rearing—her own children and those of her husband's relatives, the boys who had suddenly appeared in the household.

So, when Vonnegut quit GE (a regular *Mad Men* milieu), he was aided in his career building not only by his wife, but also by a male acquaintance he had made during his abbreviated tenure at Cornell, Knox Burger, a more literary type who shepherded Vonnegut's writing life in different ways for a number of years, as editor, publicist, and general booster, at a variety of different publishers where Burger worked over the years. When Burger became an agent in the late 1960s, though, Vonnegut, at the eleventh hour, declined to be his client. Another man, Seymour "Sam" Lawrence, recharged Vonnegut's career and standing as an author. Lawrence knew how best to turn him (and other authors he published) into a product, giving him status plus marketing savvy. Vonnegut cut Lawrence loose, too, after Vonnegut had reached the apex of his celebrity orbit and was, in the years that remained, unlikely to fall from it.

The book that put him in that high orbit was, of course, *Slaughterhouse-Five*. This is Vonnegut's most successful novel and it took him many years to find a way to write it. Emotion recollected in tranquility, more or less, though Vonnegut's life was never tranquil. There is another biography out now, by Gregory D. Sumner called *Unstuck in Time: A Journey through Kurt Vonnegut's Life and Novels* (no one in the title business seems to like the junior), and covers the critical and biographical ground of the books themselves. Shields's book is best read by those who already have some familiarity with Vonnegut's work. Nowhere in it does Shields remark on the almost unavoidable comparison between the beginning nonfiction section of *Slaughterhouse-Five* and the Custom House prologue to Nathaniel Hawthorne's *The Scarlet Letter*. It's not the only comparison that can be made between those two books.

Vonnegut became a millionaire somewhat suddenly, though previously he had lived in a haute bourgeois bohemian style (the big house on the Cape, trips to Europe), though, at times, resorting to eating cereal at home. Again, it was Vonnegut's own version of his extended family's life, great wealth gone, but the accouterments of the rich were still implanted in his psyche. As a boy Vonnegut would go off in the summers to a family compound at Lake Maxinkuckee in north central Indiana. It's not every kid whose hometown (Indianapolis) is so studded with edifices and evidence of his family's mark and influence. I, but apparently not Shields, have always thought that the name of the lake itself (Maxinkuckee) was the progenitor of so many of Vonnegut's quirky monikers for his characters.

Another man, Don Farber, handled the Vonnegut money after it began to come in in great gobs. And Farber seems to have done a good job. Vonnegut was never guilty of gaudy conspicuous consumption. An affectionate uncle had given Vonnegut a copy of Thorstein Veblen's *The Theory of the Leisure Class* when Kurt was fairly young and some of the critique had stuck.

But Vonnegut's life overall, according to Shields, is yet another American account of the old adage of money not bringing happiness. For those of us who want to differ, I could only think of how unhappy and less productive Vonnegut's life would have been had he not been rich for almost half of it. Which brings me to my second brush with proximity to the man himself.

II

Near the end of 1976 I went to, or, rather, crashed, a party held at the Strand bookstore, at Broadway and Twelfth in Manhattan, one of the few independent bookstores that still flourishes. The party was for the publication of a book filled with Burt Britton's solicited self-sketches of "book people" (*Self-Portrait: Book People Picture Themselves*, Random House, 1976). Britton worked at the Strand then, in the review books section down in the basement, which I had made use of when I wrote reviews for *The Nation* in my early twenties while in graduate school at Columbia, selling my review copies for a quarter of their price, which the Strand then sold for half their price. Britton had been collecting spontaneous portraits of mainly writers for many years. It was a by-invitation-only party and I heard it was happening because my friend Craig Nova, whose self-portrait was in the book, told me, adding he wouldn't be going himself. I volunteered to take his place.

I showed up after the festivities were underway and happened to arrive right behind Fran McCullough, who was Craig's editor at the time. When the doorman inquired who I was, I replied I was Craig Nova's substitute and Fran McCullough turned her head and looked at me strangely, but I was let in. I'm not sure any other party I've attended since has matched the density and makeup of this particular gathering. It was book people: only authors and editors and publishers. Hardly any civilians. I would say none, but there's always an exception.

Earlier that day I had been talking to my editor at Random House about an anthology of mine it was publishing, *On the Job: Fiction about Work by Contemporary American Writers.* She hadn't mentioned the party to come that night, and when I saw her later in the crowd she looked surprised. Back when I had proposed the anthology idea to her, I heard from a mutual friend that she later had said, How can we steal the idea from him?

But I was enjoying myself at the party, because, as my coworkers in the South Bronx used to say when we congregated together to avoid some unpleasant task: one grenade could get us all. All of literary New York City was in attendance, it appeared. The Strand had put up a very large stretched blank canvas for the guests to sign. There were around seven hundred self-sketches in Britton's volume, starting with Edward Abbey and ending with Paul Zweig, with everyone else (but me) in between. And it looked like most everyone had come. I, nonetheless, signed my name to the crowded canvas, appending, "who is not in the mainstream," and after I walked away, a very pretty young woman appeared, halting my stroll. She wanted to interview me, beginning with who I was. I forget what publication she was from (it was an obscure one), and I continued walking away from the canvas (it was about twenty feet long), with her tagging along. Then I stopped and told her, "You don't want to interview me, you want to interview him." Standing next to me by then was Kurt Vonnegut and standing next to him was Richard Yates. "Yes, not me, I'm not famous enough, but he is," I said, pointing my drink-filled hand at Vonnegut, "and he," I went on, "can introduce you to him," indicating Yates, "who is even more famous." Vonnegut and Yates, who loomed above us, both being taller, looked down at me bemusedly. I was, after all, handing over a lovely young woman with demonstrated literary interests to them. But, I didn't realize till I read Shields's book that I unintentionally stumbled upon one of Vonnegut's central pet peeves: that he lacked the literary cachet of other famous writers. Because, truly, that's what I meant when I told the young woman (she was, likely, my age at the time, or a bit younger) that Yates was more "famous": in a literary way, that is, famous to other writers, not the masses.

Yates's and Vonnegut's careers had almost opposite trajectories: Yates's first two books, the collection of short stories, *Eleven Kinds of Loneliness* and the novel *Revolutionary Road*, were huge literary hits, whereas Kurt Vonnegut's first two books (*Player Piano, The Sirens of Titan*) were largely ignored and considered low status "science fiction" volumes. I had put a Richard Yates story in my anthology-to-be ("Wrestling with Sharks"), but I hadn't put any story by Vonnegut (never having read any of his short fiction, his "hack" work) in it, though I'm sure if I looked now there would be a "work" story that qualified.

Things, of course, rapidly changed for both of them. But that night in 1976 they were in many ways literally and figuratively next to each other. By the ends of their lives, Vonnegut had become a personage, a "spokesman for a generation," and Yates had become a broken, practically penniless, specter, dragging along an oxygen tank, dying ignominiously in Alabama, after teaching for a semester in Tuscaloosa. Vonnegut, too, had died ignominiously, tripping over his tiny dog's leash, but, nonetheless, most everything else was different.

Both authors, though, did share another critical thing: the same publisher, Sam Lawrence, who stuck with Yates till the end, whereas Vonnegut had bailed from the man who had helped create his literary reputation.

At the Strand party, there was another major figure of Vonnegut's life, Jill Krementz. She wasn't yet married to Vonnegut then, but they were involved; she figures as an *éminence grise* in Shields's book. I knew of her because she had taken photos of all the fashionable contemporary authors during the last few years, and I was not fashionable. She was not hanging with Vonnegut and Yates, but was in the middle of the room, talking intimately with Anatole Broyard. Broyard, at the time, was a daily book reviewer for the *New York Times* and he played a role in both Vonnegut's and Yates's literary lives, mainly by writing vicious attacks on their books. But that was Broyard's métier in the review game. Toward the end of his reign at the *Times*, Broyard reviewed first novels by a series of attractive young white women and excoriated them all. It became a sort of comedy sketch, all those bad reviews coming one after another of good-looking young white female authors.

Broyard was one of the last famous cases of "passing," a black American posing as "white"; there had been rumors for years of Broyard being a "mulatto," and he threatened anyone who publicly passed them on in print; and no one wrote of him "passing" until after his death in 1990. But he and Krementz were conspiratorially conferring, two heads of luxuriously glistening black curly hair, leaning into one another. Broyard must have had a bad and ongoing case of self-hatred raging in him. He had wanted to be a "writer" and had published a few short stories early in his life, but never completed a novel. Book reviewers who are frustrated writers tend to be, often, hostile generally to novelists who do well.

That night I didn't mention to Yates that his story was going into my anthology, nor did I mention to Vonnegut my ties to Barnstable.

Yates died in 1992 and got his biography in 2003 (*A Tragic Honesty: The Life and Work of Richard Yates*, by Blake Bailey, Picador, 2003). With publication of the Vonnegut biographies, especially Shields's, in 2011, I wonder if we are nearing the end of this sort of writerly attention. It's hard to picture biographies of the current crop of literary "stars"—for practical reasons, the death of letter writing and the birth of email, but also because there are no more literary stars of the Vonnegut sort. No one plays that role in the wider culture anymore. As my young Random House editor, a harbinger of things to come, might have said back then, it's all dog eat dog, everyone for one's self. There are successful writers today, of course; some even try to aspire to celebrityhood. But not culture heroes, not role models for the aspiring young. It almost takes a fatwa to create one and even then there's no guarantee. Perhaps the number of solely literary biographies will diminish (fewer PhDs in contemporary American literature being made, too), though celebrity bios will doubtless continue unabated.

Vonnegut did not want to be a role model, and, indeed, was not who his young admirers thought he was—an antimaterialist noncapitalist—but a man who still preferred Brooks Brothers' suits and most of the male prerogatives of the post–World War II era. Indeed, it was only his own gnawing about not being accepted as a "real" writer, on his terms, that gave him some empathy for the disenfranchised and underpraised.

And, again, Vonnegut was predictive: he was antiwar by experience. As terrible as Dresden's aftermath was, what is truly shocking in Schields's telling is how Vonnegut's unit was outmaneuvered and the subsequent details of its pathetic surrender, which led Vonnegut and others to their POW service in Dresden.

In an essay, "Torture and Blubber," which appeared in the *New York Times* in 1971 and which Shields quotes, Vonnegut wrote:

> Simply we are torturers.... Agony has never made a society quit fighting, as far as I know.... One wonders now where our leaders got the idea that mass torture would work to our advantage in Indochina. It never worked anywhere else. They got the idea from childish fiction, I think, and from a childish awe of torture.... But children believe that pain is an effective way of controlling people, which it isn't—except in a localized, short term sense. They believe that pain can change minds, which it can't. (292)

Unfortunately, life became even more absurd than Vonnegut thought it could and, post 9/11, torture began being spoken of as a virtue by the leaders of our country, primarily those in the Bush II administration.

Vonnegut used his literary celebrity by serving a number of do-good literary organizations, such as PEN, as a spokesperson. Books continued to be written, or assembled, and more nonfiction infiltrated the fiction (as autobiography has in this piece of criticism—creating a mixture of things, that is). Richard Yates, too, kept writing till close to the end (he left an unpublished novel). When he died in 1992 Vonnegut offered an affectionate tribute, but, with the exception of *The Easter Parade*, which sold well in a Book of the Month Club edition, none of Yates's late novels made their advances back, which left him in dire need of money. But not Kurt.

The why of that is telling. Vonnegut, for all his savage critiques, is an entertaining writer, often silly, which certainly was attractive to his young readership. Yates, though equally excoriating, is not given to humor other than the gallows sort and his gray, wrenching novels could only summon (without Book of the Month Club help) sales of ten thousand, or less. Vonnegut was comedy, Yates was tragedy.

In the universities, during this period of the late seventies onward, the teaching of creative writing changed, too. Indeed, there had never before been so much study of literature (poetry, short stories, and novels) with the intended purpose of students writing actual literature themselves. In the older past, university English departments taught students how to read and understand literature and only as a by-product did a handful of students end up writing it themselves.

And the growth of MFA programs produced a new generation of creative writing instructors. Not the "visiting writer," but the full-time faculty member, dealing with various committees and all the other tasks of any other academic. If one was lucky, your fate wouldn't be traipsing from one university to another as an "adjunct," but becoming tenured and perhaps moving upward if some institution offered you a chair. Vonnegut only came face to face with one aspect of the new age of creative writing when he taught, very briefly, at Smith, shortly before he died. The women students drove him from the classroom because he was so politically incorrect.

Today, the humanities as a whole could be said to be housed in various Arts and Entertainment Departments. It would be hard to say that Yates's novels qualify as entertainment, except in a profound, classical tradition way. Vonnegut's books were able to straddle this new divide; they entertained the reader, especially the younger ones, while instructing them enough to pass muster. That was Isaac Bashevis Singer's definition as reported by Richard Russo: "The purpose of literature is to entertain and to instruct." The difficulty, of course, is to find those who can be entertained by, say, advanced calculus. Yates's readers could be among them. Wherever they are, they are not that many, only, alas, existing in the thousands. But Vonnegut has reached much higher numbers, since he fulfills Singer's prescription.

Though, these days, Singer himself is entertaining fewer readers. And since so much writing (not just by the students but by their author professors) is housed in universities, more particularized divisions have appeared, the traditionalists versus the cerebralists, those who favor something that smacks of narrative realism, or those who favor narrative as an exercise of the mind. A bit of calculus-loving helps with this sort of literature, too.

This has always been the problem, the tussle between the popular and, for lack of a better designation, the hyperliterary: literature for the few, not the many. At the commercial level, it is often easier to divide up authors. But some have written their way, by determination, into the literary canon. Take the example of Stephen King, another genre writer, like Vonnegut, who exceeded his genre and finally published a story in the *New Yorker*, something Richard Yates desired to do, but never accomplished—except, alas, posthumously, during a brief boomlet for *Revolutionary Road*, and things Yatesian, in the early 2000s. Vonnegut breached the *New Yorker*'s walls with a poem while he was alive.

King is doubtless an exemplary fellow (and certainly there will be biographies of him), and the literary world has caught up with him, though "caught up" doesn't capture the process. The literary world has in some ways surrendered to the world of celebrity, under the spell of great forces and circumstance, the sort that caused Vonnegut's regiment to surrender during the Battle of the Bulge. Tens of thousands of men, according to Shields, were suddenly turned into prisoners, marching down foreign roads.

That comparison on my part is, of course, an inappropriate exaggeration. Overall, Shields's biography is well worth reading if you have any interest at all in Kurt Vonnegut. It also covers well, though not overly consciously, the changes those pivotal years brought about. The test of any author for a reader is whether any words of the writer have ever "seeped into your soul," as Edward Dahlberg once put it. Often, they are not the author's most profound remarks. In the case of Richard Yates, I have regularly quoted the axiom found in his early short story "Builders," in his collection *Eleven Kinds of Loneliness*, "I didn't have time to write you a short letter today, so I had to write you a long one instead."

The oddity of that—spoken by Yates's bumpkin-ish cab driver character, Bernie, someone who desperately wanted to be a writer (though I doubt he read much Pascal, who originated the thought)—is that it is a version of what would be held against Yates's last novels: that Yates was too much a craftsman (especially by Anatole Broyard in the *Times*), that the novels were too well constructed, with too much attention paid to style.

But the old saw (not enough time to write you a short letter…) contains the nub of the problem, as well as does the notion "entertain and instruct." In Kurt Vonnegut's case, the line I think of often is one I can see in my mind, since I know the artifacts that produced it. I can't remember which book it's from, but it describes the flagpole swivel snap hook which is tied to the rope that the flag ascends and descends on, how it bangs against the metal flagpole in front of a school at dusk, making a melancholy noise that means it's "dinnertime everywhere." I know the school in West Barnstable, I know the flagpole, I've heard the sound it makes. But the feeling Vonnegut's image captures—for those who do not know that specific pole, but know at least one—is surely an emotion that instructs and entertains. And, over the years, every time I hear that sound I think of Kurt Vonnegut Junior.

Notre Dame Review 34 (Summer/Fall 2012)

Up Against the Workshop

■ Anis Shivani. *Against the Workshop: Provocations, Polemics, Controversies*. Texas Review Press, 2011.

Anis Shivani, a poet, fiction writer, and critic, has always stood out for me in one singular way: he's a voracious reader, a reader of actual books, one of a vanishing breed, a throwback to an earlier generation, or so it seems in these dire and dismal digital days.

However he manages it, Shivani's existence appears to be full of reading and writing; more writers than I care to count are not extravagant readers, but fairly selective readers. And one always hopes for readers who are not writers themselves and I'm sure some such individuals can be found somewhere. (Where, oh, where?) But Shivani, by all evidence, devours books.

And I am always happy to discover such a person; if the world had more Shivani-type reader/writers, writers would have much less to complain about.

Indeed, anyone who pays attention to the contemporary literary world has complaints and Shivani rose to notice, at first, as an attacker of MFA programs. In this regard, he was a Johnny-come-lately, since a variety of MFA bashers (the list is long—more on that later) had already staked out that territory, but, somehow, equipped with cultural blinders and the certainty of a Conquistador, Shivani has claimed the territory as his own. One of the most common sins of our time is just this sort of intellectual dishonesty; usually it is brought about by ignorance: this is the first... no other writer has..., etc. Absolutes are hurled about in the real world and one can see, at least, their use—but, in the literary world, absolutes are more than quarrelsome. They're downright foolish and the tool of the under-read, usually wielded willy-nilly by book reviewers.

Shivani had gained a perch on the news and opinion aggregator the *Huffington Post*, and he had published a piece (with photos) entitled "The 15 Most Overrated Contemporary American Writers." Needless to say, Shivani had begun to see the career advantages of controversy, and he had met the paradox head on: that in order to gain an audience (or eyeballs, as readers are called on the web) one must join them in order to beat them, and to attack the well-known is always more profitable than damning the obscure. The chief mystery in the literary culture is how one acquires an audience, actually gets read and considered.

One argument that can be made is that creative writing programs have kept alive contemporary literature in English departments across the land; and, subsequently, it is the avant-garde that has retreated to academia, not the sort of literature MFA programs are condemned for producing ("cookie-cutter," "bland," etc.). The contemporary fiction writers often taught in English Departments (by PhDs, not the creative writing faculty) are the avant-garde-ists, the so-called cutting-edge types. The Fiction Collective, which began in the early 1970s as a publishing venture for fiction writers formerly published by commercial houses, but who had been abandoned by them because of insufficient sales, is now, in its new incarnation as FC2, mainly the home for experimental writers above all. In the beginning, it wasn't so much an aesthetic opposition, but a commercial one: sales versus art. Now it is a war between art and art, between hipsters and, for the lack of a better antonym, the traditionalists, though, since the avant-garde itself has such a long tradition, it, too, is comfortably familiar. The avant-garde finding a home in the academy is more troubling than the fecund proliferation of creative writing programs.

But Shivani's advantage is that his attacks are all over the place; he is, in the main, a champion of the global, not the parochial. Of course, that is the real point. And, I assume, eventually, the globalization of literature will become his primary subject. In *Against the Workshop* he makes a stab or two at it. But, unfortunately, Shivani does seem to echo the outlook of Horace Engdahl, the permanent secretary of the Nobel Prize in Literature, who, in 2008, told the Associated Press:

> There is powerful literature in all big cultures, but you can't get away from the fact that Europe still is the center of the literary world...not the United States. The US is too isolated, too insular. They don't translate enough and don't really participate in the big dialogue of literature.... That ignorance is restraining.

Shivani shares this worldview, more or less. One of his favorite authors, if not the favorite, is Orhan Pamuk, who has already won the Nobel Prize. And Pamuk writes about a world Shivani is familiar with. If that's not parochial, what is? But take a look at the last few years of the *Best American Short Story* volumes. Half of the stories are set elsewhere than the USA; a number of the writers in the volumes are transnationals. The evolution that has occurred in the literary world is the same that has taken place everywhere: we are the victims and the beneficiaries of globalization.

Shivani may be native born (Texas?). This biographical information is, curiously, harder to pin down than it should be, but, nonetheless, Shivani has assumed the persona of a transnational. He went to Harvard and studied economics; at least, he has a bachelor degree in economics. It's a bit much for him to bash MFA programs just because he never went to one. It appears, oddly, that he has never had much formal study of literature. I may be wrong, but his tastes do share the eccentricities of the autodidact. Certainly, when it comes to surveying the national American literary landscape, he does display a number of blind spots. A handful of the early bashers of MFA programs are those that helped create them; theirs was a case of self-hatred, not an uncommon affliction of American writers. One only needs to consult Mark McGurl's 2009 book, *The Program Era*, to become acquainted with some of that history; Shivani mentions the book in his preface, so, he seems, post facto, or post these essays, to have encountered it. Or, perhaps, he's kept up with the 2010–11 exchange between Elif Batuman in the *London Review of Books* (which largely takes the Shivani view, though more judiciously) and McGurl in the *Los Angeles Review of Books*. But there is no mention of the 1994 book by John Aldridge, *Talents and Technicians*. Or, two years later, the 1996 book, *The Elephants Teach*, by D. G. Myers.

But Shivani takes the-fish-in-a-barrel approach, since the barrel is big and there are so many writing programs in it. Who could ever attend an Association of Writers and Writing Programs (AWP) convention of the last few years without being filled with dark, troubling thoughts?

The concluding piece of *Against the Workshop* (a "Pushcart Prize winning essay"! boasts the cover), "The MFA/Creative Writer System Is a Closed, Undemocratic Medieval Guild System that Represses Good Writing," Shivani throws down his bolts from his high-school-stage-set of Olympus, again, not crediting, or quoting, from all those who have come before, speaking out against the system he decries; he maintains a Captain Renault–like indignation: I'm shocked, shocked, etc. What good would it do him if he acknowledged he was at the end of a long queue? Better to jump the line: "Medieval guilds were endowed with the right to combine and make their own regulations—precisely this impetus is behind the MFA system's retreat from the world of unabashed capitalism (also known as 'reality' in the industrialized world)."

Well, I guess that's his Harvard education coming into play, all those economics classes. And one does need to be a rank conservative at heart (or just wrong) to think writers in the USA have retreated from the world of unabashed capitalism, "also known as 'reality.'" One of the dispiriting attributes of Gen Xers and millennials is that most of their heroes are capitalists (see Steve Jobs, etc.). Unfortunately, the MFA system is not a guild system, except accidentally, here and there. Too bad Shivani didn't go to Yale, instead of Harvard; he could have taken (perhaps) Harold

Bloom and suffered the anxiety of influence, rather than the anxiety brought on by too many MFA programs. Though the growth period of the MFA world was during the last three decades of the twentieth century and the rise of organizations such as the AWP and Poets & Writers mirror those dates, the singular place where the "guild" system critique has some legitimacy, the Iowa Writers' Workshop, opened its doors in 1936 and has produced the longest list of writers who have attended, and writers who have helped other writers, over the years. So, if the contemporary problem that Shivani recently has noticed began before World War II, I would think it is a larger phenomenon than he has even begun to admit or understand; in the essay he acknowledges that Iowa's program "existed," but blames everything else on the "sixties scene."

According to Shivani, "writers" want to run from the "market economy." He claims, "If they could create a self-sufficient guild, they would be removed for its vicissitudes." He seems to have the same economic and political analysis as Eric Cantor, if Representative Cantor was a literary critic, and not the Republican House majority leader. It may be the case that Shivani started out so far Left he became Right.

The growth boom throughout the 1970s and '80s of MFA programs was a creature of capitalist exploiters, wanting to have more cheap labor (or, in a few cases, such as Columbia, high tuition payers) available. MFA programs were the canary in the coal mine, prefiguring the current situation where adjuncts, graduate students, do so much of the teaching in American universities, especially the basic writing classes offered everywhere.

Shivani names some of the backscratchers who come and go (and those who came and went) over the decades: older writers helping out the careers of younger writers. This is unavoidable and, for the most part, laudable. The history of literary communities is friends helping friends, the acquaintanceship bias that is always worth something. It's an economic premium, which Shivani should know about. Shivani's MFA program bashing is his version of attacking the one percent, the fashionably elite and overpraised. The production of fame is most often a high capital production here in the states, which requires the right publishers and the helpful collusion of the few gatekeeping publications that matter in that machinery. I'm all for attacking the one percent, wherever it's found (Occupy AWP!), but attacking the overpraised these days is just one more bubble in our bubble economy that can be all too easily popped.

Against the Workshop is a hodgepodge, but that is shared with any number of miscellanies. (I was under the delusion that he was going to produce a coherent monograph, like *The Program Era.*) Alas, Shivani has a fondness for one literary form, one often used by amateurs, where the author assumes the voice of another to perform self-surgery on the presumed speaker. It's a form of parody, I suppose. The first example, unfortunately, begins the volume (page 1, after a preface, and an introduction by Jay Parini—who is later praised in the book; Shivani, no matter how assiduously he attacks log rolling, is not immune to favoring writers he knows personally), an epistle "written" by Aylesha Pane (an agent) to Preeta Samarasan (her client). If you don't know who these people are, well, you don't know. And, late in the volume, in a review of *The Best American Poetry 2007*, the voice of that year's editor, Heather McHugh, is employed. Shivani has no talent whatsoever for this sort of thing; and both pieces only bring to mind cringe-inducing words like *jejune, sophomoric, childish.*

In these and other weaker outings contained in the volume Shivani sounds like an MFA basher who has been spurned from some program he had applied to. In the concluding essay there is this sentence of complaint: "You may pay a few thousand dollars to attend Bread Loaf as a 'paying contributor' and soak in the mystery surrounding the über-masters, but you may never become a scholar/fellow/waiter unless you are a certified member of the guild." (But, in this case, it is likely he knows whereof he speaks, since in Shivani's 2009 book of short fictions, *Anatolia and Other Stories*, there is a tedious tale set in a Bread Loaf–like summer literary confab, a sour-grapey account and the least commendable story in the volume.

While reading *Against the Workshop* I kept finding myself wishing that Shivani had gone to some graduate program, more pertinently, some PhD program in literature (coincidentally, Batuman's central point: PhD jingoism), so he could put his intelligence to some coherent use, rather than presenting us with this sort of volume that is so full of internal contradictions that one wonders how an author as smart as Shivani obviously is could have missed them himself.

Notre Dame Review 33 (Winter/Spring 2012)

The Media Burglary and the Media

■ Betty Medsger. *The Burglary: The Discovery of J. Edgar Hoover's Secret FBI*. Alfred A. Knopf, 2014. Vintage paperback, 2014.

Communicating with an old friend from the Harrisburg days of 1972, I mentioned a review I was writing for the *National Catholic Reporter* of Betty Medsger's new book, *The Burglary*, which is focused on two main events: the Media, Pennsylvania, FBI office burglary of 1971 and the FBI's response to it, though, along the way, the book manages to cover most of the history of the Catholic and religious resistance of the anti–Vietnam War era.

"It's clear," I told my friend, "that she never read my Harrisburg book, which came as a surprise."

"Then why are you reviewing her book?" he asked.

"Well," I replied, "because I want to review it and everything I am putting in the review I believe."

Reviewing is a genre, insofar as there are conventions that are attached to the form, traditions that carry the weight of repetition, solidified into something like rules, though, really, there are no rules. Reviews do tend to conform to the publications they appear in and the writers often take on not so much the style of the source, but at least the manner of the periodical, how it does things. Like everywhere else, you can stretch the margins, but usually you are aware of them. Length also plays its rigid role.

My editor wanted 750 words and I ended up with 900, about as tight as I could make it, but I certainly had a lot more to say about *The Burglary*, so I am saying some of it here.

I haven't seen Betty Medsger in over forty years. The last time I saw her was back in Pennsylvania at an event I only have the dimmest recollections of, even to how I got there and why I attended. It was a conference of sorts and I was invited, which doubtless was a novel experience for me back then circa 1973. I can't remember if I did anything at the conference, or who paid for my travel—most likely myself, I think—but it was billed as a law enforcement confab, attorney generals, or chiefs of police, or something odd enough to make me think back then, Why not?

Betty Medsger was there, along with Ben Bagdikian. They both had left the *Washington Post* and were headed for the West Coast. I do remember being in a car with them, talking about the previous evening's featured speaker, the head of the Gallup Poll organization at the time, and I was joking, mainly for Betty's benefit, that 42 percent of the audience had found it adequate, 22 percent had found it run of the mill, 18 percent found it boring, 8 percent liked it, and 8 percent hated it. (I didn't actually go on that long.) Betty laughed—neither she nor Bagdikian had heard the speech, coming in just for this day, one or both of them being slated to do something at the conference. Bagdikian gave me a sour look, miffed that the much younger man, myself, was making Betty laugh.

It was then I asked her why the *Post* hadn't reviewed my Harrisburg book (*The Harrisburg 7 and the New Catholic Left*, T.Y. Crowell, 1972), one of the few publications that hadn't, and she told me that when it arrived she brought it to the attention of the book editor and he said, "We've already done those books"—those books, I thought then, being Jack Nelson's (with co-author Ronald Ostrow) book on the trial, *The FBI and the Berrigans*, and one other book on the Berrigan brothers.

But, it turned out, those books were reviewed separately and the only one on the trial was Nelson and Ostrow's volume. And it was Betty who wrote the review, a not entirely complimentary one, which I didn't track down at the time, but have finally read, some forty-plus years later. Some of her ideas enlarged on in *The Burglary* were evident even then, though her musing in the review—"Surely an exploration of how 12 middle Americans in rural Pennsylvania came to vote 10-2 for acquittal would be significant"—did wait for Paul Cowan (who, alas, died in 1988) to explore at length in a book, *State Secrets*, which came out in 1974 and was put together by himself and four other authors. And, of course, I covered—and answered—succinctly her jury question in my book in 1972.

But that encounter in the car was the last time I was with Betty Medsger, other than the three months we were sitting day after day in the press section of the courtroom of Harrisburg's federal building.

In addition, she was helpful when I came to Washington, DC, immediately after the trial, to do more research at Ramsey Clark's law firm, Paul Weiss Rifkind and Garrison, mainly going through the copy of the trial transcript they had there. Clark let me use their offices and even got me a key (which I still have). It was the early seventies and the feminist movement of the time was heating up and it was certainly needed, given the young male lawyers' behavior and their pursuit of the secretaries at the Friday afternoon parties that went on there. I was making notes from the transcripts and they were running around chasing skirts. I thought perhaps I should go to law school.

And Betty let me invade the newsroom of the *Washington Post*, which then did look more or less like the one captured in the film of *All the President's Men*, yet to come. Indeed, the Watergate burglary had not yet taken place, since it was April 1972, and Woodward and Bernstein were doubtless doing not much of general interest at the time.

What I was doing was availing myself of the *Post*'s Berrigan files that Betty let me access. Access then meant her bringing me the fat paper files and letting me leaf through them.

Of the things that have been lost with the onslaught of digitization and the internet is what I call the mandala effect (not the Mandela Effect): the arrangement of similar things that will form unexpected patterns if you place them together, often in a circular fashion, or, at least, a grouping where you can see them all at once.

This is hard to do on a computer, though not difficult to do if you have clipping files from many years spread out on a desk, which was the case at the *Post*. Computers have reintroduced a linearity to modern thinking, one thing after another, unless one prints out everything one finds and implements the older effect.

Betty was a help to my book, allowing me to despoil the *Post*'s "morgue," a term oddly no longer much used, especially given the current fascination with zombies, prompting the realization that not much history these days actually dies. (A nod here to Mr. Faulkner.) Google enlivens the undead. And Medsger is quoted in my book, as "B."—any reporter I quoted I usually identified by the first letter of his or her first name (and she is thanked in the acknowledgments of the first edition).

But when I finished reading *The Burglary* it was clear she hadn't read my book at all. And that is the kindest assessment. Otherwise, she would be guilty of an overt act, harking back to the Harrisburg trial language of how to prove conspiracy. In this country, as I've pointed out before, the most effective act of censorship is to ignore. It's capitalism's weapon of choice. Heaping scorn on something just brings it notice. To not mention it at all is the way to go, beckoning oblivion.

It's always hard to be written out of history, especially if you've written history. But my Harrisburg book is absent from *The Burglary*'s bibliography, and every other page, including a list found on page 546, of books that "have noted the significance of the 1971 Media burglary." It's a long list. And it includes Jack Nelson's book, which came out at the same time as mine.

Of course, in my book, I quote from the Media papers, and indicate their significance. I still have a set of the Media papers—they were well circulated by early 1972—and for whatever reason (most likely people we had in common) I was contacted by Frank Donner, the author *The Age of Surveillance* (1980), working at Yale at the time, for a copy of what I had, which I collegially agreed to do at a cost of nineteen dollars for the duplication. He was to pay me upon receipt, which he never did. Nineteen dollars was a big deal to me back then when I was writing the Harrisburg book, living on roughly three hundred dollars a month.

And I was certainly stung to be made invisible in *The Burglary*, since it was clear to me—and I made it clear in my review—that Betty's book will become a standard text for the subject, outfitted as it is with notes, bibliography, etc., and published by America's fanciest press, Alfred A. Knopf. (My disappointment, though, didn't affect the review, which appeared on July 2, 2014, and can be found here: https://ncronline.org/books/2014/07/reporting-anti-war-catholics-and-fbi.)

Not that this hasn't happened before. Many books have appeared over the years where my book is absent from the bibliography. A lot of this neglect can be blamed on the lack of an index in the first edition, which, as most historians will admit, consigns your work to only obsessive specialists of the most narrow sort who will wade through an entire book they haven't yet read. This would be almost no one. Though the current attempt to digitize all books would change this.

I was under the spell at the time I wrote the book, I suppose, of Norman Mailer, who hadn't had any index for, say, *The Armies of the Night*. In 2012, when the Harrisburg book was reprinted, I made sure it had a solid index, though that edition's appearance evidently managed also to pass Betty by.

Ah, well.

As I wrote in my original review, the Media burglary had its truncated moment in the sun, because, among other reasons, so many secrets were beginning to be exposed at the time.

During the Harrisburg trial, which began not quite a year after the Media burglary, Daniel Ellsberg showed up at the courthouse, mainly because his lawyer for the case prompted by the Pentagon Papers revelations, which had come a year before the Media burglary, was Leonard Boudin, one of the principal Harrisburg attorneys. Ellsberg's trial had yet to begin.

The Pentagon Papers release, in the summer of 1970, was the first unveiling of insider behavior, followed fairly quickly by the even more damning White House tapes, which were to trickle out a year after the Harrisburg trial ended. The White House tapes were, in a way, more devastating than the Pentagon Papers release, because they showed Americans how their leaders actually talked to one another, whereas the Pentagon Papers, put together by "experts," were actually a higher form of literacy than the pedestrian and profane utterances taking place in Nixon's Oval Office.

Two items in the Media papers became part of the popular culture. The first more prevalent than the other: an "FBI agent behind every mailbox" is how it was often put. Hoover and his underlings were happy to generate general paranoia. The other took longer to uncover, the all-caps CONINTELPRO notation found on one FBI routing slip. It couldn't be reduced to a bumper sticker.

Speaking of paranoia, when a large and boisterous event was held in Harrisburg in April 2012 to memorialize the fortieth anniversary of the trial, I was approached there by a former Pennsylvania state official who had testified at the trial for the prosecution and he claimed that it was well known among law enforcement at the time of the trial that the Weatherman would set off a bomb at the trial's end if the defendants weren't acquitted.

Paranoia traveled both ways in those days, top down, from Hoover to the FBI agents and on to other law enforcement entities and hangers-on.

One difference between establishment and anti-establishment journalism of that period (a veritable golden age compared to today) was illustrated by the facts that emerged following the decoding of CONINTELPRO. As I put it in the *National Catholic Reporter* review: "Indeed, *The Burglary* is a demonstration of what establishment journalism could and did accomplish back then, as opposed to the rougher sort of new journalism that flourished during the 1970s and '80s—Tom Wolfe, Hunter Thompson, et al."

No one in the antiwar world was surprised at all by the revelations of the Media papers. It just verified what we all thought at the time. Establishment journalists were the ones claiming to be surprised or shocked. That is why the Media papers among activists just came and went. Been there, done that. But establishment journalists stuck with them, being on the surface less cynical than the tribe of younger, fringe, anti-establishment writers. But it took a couple of years to reveal to the public the nature of CONINTELPRO. As Medsger writes: "It was the persistence of Carl Stern, a legal affairs reporter for NBC television, that led to CONINTELPRO being exposed."

Stern filed a Freedom of Information Act request (after finally noticing the term in March of 1972), and, after being refused access, he sued the Department of Justice and the FBI in federal court. Back then, this sort of "persistence" could only be bankrolled by a large news organization like NBC. Today, alas, individuals are just as likely, if not more, to resort to the courts to discover facts that the networks and the few large newspapers that still exist might be thought to uncover.

The FBI, however, noticed the CONINTELPRO leak immediately and back in 1971 Hoover changed the name of the program in order to make it disappear, though the behavior did not change. One ancillary result of Stern's persistence was the Church Committee hearings in 1975. Before then, Sy Hersh reported in the *New York Times* in late 1974 about the CIA's actions against the stateside antiwar movement.

Hersh is a special case, a fringe reporter elevated to establishment rank by his freelance reporting in 1969 of the 1968 My Lai massacre. Though, apart from Hersh's articles, it was the photograph of the bodies of women and children and old men in the ditch, distributed widely as a poster, that made My Lai infamous. (In our increasingly aural-visual age, photographs still play a larger role in the culture than prose—consider Abu Ghraib.) Nonetheless, Hersh became temporarily attached to the *New York Times* and then his long career of high-end muckraking finally forced him back to the fringe. Though he still publishes in respectable places, the establishment press treats him as a gadfly.

CONINTELPRO was begun by Hoover in 1956. It was his id on fire, being in all ways as twisted in its methods and results as he was. He was especially manic regarding the civil rights movement and African-Americans' struggles for justice. Medsger's book, as I noted in my original review, is rather gentle on the man. Indeed, she takes the high road most everywhere. She began as a traditional journalist and, for a variety of reasons, she remains in a number of ways its champion. *The Burglary*, for all its seamy revelations, is a genteel product. If I wanted to be a sexist pig I could call it ladylike, not a term much in use these days. But it is more a matter of good manners. Since the world now has a million "journalists" on the internet, it is a rowdy world indeed and the current atmosphere makes a book like *The Burglary* seem more of an anachronism, and a welcomed respite.

But one of the oddities in a book so complete is its treatment of William Davidon, the instigator of the Media heist. The first chapter begins, "In late 1970, William Davidon . . . ," and the second chapter starts, "The story of the Media burglary begins with William Davidon." But Davidon remains a mysterious figure, insofar as there is little about his growing up, his young adulthood, his career as a physicist. He appears, more or less, fully formed, a "mild-mannered physics professor at Haverford College." A transcribed oral history interview with Davidon is available online through the American Institute of Physics (http://www.aip.org/history/ohilist/32356.html) and contains the most information I could find on Davidon's early life, little of which found its way into *The Burglary*.

He is the first cause of the Media event and his background reminds me of a number of figures involved in the anti–Vietnam War resistance period. He seems a thoroughly establishment figure, a Navy veteran, his degrees from the University of Chicago, work in the defense industry/academic conglomerate—mainly at Argonne National Laboratory outside of Chicago, a younger Greatest Generation figure, similar, actually, to Philip Berrigan, but of an entirely different stripe, a Jewish intellectual, a scientist with pacifist tendencies, worried about nuclear proliferation immediately after the end of World War II, but, nonetheless, in the belly of the beast, working at Argonne. Like Daniel Ellsberg, Davidon was an insider who decided to become an outsider, but retaining connections to both worlds.

Indeed, Davidon and two other unindicted co-conspirators of the initial Harrisburg indictment met in the White House two days before the Media burglary. Medsger covers this well in her book, but the confluence is still astounding. Davidon was used to traveling in august company, PhDs everywhere, and certainly wasn't cowed by the pomp and circumstance. Henry Kissinger, after all, was a professor, more or less, elevated to a mass murderer, given his rise to a position of power. But, as Davidon doubtless thought or felt, they were all mass murderers, the scientists who manufactured the A-bomb, and he was one of them—if not directly, at least by occupation. Troubled over nuclear proliferation, Davidon was an early member of the Federation of Atomic Scientists, American Friends Service Committee, Society for Social Responsibility in Science, National Committee for a Sane Nuclear Policy (SANE), and other peace groups.

In the oral history conducted by Patrick Catt in July 1997, Davidon says the following about the White House meeting and his pre-disclosure remarks (he died in 2013, before all the publicity began around Medsger's book) about the Media burglary:

> Henry Kissinger I think, liked to think of himself as a maverick and independent person who could do as he pleased. When Hoover made these charges that a group of people were claiming to kidnap him, I think he took it as somewhat of a joke. And through a whole series of events he kept saying he was open to a group of people coming and talking with him about the war, but he wouldn't talk about the charges for kidnaping. So all of those who met with Kissinger were among those that one way or another remained in this indictment. But we went to talk about the war. As a I commented publicly at the time, contrary to some, he's a good listener. He listens to what people say and responds without giving routine responses. That is a number of issues we raised concerning the U.S. policies in Vietnam. One of the immediate ones was there had been threats, what we perceived as threats to use nuclear weapons. He tried hard to dispel us from thinking there was any serious consideration to the use of nuclear weapons. So it was sort of, to some extent, fun and games and the novelty of being in the White

House with Kissinger with people who were being accused of plotting to kidnap him. And also, particularly Tom Davidon [sic, Davidson] and myself were trying to sort of test the situation. We came with briefcases stuffed with irrelevant stuff to see whether or not we'd be searched when we came into the White House. And in the middle of the meeting I excused myself to go to the bathroom. I wanted to see would I be followed in the White House if I went to the bathroom. There's that fun and games aspect of playing with the White House, testing the limits. The substance part of it was talking with Kissinger, and then using that as an occasion to afterwards talk with some columnists about what went on, and about why we were talking about our views on the war with Kissinger.

CATT: Were you followed?

DAVIDON: Not to my knowledge. Our briefcases weren't searched. You could have brought anything in. As far as we could tell we weren't followed.

CATT: This says March 8, 1971, media.

DAVIDON: There was a burglary of the FBI office in media [Media, PA]. My role in it has never been made public, and I won't make that public now. The public part of my role in it was a couple of days later I received in the mail a packet of materials that were taken for media. I presented them at a meeting—I'd already been scheduled to give a talk to a group of ministers and I presented this information and a number of newspapers and magazines picked up on that. And that sort of began the publicity from that media burglary. So I was sort of known as somebody that was involved. And also when people—there were mailings to various newspapers from the group that took the materials. And when individuals from different newspapers wanted to get more material, I sort of became a contact person. People would contact me and say they would like information and I would tell them I would try to get it to them. And often they would end up with materials. So I was clearly linked within some way.

And that's one of the things when the FBI and the Freedom of Information Act, all the stuff they gave me made no reference to media, and I was convinced that they must have stuff in their files concerning media. So when I was talking to this guy in the FBI [! — W. O.], I said check under what the FBI refers to as medburg, media burglary, see whether my name comes up there. I think I already

> mentioned he called back a short time later all enthusiastic. "Yes, yes, your name came up lots of times." [!! —W. O.] And there's a whole new packet of materials.

One of the mysteries of the Media burglary was why no one was "caught." As described by Medsger, the FBI continued to be clueless till the end, but I find that hard to believe. The bureau may have had a list of possibles—even I knew in 1972 the burglary was done by an unnamed segment of the East Coast Conspiracy to Save Lives, mainly Catholic activists. But, in this case, it turns out, led by a Jew. The Jewish/Catholic connection in the peace movement was as prevalent back then as it was, is, in the labor movement over the decades.

The Harrisburg jury was deliberating for a week and during that time, the end of March, beginning of April 1972, there was an "action" in nearby York, Pennsylvania:

> CATT: Then December '71 question mark. Made hundreds of bomb casings unusable at AMF plant in York, PA.
>
> DAVIDON: The question mark is just the date. I don't remember the date for sure and looking at defining the methods making it a reconstruction of that date. But this was York, Pennsylvania, was American Machine Foundry produced these bomb casings, 500 pound casings for the Navy. And they're just sort of kept in the railroad siting [sic, siding]. Most people in this immediate area went there and stripped the thread. They have a part that screws together. You strip the threads so they had to be re-machined. They couldn't be used then. So it was partly delaying the use of these bomb casings, but partly again, making more visible opposition to the war.
>
> CATT: I want to say, and the government's response to this?
>
> DAVIDON: As far as I know, nothing. I was never in any way contacted or investigated. I'm sure there must have been some sort of investigation, but nothing that affects me in any way.

This was a curious event. Medsger discusses it on pages 440–41 of her book. Yet another packet of papers and a release from the Citizens' Commission to Demilitarize Industry (a similar name to the Media group) claiming that it also was responsible for the Media burglary delivered to a few journalists. My friend from Harrisburg wrote about it in the *Harrisburg Independent Press*, one of many alternative newspapers popping up in cities across America at the time, though this one was, more or less, an offshoot of the Harrisburg Defense Committee, the March 30–April 6, 1972 issue:

> First word of the sabotage came Sunday night when, according to the Harrisburg Defense Committee, Ted Glick [an original Harrisburg defendant, but severed from the trial, since he wanted to go pro se, —W. O.] found seven plastic tops that had been removed from the [bomb] casings and copies of a press release from the Commission in his car. Glick distributed the releases to reporters, and two of them—Sue Gowen of *United Church Press* and this reporter—followed a map that came with the release and arrived at the scene of the sabotage about 1:30 a.m. Monday.... Our inspection of the area was interrupted by company guards, who threatened us with arrest for trespassing and took us to the plant gatehouse for questioning. We told them of the Commission release, giving them their first indication of the sabotage.

What is always provocative about such actions is not the vandalism involved, but how easy it was to accomplish. The recent Oak Ridge Three case of 2013 is a contemporary example. Even at a so-called National Security Complex in Oak Ridge, Tennessee, an octogenarian nun and two elderly male companions were able to spray-paint antinuke slogans on a building after gaining access by cutting through chain-link fence. They're all still serving time (see "The Oak Ridge Three" in part 2 of this volume).

And the other prominent thing shown by such actions is the ubiquitousness of the military-industrial complex, all the large corporations that produce consumer products, as well as armaments and other war material, in this case, an AMF plant nearby Harrisburg. Americans give their most tacit support to one form of socialism in this country, usually unacknowledged, the military and the industries that support it. The military is so socialist an outfit all their members even wear uniforms, yet the public does not see the connection.

Nonetheless, William Davidon continued to cause mischief, and the FBI didn't seem to care. Why? What was going on? If I was of the Graham Greene, or John le Carré stripe, I would tag Davidon as the perfect deep agent, or double agent type, cloaked as he is with so many high-status establishment credentials.

I don't really believe Davidon was in anyone's pocket, but it is curious. In the same vein, we have the current secretary of state, John Kerry. As I have pointed out over the years, the Vietnam War (the *causa belli* of all the antiwar actions discussed here) was so strange that the most effective antiwar group turned out to be the soldiers who fought the war itself, the Vietnam Veterans Against the War. It can't get any weirder than that. And John Kerry became the group's most prominent member, uttering the line before Congress in 1971, one of the most famous sentences of the period, "How do you ask a man to be the last man to die for a mistake?"

That sentence, of course, is only said now with bitter irony, coming as it did from Kerry's mouth. There always has been a tendency to co-op certain organizations for the benefit of, well, the powers that be. Gloria Steinem is an example, given her early history with CIA-supported organizations, all the Redstocking and *Ramparts* magazine charges she dealt with in the mid-1970s. I'm not questioning whether or not Steinem had, as it was put at the time, "continuing ties" with the government, but she certainly mainstreamed feminism, made it comfortable for the establishment, in the way John Kerry mainstreamed the denouement of the Vietnam protest movement.

And during the war, and after, it was the military that promulgated the false stories of wholesale disrespectful treatment of soldiers by civilians, the so-called spitting tales and worse. Those efforts were so successful that, as recently as November 1, 2014, Maureen Dowd began her Sunday column ("A Cup of G.I. Joe") in the *New York Times* with this sentence: "When I close my eyes, I can easily flash back to a time when it was cool to call people in uniform 'pigs' and 'baby killers.'" The military itself, back in the late sixties and early seventies, was happy to engender the us-against-them atmosphere, even after the war, which certainly plays a role in the current thank-you-for-your-service mantra heard these days.

It's a matter of gaining, or not losing, social control. Even though the country has been fighting a number of wars, there is no antiwar movement that is in any way equivalent to the 1960s and '70s period. And that is not an accident.

Historians have debated the effects of the antiwar movement of the Vietnam era, what role it played in "ending" the war. The antiwar movement did a lot of things, though, given LBJ's dour view of possible success of the entire enterprise and Nixon's long-held intentions of getting out of the conflict, his "Vietnamization," similar to our training of the Iraq army—and as successful—the military realized its options were limited and grim all along.

What the antiwar movement helped fuel was the social change going on in the country during the sixties and seventies, the shift from the post–World War II world of mom, dad, 2.4 kids, a car in the garage, the age of conformity, etc. All the cultural change that was to occur was supercharged by the protests in the streets, by the highs and lows of the variety of antiwar actions throughout the period. The Resistance, as it was called then, was just that, resistance. In the late 1960s and early '70s, though, it was never seen as the limiting thing it was: born to merely slow down the war machine, to create friction, so all the bad that could happen might be checked. It provided moral ballast to somewhat restrain our government's worst instincts.

The protest movement covered in *The Burglary* was largely a white world. There was a paradox at work, insofar as the civil rights movement that preceded the antiwar movement affected most of the leadership of the antiwar movement, and the transformations and conflicts within the civil rights movement played out its own version of nonviolence versus violence, Martin Luther King Jr. versus the Black Panthers. Some white protest groups that combined both issues were more likely to become, or promote, violent tactics, not peaceful ones. Like the Weatherman, which, given its ironic history, in its last manifestation finally mimicked the clownish Symbionese Liberation Army, and devolved into a mere gang of black and white bank robbers. But the lurid history of slavery, and the treatment of American blacks, was often the motivation, or excuse, to adopt violence as a tactic during the antiwar years.

The reception of *The Burglary*, the reviews and attention it has received, replays some of the debate in the analytical, pundit, and activist community. The *New York Times Book Review* critic, David Oshinsky, writes: "Throughout the book, the burglars are portrayed as devoted followers of civil disobedience and nonviolent resistance. But one of the tenets of such behavior is to take responsibility for the act."

The *Wall Street Journal*'s review, by James Rosen, of Fox News, attempts to correct the text, pointing out the "famous break-in"—the Watergate one—took place in the office building, not the hotel. (Most journalists use the term "complex" when writing of the Watergate, to avoid specificity and yet remain correct.) Rosen also states Medsger mangles the "Huston Plan" discussion, not clearly seeing John Mitchell's role in the fiasco. It is certainly amusing to see someone defend and praise John Mitchell.

The *New York Review of Books* used Aryeh Neier for its review. I was hoping for Garry Wills, since I knew he had read my book. But no such luck. Neier, for many years, was the director of Human Rights Watch and, as normally holds for reviewers, he spends a lot of time contemplating his main interests, foreign surveillance, which leads to Edward Snowden. Snowden figures in the *New York Times Book Review* notice, too, as he does in Medsger's book, at its end, the penultimate chapter, "The NSA Files." Oshinsky, in the *NYTBR*, writes, "The problem is that, unlike Snowden, these burglars committed a serious felony on the suspicion that a government bureau was engaging in nefarious activities; they had no evidence in hand."[!] And: "Would their actions have been equally heroic had they come up dry? Where Snowden and the Pennsylvania burglars do converge, however, is in their decision to evade capture."

Putting aside the lack of evidence "in hand"—more was known about the illegalities of the FBI than Oshinsky lets on, as Neier points out in his *NYRB* review (he cites an early 1950 book, *The Federal Bureau of Investigation*, by Max Lowenthal)—Snowden may have evaded capture, but he certainly exposed himself to the world, not a thing the Media burglars did till John and Bonnie Raines spilled the beans to Medsger decades later.

Actually, only after that news became disseminated, did the eighth burglar come forward. Medsger got cooperation from seven of the eight participants for her book, though three wanted to remain anonymous. (The eighth participant—Judi Feingold—tells her own story in an epilogue to the paperback edition.) And at least one researcher, beyond Medsger, knows the identity of one of burglars who did not want to be publicly identified, she being a woman who was also a member of the acquitted Camden Twenty-Eight protest crew.

Regarding the NSA revelations and what attributes Snowden shared with the Media burglars, it is clear that Snowden was alarmed about what the government was doing and sanctioning. He certainly had the evidence "in hand." Snowden, however, is more in the vein of Daniel Ellsberg, though, clearly, not so far up on the pecking order as Ellsberg was in the insider world. The common phrase, *the military-industrial complex*, is an augury of the more wholesale privatization of the military side of that conjoining since the Reagan administration, and Snowden, after starting in government agencies, became a contractor and is one example of many of how that relationship bites back.

Snowden, in a number of ways, was in the same position as lower-level scientists working on the creation of the atomic bomb. I suppose that is why establishment figures want to consider him a "spy." But, as is the case with the Manhattan Project, it was the science that was leading the way, in control, and drove the outcome. Scientists saw what they could build, so they went ahead and built it. The science itself was a Siren's song.

Today, the computer world's technology has become so potent and avaricious that, like the destructive capabilities of nuclear weapon building, its reach and size outstrips what common sense would require or allow. Everyone involved followed the science and let it multiply. Then they put it to use.

Like the atomic bomb, computer technology is a matter of putting the cart before the horse. Indeed, the cart has been dragging the horses along for quite a while. In the nuclear world, though the H-bomb was created and exploded, even scientists wanted to scale down production, make the weapons smaller and more manageable, even to developing the neutron bomb, no destruction, only death. And, to sell some domestic use, the history of the nuclear energy business remains open, sort of, to inspection, a testament to scientists' attempts to make their dark knowledge palatable. (Ironically, it was the Three Mile Island nuclear power plant incident of 1979, near Harrisburg, that replaced the Harrisburg trial in the popular imagination as that city's most famous modern event.) And there's nuclear medicine, too!

Though the military began the computer age, its enthusiasts and inventors have been more successful at finding ways to rope in the general population and make the technology indispensable. That there are dangers associated with it—assaults on both privacy and security—are taken as mere unavoidable by-products.

Snowden was the technician who had access to documents, though, in his case, the document dump was—in the computer-age way—enormous. This sort of thing has been in the public realm for some time. The Falcon and the Snowman case happened in 1977, bringing to public notice TRW's role in defense work. What do "spies" want? In the case of the Falcon and the Snowman it was a wacky plan of two young friends to reap profits from selling "secrets" to the Russians (or Soviets back then).

Typical spies either want money or ideological glory. The non-spies, Snowden, Ellsberg, Bradley (now Chelsea) Manning, the Media burglars, all wanted to inform the public and were overexposed publicly. Only the Media burglars remained in the shadows—till now.

The NSA is the alpha dog of computer overseers, purports to be in control of it, if the word *control* in that context means anything anymore. We live in a world where the amount of things to read outstrips any science fiction writer's imagination and, at the same time, reading comprehension of the young continues to decrease.

Now, thanks (not the right word) to Amazon, every book ever printed is available to buy, enlarging beyond measure the competition for any individual author. The one percent might have been made famous by the amorphous twenty-first-century protest group, Occupy Wall Street, called upon only to appear and hang around, but our ninety-nine- and one-percent world can be applied to any number of social constructs, not just current economics. And that 99/1 is so close to 9/11 (and 911) is one reason why the trope sticks.

I am not sure even *The Burglary* in both editions will reach one percent of its potential readers. Historians tend to dismiss the Catholic Left protests of the Vietnam era as sideshows—even the larger protest movement gets downplayed as not instrumental in ending that war. It was the serious people, they believe, who ended it, those serious people being, of course, the same people who started it.

And we are now entering the period where the actors of such events are dying off. Then it will really become "history," the past being a place as mysterious as the future, open only to interpretation and speculation.

Medsger's book comes at the right time. As does a recent documentary, *Hit & Stay*, which interviews a number of figures who were involved in the same draft-board-raiding events her book covers. It is becoming a digitized world and it is good these people have been thus preserved, now being able to move forward into the technological future.

Medsger does make one mistake about the Harrisburg case that no one, likely, but myself would notice. On pages 313–14, she writes, "The Harrisburg trial had ended in April 1972 in a hung jury. Once determined to win this case designed to protect Hoover's reputation, Department of Justice officials decided not to retry the defendants when, even in deeply conservative Dauphin County, they did not get convictions."

But, of course, the prosecutors did get convictions, on the so-called contraband counts, the smuggling of Elizabeth McAlister and Philip Berrigan's sad and hopeful letters taken in and out of Lewisburg penitentiary, counts 4–10. Even in Paul Cowan's long piece about the jurors, resulting from interviews conducted after the trial, "Harrisburg, Pennsylvania: Ballad for Americans," and reprinted in his 1979 book, *The Tribes of America*, Cowan doesn't, apparently, question the jurors about the compromise they reached in order to convict Berrigan and McAlister on the contraband counts. It is a peculiar omission. Cowan offers up the majority of the jurors as citizen heroes, though the 10-2 vote for acquittal came about not because of the common sense they showed so much as the weaknesses of the government's case and the odiousness of its chief witness/informer.

There was a period over ten years ago where I had been obliged to write a number of letters to editors of various periodicals correcting some distinguished person's reference to the Harrisburg Seven case (including the *New York Times*) that claimed defendants were "acquitted" at Harrisburg. No one was acquitted at Harrisburg.

Medsger doubtless meant the defendants, all seven, hadn't been convicted on the major conspiracy and threatening-letter counts 1, 2, and 3, those at the heart of the whole tangled web that had festered in J. Edgar Hoover's disturbed mind. On those counts the jury was hung. That's the trouble with history. It's hard to get things right. She should have read my book.

Notre Dame Review 39 (Winter/Spring 2015)

Days of Rage

■ Bryan Burrough. *Days of Rage: America's Radical Underground, the FBI, and the Forgotten Age of Revolutionary Violence.* Penguin Press, 2015.

The Vietnam antiwar movement of the 1960s and '70s was a mixed bag, populated by individuals who were pacifists, socialists, activists, young, old, mainly white, but with strands of people of color, since its roots, though tangled, were deep in the civil rights movement that preceded it. *Days of Rage*, though, is not mixed at all. It covers only the violent side of the antiwar movement, beginning in 1969 with Sam Melville, "the man who started it all," a white, thirty-something, long-haired New York City bomber, famously gunned down two years later during the Attica Prison revolt. It's a curious place to begin, but one must start somewhere.

Bryan Burrough has published five other books, three covering financial figures, one on NASA, another on the early years of the FBI. He is an odd author to tell this tale, given his attachment to the magazine *Vanity Fair* (he effusively thanks its editor, Graydon Carter, "the best in the business"). *Vanity Fair* has perfected a sort of celebrity journalism featuring the rich and the powerful behaving badly. There's a lot of that going on. But *Days of Rage* doesn't escape *Vanity Fair*'s personality-centric style. The book lists a "Cast of Characters," fifty-four people, members of six groupings Burrough's assembles, such as the Weather Underground, the Black Liberation Army, the FALN (Fuerzas Armadas de Liberación Nacional Puertoriqueña), and others, some little known. Given the span of history covered by the book (roughly from the late 1960s to early 1980s), this is actually a small amount of people; Burrough seems to ascribe to the theory that history is driven by individuals, rather than so-called larger forces.

Indeed, Burrough's object, he states, was to write a "straightforward narrative history of the period and its people." He means to keep his judgments "to a minimum." Earlier, he criticizes John Castellucci's dense book on the Brink's robbery of 1981, *The Big Dance*, for being "so loosely structured it is often hard to follow."

The world of the not-loosely-but-tightly-structured, straightforward narrative, is meant to be fast-read history—if any book of nearly six hundred pages can be said to be read fast. A number of odd revelations stand out with this method.

Burrough alternates white groups followed by black groups and Puerto Rican groups (the FALN), then mixed racial groups, concluding with the strange (though all the stories are strange) account of two white couples, plus children, merry bombers, and eventual cop killers.

Being so schematically structured, *Days of Rage* presents the white/black/ Puerto Rican worlds as separate, occasionally invaded by the practically all-white FBI, and other law enforcement groups with sparse minority representation, looking for the diverse underground perpetrators. Burrough thus sets up, perhaps unconsciously, a weird race-based story. Succinctly put (which he seldom attempts, brevity-being-the-sister-of-art not being his strength), he shows that the white radicals went to college, the black radicals went to prison, and the Puerto Ricans did a bit of both, for their sessions of radicalization.

That's the trouble with fast-read history; it often leaves out nuance. Burrough's caused cause for all the depicted mayhem is white students' guilty solidarity with black struggles: "What the underground movement was truly about—what it was always about—was the plight of black Americans." He downplays the Vietnam War, the draft, etc.; but the history is more complicated than he allows. He never notices, it seems, that righting wrongs heaped upon black Americans was not so much the reason for the conduct described as it was a justification. Not coming from the generation he writes about, Burrough misses other motives, including the effect of the Holocaust, being fitfully revealed as these kids grew up, on their consciences.

So, beyond the great "man" theory of history, we get the violent theory of history, which is that nothing of importance happens in the world without violence. It's the "American as cherry pie" analysis of social change, from the street philosopher and former head of the Student Nonviolent Coordinating Committee H. Rap Brown, whom Burrough's quotes. In *Days of Rage* you will read the Top Ten quotes of the era; he doesn't miss those beats. His book has been assembled from research, other people's books, a lot of memoirs, and a few important interviews he undertook with prominent movement veterans. This is the method of magazine journalism, yet Burrough's most important contribution is those interviews—especially the ones with Liz Fink (*nomen est omen*), a radical lawyer active in the circles described since the late 1960s; Cathy Wilkerson, the Weatherman who survived the 1970 11th Street townhouse explosion; Ron Fliegelman (Burrough's chief scoop), Wilkerson's partner in crime and father of her child; and a few peripheral others, plus a handful of talky former FBI agents.

From a writer of three books dealing with the modern financial world, I was surprised Burrough didn't have any sort of political economy analysis to offer, even of the Freakonomics sort: Why were all those college kids able to drop things and run off to protest, both in the civil rights arena and the antiwar movement? He still doesn't seem to know. It's the economy, stupid. The 1960s and early '70s still had enough surplus capital floating around to allow for youthful leisure, this being before Ronald Reagan made sure all that money went into the right hands. It's one of the larger forces Burrough neglects.

Burrough keeps saying throughout, in one version or another, that the world the underground bombers occupied, began to "change." No one cared anymore, "America yawned."

The book ends with a *Where are they now?* epilogue. I enjoy that sort of thing as much as anyone, but still there is no hard reckoning of how the world changed. That might have forced the author to make "judgments." But, Burrough should know: his most recent previous book is titled *The Big Rich*.

Days of Rage is full of period highlights and if one is well versed in the history Burrough doesn't cover, it's easy to add context. (The name Berrigan isn't found in the index or the text, though Burrough refers once to the "Catholic underground," though that too missed the index.)

Fresh ruminations, though, can arise from his depictions: 1) The black, violent revolutionaries were among the first to be globalized, to travel abroad, to see their plight in a geopolitical context (see Malcolm X, Eldridge Cleaver, etc.); and 2) As the underground and the bombings continued for over the decade of the 1970s women became more central—yet still at the beck and call of the men—their feminism increased but remained paradoxical because of what they would let the men get away with. An early form of this was Weather-woman Bernardine Dohrn's hybrid persona of sexpot and conflicted protofeminist. This internal volatile dynamic finally helped implode the remaining straggling violent groups.

Heavy on facts and light on analysis, readers not familiar with this material will read *Days of Rage* chiefly as a lurid tale, a text-movie unspooling before their eyes: the sexual revolution as adapted by radicals, the boyfriend/girlfriend world of political motives and decisions (though Bill/Hillary are not discussed), the fun of blowing things up ("Made it, Ma! Top of the world!"), thrills and chills, the Patty Hearst circus revisited once again, wild ironies on display and jaw-dropping episodes of coincidence, how drugs fueled so much of the late violent manifestations, and all along the "feckless" FBI fumbling through. Burrough, preposterously, speaks admiringly of J. Edgar Hoover, but the FBI doesn't come off well, as usual, in this account. But, however flawed, I hope *Days of Rage* secures a wide readership, especially among the uninformed young.

Though Burrough's book doesn't tell you, the Black Panthers' outbursts led to the militarization of our country's police forces. The flirting with violence of the Catholic Left led to the Catholic Right's attacks on abortion clinics and physicians. History was upended; those most prone to violent protest switched sides.

Burrough's central thesis is that all this past has been "forgotten." But by whom?

America's talent for forgetting can be salubrious. The problem is not what we forget, but what we remember. That propensity produces many grim examples, one being what the recent stars-and-bars-waving young killer, Dylann Roof, chose to remember in Charleston, South Carolina. He murdered nine—no radical bomber in *Days of Rage* killed nine people at once. Look out for what you remember.

National Catholic Reporter, October 23–November 5, 2015

Patty Prevails

■ Jeffrey Toobin. *American Heiress: The Wild Saga of the Kidnapping, Crimes and Trial of Patty Hearst*. Doubleday, 2016. Paperback, Anchor, 2017.

There has been a recent spate of books about radicals of the 1970s: *Days of Rage* by Bryan Burrough, a compendium of most of the violent revolutionary groups active during the period, came out in 2015 and Betty Medsger's *The Burglary*, focusing on the FBI and the largely Catholic band of the East Coast Conspiracy to Save Lives that busted into an FBI office and made off with its files, appeared in 2014. My own *The Harrisburg 7 and the New Catholic Left* returned to print in 2012 with a new, long afterword, forty pages in manuscript covering forty years, bringing up to date the participants and their outcomes. Doubtless, these volumes serve as a soothing counterpoint to our own continuing conflicts: surely, this too will pass.

Now there is Jeffrey Toobin's book about Patty Hearst, *American Heiress*, her notorious kidnapping in 1974, which brings up a number of issues about nonacademic works of history, one being whether or not the author needs to have been on the scene when dealing with the not-so-distant past.

It brings to mind some version of Orwell's 1944 remark about history being written by the winners. Or, in the cases mentioned, some species of journalist, adept at narrative, wanting to turn history into story, making the product, as some of the blurbs say, a book that can't be put down. Orwell's line carries the implication that such history may well be false. In the case of the Hearst kidnapping, that remains a central question since there are completely contradictory accounts available. See Patty's own version in her ambiguously titled *Every Secret Thing* that came out in 1982.

Toobin aims at setting the record straight, letting the discerning reader decide. Popular history has taken a beating during the last quarter century from television's view of journalism. Such shows as *Dateline* have created a new genre, a mix of truth and falsehood, keeping the viewer in the dark, the discovery scene saved for the end, a version of the mystery, gumshoe novel. News has long been turned into entertainment. History is now written by entertainers.

The Hearst case made that clear from the start. It certainly was entertaining. Who could make this stuff up? The Hearst imbroglio, unfortunately, rivaled another more somber event in American history, the assassination of President Kennedy, insofar as the killing of Lee Harvey Oswald on television raised the bar for both spectacle and contradictions, fueling conspiracy literature long into the future.

Kennedy, of course, was also American royalty. The Hearst case, though, was the profane version of a dynasty's entitlements. Oswald being gunned down was replicated in the burning alive of the core of the kidnapping perpetrators, the ragtag Symbionese Liberation Army (SLA). This was the first modern example of an American police force using immolation as a tactic. (Burning buildings in urban riots didn't count.) It was followed by the Philadelphia air force burning down a couple of city blocks in 1985 and the Branch Davidians cleansing by fire in 1993. In 2016 there has been the subset example of death-by-robot bomb of the Afghan-vet cop killer in Dallas.

Toobin is not new to sensational contemporary history. He was in the thick of things for the O. J. Simpson trial. Toobin's reporting back then helped O. J. walk free, by helping to broadcast, very early on, the total unreliability and more than latent craziness of the prosecution's most prominent witness, the bad cop Mark Fuhrman. Indeed, though that trial and Toobin's subsequent 1996 book, *The Run of His Life*, share a remarkable number of personalities, Toobin can hardly bear to speak about it, as if he is still guilty over his zealous aid to the Simpson defense. In *American Heiress*'s final pages of recapitulation of where-are-they-now he doesn't even note that O. J. finally resides in prison because of a spectacularly lesser crime (burglary, assault) than the slaughtering of two people.

As I may have pointed out before, nonfiction often turns into fiction not for what is there, but for what is left out. Toobin knows a lot about the Hearst case, and his account required quite a bit of labor. A new generation of readers will profit from its pages.

The radical rampages of the late 1960s and throughout the 1970s were an offshoot of globalization, a term not much used at the time. "Bring the War Home" was a slogan back then and, indeed, that's what happened. By the time of the rise of the SLA (brought about, largely, by the contemporaneous do-good movement outreach to the California prison system), things had quieted down a bit, and the Johnny-come-lately group seemed, in most ways, superfluous. The SLA's killing of Marcus Foster, the African-American California school administrator, well described by Toobin, was generally denounced by far left groups. But kidnapping Patty Hearst seemed to resurrect the SLA's reputation. For a group of less than ten individuals, they showed irrepressible native entrepreneurial power. They all, especially their one black member and titular head, Cinque, had ambition and big dreams. Their folly was fueled by good old American ambition and get-up-and-go.

Toobin credits the Tupamaros of Uruguay as the SLA's "model" for the kidnapping: "Kidnapping as opposed to murder—this was what passed for moderation in the SLA." Toobin, or the SLA, needn't have gone to Uruguay for their model, since, during the first three months of 1972, there was the well-covered Harrisburg trial in Pennsylvania, of seven radicals, six of them Catholics, who were charged with plotting to kidnap Henry Kissinger, at least as famous (but perhaps not as much in California) as Patty Hearst. This is often the trouble with popular history written far after the fact; it leaves out many things that eventually disappear from recorded history. Kissinger, of course, wasn't kidnapped, which leaves Toobin correct when he writes, "No one with a famous name had been kidnapped in the United States since Charles Lindbergh, Jr. was seized and murdered in 1932." But Henry Kissinger's alleged wanna-be kidnappers were certainly well publicized.

Another thing largely gone from popular memory, nothing that Toobin concentrates on, was the fact that Patty Hearst was a Catholic, and her mother a fierce one at that, sending young Patty to a number of Catholic schools, where, no surprise for a woman of her generation, she turned rebellious.

As the Jesuits once told me, allegedly quoting St. Francis Xavier, spoken in the sexism of the day, "Give me the child until he is seven and I'll give you the man." Well, the same goes for Patty Hearst. It's instructive how many Catholics play roles in *American Heiress*: attorneys, radicals, FBI, journalists—the parade of Catholics is practically nonstop.

Patty's bodyguard and eventual spouse was picked by her Catholic attorney because he was married, and then, after Patty found him a divorce attorney, he became her first and only husband.

"He was married with two young children and had been named the Catholic man of the year in public service by the Archdiocese of San Francisco," Toobin tells us of Bernie Shaw, the lucky guy. And this sort of line pops up frequently in Toobin's account: "Patricia had said 'Olmec monkey,' not 'Old McMonkey.' (The FBI transcribers, like many people in law enforcement, were probably Irish Americans.)"

Catholics everywhere—which brings me to Patty's "brainwashing" defense that did not succeed. *Brainwashing* became a popular term at the time of her trial, soon to be followed by the Stockholm Syndrome (now it would be *radicalized by the internet*), which did not come into popular use till a few years later, though the brainwashing notion did help her get a commutation from Jimmy Carter and, eventually, a pardon from Bill Clinton. Her pleas were enhanced by the over nine hundred deaths of Rev. Jim Jones's religious-cult followers in Guyana in 1978. Jones, too, had wandered into the Hearst-case orbit, volunteering to aid the "free food" fiasco that Patty's father brought about.

As Toobin points out, a number of people had been transformed by the events of the previous decade, a frenetic time of change in this country: other white members of the SLA, countless young throughout the country, even Patty's father, Randolph Hearst, though not evidently her mother, Catherine—the Hearst's marriage disintegrated by the end of the trial.

Patty's change was more a religious conversion than any sort of brainwashing. She was ripe for a change, living with the hapless Steven Weed, everyone's favorite whipping boy (including Toobin's), her former tutor and high school catch, meaning, as a high school student, Patty set out to snag him and she did. Hard to picture any of that going on today.

But Patty continued to rebel, especially at the dull domesticity of Weed and his un-evolved, soon-to-be retrograde sexism, at the midpoint of the 1960s and '70s women's liberation movement (so-called second-wave feminism).

Patty's deprivations while kidnapped would have appealed to, say, Mother Teresa: Patty's closet a cave, her diet an eremite's bland repast, her torments a veritable dark night of the soul. And, though Toobin doesn't follow this (my) analysis, she turns the table on the SLA and they eventually become her disciples.

Why Patty escaped immolation in the televised house conflagration was that she and the married SLA couple, the always quarreling Harrises, were allowed to go out and run errands, taking Patty along that fateful day, over the opposition of some of the gang. But Patty's wishes prevailed: out of the squalid quarters they all occupied into the sunshine and fresh air that eventually saved her life. She continues to prevail today.

Notre Dame Review 44 (Summer/Fall 2017)

Richard and Roger

■ Alice Goode-Elman, ed. *Complete Poems of Richard Elman 1955–1997.* Junction Press, 2017.

Richard Elman's posthumous nonfiction book *Namedropping* was one of his best, as was his last novel, *Tar Beach.* Elman (1934–97) authored, by my count, twenty-four original works, the majority fiction. Along the way, he published four volumes of poetry, the first in 1975. Now his widow, Alice Goode-Elman, has, as many would say, lovingly put together a *Complete Poems* that runs 528 pages.

Namedropping (1998) was well named. It was a compendium of what passed for short biographies, and hence mirror-image autobiography, of many well-known figures, mainly writers of various sorts. At the time of its publication I supplied a blurb: "Richard Elman's *Namedropping* is the most refreshing of rogues' galleries, for all its rogues are articulate and accomplished. Here is a memoir in the form of biography, in the tradition of Ford Madox Ford, another learned and provocative man of letters. Elman is funny, irreverent, and, most of all, generous of heart."

Cruelly, at least I thought it cruel, the *New York Times Book Review* gave it a very positive review, which may have, or may not have, generated library sales. Nearly twenty years later the book still hasn't aged, but the literary world has changed utterly, even though that change certainly was well underway by 1998. Here is a bit of the *NYTBR* review by Lee Siegel:

> On the basis of these astute and entertaining pieces, it's clear that Elman had what Keats called negative capability—the ability to enter into other people's moral natures while suspending moral judgment—in abundance.... *Namedropping* is a slight but mostly absorbing collection. On the one hand, it offers some delicious gossip as a form of social history.... Mingled in with the gossip are tart and satisfying remarks like this one about Hunter Thompson, who once took Elman on a terrifying nighttime motorcycle ride: 'All I ever learned from his depictions of Las Vegas and political conventions I knew in kindergarten.'... The really peculiar and riveting and exasperating quality to this collection is that for all Elman's many disappointments, he seems never to have lost his

illusions. There are penalties for that, and though they might be unfair, they are not always undeserved.

As I was saying, why the review was cruel was that Richard was dead and he would never get to read it. Everyone likes praise. And some are more likely to get it after they die. The *NYTBR*, by 1998, was more or less standing alone, and wielded a great amount of influence, both in sales and reputation. Richard had slipped into a hiatus of attention late in his life, mainly through the 1970s and '80s, though gradually his standing was being resuscitated and the daily *Times* also reviewed *Tar Beach* in 1992. If you have a long career, you may be taken seriously for a while, but generations change, new "blood" flows into publications, and if you haven't produced big sales you are more likely to be forgotten, or ignored, by the newbies. And when your cohort begins to die off, or retire, the younger generation has its own people to praise and promote. Other large forces are at play, too.

Indeed, I have always contended that the golden age of reading peaked at the end of the 1960s and then technology (VCRs, cable, eventually the all-consuming computer and its unholy offspring, the internet) slowly chipped away at the national pastime and reading became another vanishing ability, especially reading so-called literary books, eroding the numbers down to, say, the amount of people who could play satisfactorily a musical instrument in the 1960s, a small percentage of the population.

Newspapers across the country have all, more or less, thrown overboard their literary book review sections, which, of course, give the very few (one? two?) that remain, a great deal of power. Authors have become overpopulated mice in a cage, resorting to cannibalism, as I witnessed as a small boy viewing a failed experiment run by an uncle when he was a hospital lab researcher.

The internet, of course, is now the Tower of Babel come to electronic life, where everyone speaks, "writes," sounds off. To reverse a Norman Mailer remark, the magnitude of the machine, the paucity of the result.

Back around the time of *Namedropping*'s publication, I used the phrase *person of letters* to describe the old tradition of the *man of letters*, given that many thought the latter phrase sexist. Unfortunately, *person of letters* is not a fluent coupling (doesn't roll off the tongue, or anything else) and, these days, would not be appropriate, either. It would have to be she/he/they of letters, or some such. Language itself is taking a beating, since there are now words that some want no one to say, use. Richard was a true fellow of letters, in any case. Or guy of letters, since "guy" is now used androgynously, at least on TV, to include whoever is sitting around a table, male, female, whatever. "Thanks, guys." The whole idea of "man" of letters has been devalued in any case, taking on the patina of being a jack-of-all-trades, a pen for hire, talents spread too thin. And the phrase exudes an odor of *belle lettres*, not a scent the current generation finds enticing.

Richard wrote in all genres, aping those nineteenth-century authors who wrote most anything they wanted, or could. Specialization became a post–World War II phenomenon. Why that is, was, isn't entirely obscure. Though I won't spell that out here. Let's just say being a person of letters was seen as a dead white male thing, though a woman author, or two, or three, also practiced the do-it-all trade, but the preponderance was male. Richard, alas, is now a dead white male, so he fits the bill.

A great number of predominately prose authors have written poetry when they were young, but fewer continue to write it all their lives. Another acquaintance, R. D. Skillings (b. 1937), is roughly Richard's contemporary—if Richard were still alive he would be eighty-three—and another writer in the Guy of Letters mode. Roger has published mainly prose works and his last "book," meaning the last he has finished before Alzheimer's began to claim him, is a collection of poems. Roger has been saying for the last few years that he was afflicted, but to my eyes and ears the condition has only descended upon him in classical fashion this year (2017). So his final poetry manuscript, completed, is called "Only Bones," and one hopes it will find a publisher soon.

Roger published a previous volume of verse, *Memory for Marisa Rose*, in 2003. Poems from the new collection appeared in *Tri-Quarterly* and *Virginia Quarterly Review*, among other venues. He has also published several collections of short stories, a novella (*Obsidian*), 2001, and one demanding novel *How Many Die*, also in 2001, demanding in the sense of its content, the peak years when AIDS ravaged the gay population of Provincetown, Massachusetts. Along with the language problem these days—of what can and cannot be said, and by whom—Roger's sexuality is what is hideously called heteronormative, or, worse, cisgendered, some such neologism. Find the ugliest words and you will find only politics, as George Orwell should have said. If Roger had been a gay writer, who knows how successful the novel would have been? As it is, only the lucky few have read it. But his "reputation" has rested on his short stories. Here's part of a review from *Publisher's Weekly* on one of his collections, *Where the Time Goes* (1999):

> P-town, aka Provincetown, Mass., is the common ground of the dozens of motley characters in Skillings's beguiling fourth book of short stories. Skillings, who charted the same small-town's down-and-outers in *P-town Stories: or, The Meatrack* (1980), puts inventive, colloquial language to

> satisfying use in these innovative and darkly humorous tales. Successfully employing a wide range of voices, forms and lengths (entries vary from one paragraph to several pages), he describes alcoholics falling off the wagon, gay men struggling with coming out and the havoc wreaked by AIDS. Everyone rails against conformity.... Those who stay in town battle their demons with strength, wit and a strong sense of the absurd, heading all the while for catharsis: solutions are elusive and almost always unexpected. One panacea, at least, is prescribed in "Op Ed," a cheeky take on Swift's "A Modest Proposal," in which the narrator advocates masturbation as the precursor to a reign of "joy and kindness."

Though I have spent a long time involved with graduate creative writing programs (and I invented one at the University of Notre Dame), it is still difficult to imagine what the literary life of young people we have graduated will be. I do know what the literary life has been for my generation of writers. Transformative, as they say. Transitional, as others say. There is always a lag-time between generations. But, as I have indicated above, my cohort went from the golden age of reading to a postliterate world, from a triumphantly literate world where reading and writing were paramount in the culture, to a largely aural-visual world (graphic novels, anyone?), with other oral trappings (podcasts, anyone?). The era of enormous bookstores (Barnes and Noble, Borders) is now mostly over, but they contributed in their fashion, becoming book galleries, where people went to "see" books. Then, much to the displeasure of the corporations involved, they went to their computers to buy them, if so moved, at Amazon.

Yes, people still read. I could probably count on two hands the number of people who will read this. One hopes more, but... the zone has been flooded. The number of "books" that are being published—if you just count the Library of Congress numbers—is astounding. That is because of the growth of the little presses, and their questionable offshoot, coterie publishers, where a group of friends get together and create presses. Thank God for publishing on demand!, so to speak. As I have written before on this subject, it's all Virginia Woolf's fault.

When I was finished with Columbia University's fresh MFA program in 1970, I would have never predicted that my generation of writers would end up cosseted in universities. In the late 1960s there were only a handful of "creative writing" programs to attend. Now, anything that calls itself a university has one. But I wouldn't have predicted that, even if I had been in the prediction business. There was a general decline of writing skills as the literate culture morphed into the oral culture and if places of higher education had writing programs at the graduate level they could staff many freshman (now "first year") composition classes with cheap labor, aka grad student stipends.

The problem was so acute it has carried over even to PhDs in English, the adjunct hamster-spinning-wheel, and Richard was on and off that wheel most of his life, as he pursued a living as a writer—his pen was for hire, sort of. One of his most-read novels was the "novelization" of the hit film *Taxi Driver* (1976). Since he used his own name for that it didn't help his reputation in the snobbish literary world. That changed, too. The snobbishness vis-a-vis Hollywood. Now, any association with La La Land is a plus, but not in the 1970s and '80s, when it was looked down upon.

I have had the unhappy experience of helping older writers in my life, unhappy because of the ironies involved. I procured Edward Dahlberg his last major publisher, prompting four books to appear, an ominous volume of his three early proletarian novels (*Bottom Dogs*, *From Flushing to Calvary*, *Those Who Perish*) and a new, decidedly nonworking class novel (*The Olive of Minerva*), a circumstance which led to his—and my—editor leaving publishing. (He became an agent, though, of commercial fiction.) And I secured Richard a position at Notre Dame, just as our graduate creative writing program was getting under way. Both Dahlberg and Elman had been my teachers (Dahlberg at the University of Missouri–Kansas City, Richard at Columbia). Roger was never my teacher, just my friend, and I am certain I have never done enough for him, other than publish a number of his remarkable stories and one essay, when I was the editor of the *Notre Dame Review*.

Not to make this a treatise on genre, but over the years I have told students that the material itself often seeks its own form. There are things that want to be poems, plays, stories, etc. One aspect of James Joyce's career is that in many ways he demonstrated the evolution of most writers: first a poet (*Chamber Music*), then poetry-infused prose, then what would be considered (see Chekhov, etc.) traditional short stories (*Dubliners*), then a half-first novel (*Stephen Hero*), then the typical first novel (*Portrait of the Artist*), then the flowering of the form (*Ulysses*), then an unreadable masterpiece (*Finnegans Wake*). It was a direct line upward, a multiplying evolution. Woe to those writers who tried to duplicate it.

On a lesser scale there seems to be writers who are "natural" short story writers and who have a hard time graduating to long works. Or the reverse. It seems to hinge on a worldview, a micro and/or macro inclination, seeing large or seeing small. One hopes it is all worth seeing. And, it has to be admitted, that some writers, those who remain largely unpublished, just flail around, going from one sort of writing to another, always hopeful, mostly disappointed.

What called out to Richard in his early poetry? His widow points to his early influencers in her introduction, when his poetry was noticed by his teachers during his senior year in high school. The poets Richard read are what I call City Poets, largely male, Hart Crane, Walt Whitman, William Carlos Williams, that sort. When Richard finished college at Syracuse, he went off on a fellowship to Stanford, where he had a run-in with the elegant buzz-saw Ivor Winters, who made him feel "that every impulse that had impelled me to write poems was counterfeit," he wrote in *Namedropping*. Winters, Richard claimed, made him feel that his poems were "high crimes and misdemeanors." Well, a lot of writers who persevere often encounter harsh accomplished masters in their early years (and those writers are most often in their later years). It can be helpful. What Richard may have learned from Winters is that he had more to write about than could be contained in verse.

Not that verse can't contain multitudes, etc. But Richard was outgoing, energetic, a big guy with boisterous ambition. His early work led to nonfiction in various outlets, the early novels were "historical" fiction, partly because his nonfiction was confronting the world head on, and he went a bit backward in his early novels. He had a radio career, which lasted till he started criticizing Krugerrands on NPR. NPR had veered by the late 1980s into corporate sponsorship and they liked Krugerrands. His lively commentary there ended.

The first poem in Richard's first collection, *The Man Who Ate New York* (1975) and, in this one (beyond a dedication poem, very late, written when Richard knew he was dying, entitled "Dear Heart"), it remains this volume's first. The poem ("The Man Who Ate New York") begins:

> The man who ate New York began in the Bronx,
> licked his way slowly south, toward Spuyten Duyvil.

And so on. It ends in Brooklyn. One can immediately see two things. The first, its originality. No one but Richard ever wrote: "The man who ate New York began in the Bronx." And that what is being said needs to be a poem. Even though poetry is prose, the length dictates how it is to be read and, in this case, as poetry. It's always a puzzle a reader solves, usually knowing, if not always, the length of what they are just about to read. Length often tells them what it is they are going to read.

The last poem in the collection is short. It ("The Afterlife Is Only Strange") goes:

The afterlife is only strange
to those who never had an afterthought:
When Don Juan went to hell he saw his putative father-in-law.
Don't ask me what I'm doing here, he said. Vengeance was mine. I'm
damned by that design. Things do have shapes that we depict
for them.

That was written shortly before his death and was "signed" J.H.S., standing for a pseudonym he used for a book (*Little Lives*, 1978) and other odd pieces in his life. I guess, in many ways, you turn into a pseudonym when you die.

Roger Skillings isn't dead, though, given his condition, any more new writing will be thought suspect. So, this last collection of poetry may be it, though there are other unpublished prose works finished before Alzheimer's has completely claimed him. If one wanted to put together a Collected anything for Roger, it should be the Collected Stories. He has published five volumes, the first *Alternative Lives* in 1974, the last, *Summer's End*, in 2016. It certainly has been his most used and favored form—and his most praised and known. Stories of his I published in the *Notre Dame Review* were cited in Pushcart Prize volumes and the only essay of his I published was singled out in the *Best American Essays* volume.

Collected, a volume of his stories would show his prominence in the field; he's certainly, over his long career, one of the top twenty continuous American writers of remarkable short fiction. Such a book would, like Richard's *Complete Poems*, be well over five hundred pages. As I have pointed out elsewhere, anyone connected to a creative writing program has encountered the fact that almost any writer can write one good short story. The short story, in a sub-rosa way, is the most amateur form in literature, given that even a novice can compose a more than polished example of the form. Oddly, this isn't done as regularly, or even irregularly, in poetry. Most amateur poems are bad ones and those who write them don't, almost by accident, come up with a successful one out of the blue. And no one writes a good novel by accident.

It is not a test, but short story writers who excel, and can claim the title, do so over a long length of time, over and over. Again, think of Chekhov. He, too, prospered in more than one genre, namely his plays. But other multiple genre writers don't necessarily hit the same level every time they put pen to paper, or tips of fingers to plastic keys. I could do without Thomas Hardy's poetry, but couldn't live without his novels. There are other examples.

But Roger's output and content have been long fixated on Provincetown, a village he hasn't really left in nearly five decades. Hence, he's thought of as being regional. William Faulkner actually got to Hollywood for a while, but Roger has stayed put. Richard was a traveler, often to exotic locations, a man (person? guy?) of the world, in a number of that phrase's meanings. I don't think Roger and Richard ever met (I may be wrong), even though Richard, too, spent a bit of time in Provincetown, in the usual way, during the summertime. Not so coincidentally, they both, separately, were friends with Louis Asekoff. It was Roger's intercession, his doing, that got me to contact Asekoff in New York City when I lived there, post Harrisburg. Louis threw remarkable parties then, populated with most of the active and well- and not so well- known writers in the city. At one such I was sitting next to Donald Barthelme and he asked me what I did and I recall saying, "Alas, I'm a writer."

Unfortunately, the literary world of the 1970s and '80s hasn't been well documented. At least not by any profession biographers. All the connections between writers of the time have been mostly unrecorded, given that the whole notion of "generation" has largely become passe. The irony, and another example of the triumph of the oral (aural/visual) culture, is that various musicians, singers, etc., of the period have been well documented, obsessively, their overlapping lives of great interest to biographers and fanzines, *Rolling Stone* being one of the more prominent chroniclers. Patti Smith won a National Book Award before Bob Dylan won the Nobel.

Obviously, one other difference is economic, given the profit involved, the money generated for others by those artists' work. Our modern celebrity culture began with Ronald Reagan, the first "celebrity" to be elected president and, after that the deluge. Writers, as the years went on, didn't cease to multiply, but their incomes didn't swell. Indeed, so many of my generation scattered to university writing programs around the country. And, in most every case, a few exceptions here and there, their salaries as teachers supported them.

Roger brought his "school" to him, insofar as he has been the literary glue that held the Fine Arts Work Center together over its existence, since the beginning of the 1970s. Richard, as mentioned, taught intermittently. Putting so many American writers in university settings has been a phenomenon of the last forty years, more or less. That fact is brand new, a condition that one can't find in earlier American literary history. Not that in the mid- to late twentieth century an occasional writer didn't stumble into a college somewhere. But never the wholesale housing of an entire generation of writers teaching, what? students how to read and write?

Even though conservatives constantly complain that liberals have overtaken academia (they certainly haven't overtaken university administrations, those who actually run the joints), putting a generation of writers there has, more or less, put that generation in protective custody. It was a savvy move, even though the powers-that-be didn't quite bring it about on their own. Roger's "Only Bones" is once again a chronicle of Provincetown—with a bit of his childhood Maine thrown in. As one might gather by the title, "Only Bones" is full of the dead, or the near dead, homages to what has come and gone, both fauna and flora, places and people. Its first poem sets a tone, half eulogy, half jocular send off:

Fiddler's Reach

A sloop
in early days
coming through the last elbow in the river
saw with delight
the long reach ahead.
A fiddler went out
on the bowsprit to play a tune when the wind slat the jib, knocked him
    overboard
and he drowned giving the place in time
a gay name.

Did you have to look up "slat"? To throw or dash violently. A simple bit of verse that isn't that simple. Vocabulary is often thought an indicator of IQ. But, these days, that sort of thing is suspect.

Since I'm all for parallel construction, the final poem in Roger's manuscript is called "Bird Feeder in the Rain" and here it is:

The cardinal in the privet hedge gladdened by the splashing drops cocks
    his black mask, flits tail.
Nervy, frolicsome, his lot
is not to know he's red, ephemeral in a dumb world. His drab mate
keeps her grip on the clothesline pole, husking a seed, flinging mist and
    debris. She wings off. He follows instantly.
A migrating flock of evening grosbeaks gabble and fritter with their pods,
out-battle the fat indignant jays, overfed residents, jealous of their place.
A bitter door bangs. The grosbeaks soar, one concussive, flashing arc, and

settle snug as yellow Buddhas unanswerably still in winter's spectral
tree.

It's a troubled marriage poem of sorts (that pair of cardinals, that bitter door banging); and it certainly contains nature observed meticulously, something not unexpected, given Roger's prose work, his piquant powers of observation. But the succor he takes in the ingratiating facts of the physical world is almost overwhelming. Titles of other poems in the manuscript are also somewhat expository: "Two Young Poets Drunk," "When the Genial Spirits Fail," "Faces of the Old." They, the poems themselves, all are mysteriously linked, much like the currently fashionable "novels" that are "rings" of stories, interconnected, with repeating characters, to pass somewhat fraudulently as "novels," or long, continuous narratives, sold to readers who are not satisfied with mere short stories. But, in Roger's case, these poems do function as, once again, a pictorial mosaic of a place and its denizens.

This, it should be clear by now, is less a review than an introduction to two remarkable writers, each not publicly praised and regarded as they deserve. Not that that is so singular in these times. There is a surplus of writers today, given the demand.

Both Richard and Roger are true poets, meaning their poetry is not a sideline, or whimsical offshoot, such as most, if not all, of John Updike's poetry. He could often be accused of penning light verse, a mere diversion from his many novels. Elman and Skillings are heavier than that.

But, unlike Updike, they have not entered the modern pantheon, the recognition of the literary establishment. I recall Richard's disappointment when his novel, *An Education in Blood* (1971), written and published around the time I first encountered him, did not become the success he had hoped for. Indeed, if you publish a novel that doesn't go into paperback, you've published a rare book.

And another mirage neglected older writers indulge in, is that they might be "rediscovered," brought forward to a new, eager, large audience. Alas, that would require the hardiest and rarest of humans, a critic or commentator who was a voracious reader, one who sets out to do just that. There may be a madding horde of writers, but nary any of that sort of pilgrim. Indeed, you can enter a strange, eerie world and become a writer who has published too much, and, therefore, no one is eager to spend the time actually reading so many books to chart your possible ascendancy. The only way into that nirvana is that a late book wins a big prize, such as the National Book Award, or some such.

But, as I've been claiming, we have been exiting a literary age, entering a new world, neither cowardly or brave, but different. Yet I am more than happy that Richard Elman's *Complete Poems* now exists. It is a boon to literature. Mary Karr (Mary Karr!) has provided a blurb for the volume, which begins, "Every lover of poetry will relish this gorgeous collection by the late Richard Elman." And I'm pleased that Roger Skillings's collection, "Only Bones," exists—and likely to appear, thanks to some small press—even though everything that is published now is a hostage to fortune, but these days only more so. Such complaints go back a long time, a very long time; let's say, all the way back to Chaucer and his hopeful lament, "Go little book: go, my little tragedy."

Notre Dame Review 45 (Winter/Spring 2018)

The Miracle of Dan Berrigan

■ Jim Forest. *At Play in the Lions' Den: A Biography and Memoir of Daniel Berrigan*. Orbis Books, 2017.

I first wrote about Dan Berrigan in my 1972 book on the Harrisburg Seven. He had been an unindicted co-conspirator in that case. And he showed up in town while the trial was in progress, having been finally freed from prison, sentenced for his involvement in the Catonsville Nine case, and then paroled after nearly dying from a botched medical procedure. I described him then in this way: "This Berrigan has a prelapsarian face; creatures of an enchanted forest come to mind." More followed. It's not entirely clear to me now, but most likely I was introduced, being one of a small group that surrounded him during a recess of the trial. We didn't speak directly.

But he would turn up at various events I attended, and, because of my book on the trial, he seemed to know who I was. The last time I saw, spoke, with him, was in South Hadley, Massachusetts, when I taught at Mount Holyoke College at the end of the 1970s. I walked into a local coffee place and there he was, sitting with someone I did not know. Berrigan looked up when I approached and his face took on an expression of surprise that flickered momentarily. We chatted for a bit, me filling him in on why I was where I was. It was nearly ten years since the trial, but he hadn't seemed to have aged much. He was wearing a black watch cap. I, I'm sure, had changed. Berrigan looked somewhat resigned. Not that anything I said to him cheered him up. Eqbal Ahmad, one of the Harrisburg Seven defendants, was teaching at nearby Hampshire College just then, yet another coincidence or connection. The fellow Berrigan was sitting with wasn't introduced and remained silent throughout our exchange. Who knows? This could have been a portentous rendezvous. The King of Prussia, Pennsylvania, Plowshares Eight action (GE nuclear facility, pouring blood, etc.) had yet to occur and was right around the corner (1980).

A "Biography and Memoir" does double duty for any single author, though, overall, there is more biography in Jim Forest's new book than memoir. Indeed, when finished I knew more about Dan Berrigan, S.J., than I did about the author. And I already knew quite a bit about Berrigan. Memoir, as I have noted before, doesn't come from memory, but memorandum, the recording of important events, and Forest illuminates any number when both he and Berrigan overlap. But, as the photograph on its cover shows, this is Berrigan's book.

Anyone who wants to read only one book on Dan Berrigan, this is it. And the reader will be getting many works at once: a history of the Catholic radicalism of the last fifty years, a digest of many books Berrigan himself wrote, a chronology of the social history of both the Catholic Church and the Jesuit order in America, among others. Overall, the volume amounts to a compendium, including helpful photographs and excerpts of other literature.

For nearly fifty years, the Berrigan name was most often plural. It was Dan and Phil, the Berrigans, ever since they both appeared in Catonsville, Maryland, in 1968 to burn draft files. That became the signature event of the new Catholic Left protest movement of the period. The reasons are many: the success of the 1970 play Dan wrote about the trial, using the transcript as its base, the film that appeared not long after, the inherent symbolism in the tiny immolation the nine participants sparked, echoing the war they protested and their own religious motives. An exhaustive book titled *The Catonsville Nine* by Shawn Francis Peters appeared in 2012.

Catonsville was hard to top, but many other actions followed. The documentary *Hit & Stay* (2013) is the most complete record of this sector of the anti–Vietnam War movement. It was a busy time. Forest, himself, who was part of the Milwaukee Fourteen, covers a good bit of this ground, but what is even more illuminating is his treatment of the Berrigans' childhood, Dan's years becoming a Jesuit, a long process, and the last twenty years of his life, quieted by both his own aging and the curdling of the culture. Berrigan's last appearance at a protest was Zuccotti Park during the Occupy Wall Street movement in 2011. He was there though did not speak. (Forest quotes Joe Cosgrove, "Dan's witness could not have been louder.")

But speak Berrigan did through most of this life. Previous to Catonsville, Dan, like any number of men of his generation, went from the most provincial of upbringing—poor, an abusive father—to become a worldly figure. The so-called Greatest Generation was, most regrettably, great because World War II took so many ordinary Americans, plucked them from parochial backgrounds, and introduced them to the wide world. In Philip Berrigan's case, it was his stint in the army. In Dan's case, it was the Jesuits, sending him to France, Czechoslovakia, and South America as a young man. One of the many harms of Vietnam, the war that concentrated the Berrigans' fame, was that great widening, enlightening, didn't happen with the young generation of men who fought in it.

Forest's book is consistently interesting for even those, like me, who know a great deal about its subjects. It is his intimate side of the "memoir" parts, so we see

Dan Berrigan as one of an extended family, as well as a number of his associates Forest shares: Thomas Merton and Dorothy Day, in particular. Forest's portrait of Merton is especially revealing.

There were ups and downs throughout Dan and Phil's careers as professional protestors. The largest down was the Harrisburg Seven trial, not an event they brought about. It was the product of J. Edgar Hoover and his FBI, which had turned a willing informer who shared a prison with Philip, and his love affair with Elizabeth McAlister, into a federal case. It was a large road bump in the Catholic Left's progression and reputation.

They had gained the moral high ground with the sui generis draft board raids and Hoover sought to knock them off their pedestal. The smuggled and duplicated letters of Phil and Liz gave the FBI all the ammunition required, and though the government prosecutors lost the case (hung jury on major counts, convictions of Liz and Phil on minor counts that were later voided), Hoover's intention was achieved. The Berrigans' group splintered, reformed as Jonah House in Baltimore, and antinuclear weapons became the new focus of the protestors for the remainder of their years.

Dan, himself mostly free of collateral damage from the Harrisburg case, wandered into some unfortunate controversies, centering first in 1973 on Arabs and Israel. He, not to put too fine a point on it, attacked the Jews. Forest goes through this material carefully, though he doesn't dwell on a lot of unfortunate historical material relating to the early twentieth-century Catholic Church. It was a no-win situation for Berrigan and, in this one case, he seemed to go off half-cocked, given his lack of familiarity with Israel at the time, which he corrected after the blowup. Given the natural allies of the antiwar left, this estrangement lessened his influence for a short time. (The current far left, for better or worse, now echoes most of his criticism.) The second bump was a clear-cut and vocal anti-abortion stance, just as second-wave feminism was rising. Again, to left-wing political coalitions, there continues to be the sour equation: prolife = Donald Trump.

The sibling rivalry between Phil and Dan, often commented on, seemed in later life to turn on Phil's marriage to McAlister. Dan, alone, knew of the alliance before the news came out during preparation for the Harrisburg trial, but he was never able to entirely square it with his deeply held affections for his brother. Forest quotes a letter from Dan to Phil: "I had of course in no way been prepared for this. How could I be?" It remained a betrayal, however mysterious its reasons, to Dan, not wholly understandable, since it was so far from Dan's own loyalty to his Jesuit vows.

It was a betrayal to a lot of people in the now old New Catholic Left. But, among the many charms of Forest's valuable book, are the photographs that abound in the margins. And on page 219 the reader will see one of Phil and Liz and two of their young children. Both adults look so happy.

Over the years I kept track, somewhat lazily, of Dan Berrigan. He, like Leonard Boudin, one of the principal attorneys of the Harrisburg case, kept prophesying his own imminent death, but Berrigan outlived his dour predictions. (Though Leonard wasn't so lucky; he died in 1989 at age seventy-seven.) Forest covers Berrigan's final years well, post Philip's demise in 2002, when Dan lived, for the most part, quietly, in Manhattan, not emerging much after his Occupy Wall Street appearance. Living till ninety-four (he died in 2016) was a miracle of sorts, so if Pope Francis, a fellow Jesuit, is looking for another saint—one to offset Mother Teresa—he might turn his kind eyes toward Dan Berrigan, S.J. One necessary—required—miracle already has been proven.

Notre Dame Review 46 (Summer/Fall 2018)

O'Connor/Giroux

■ Patrick Samway, S.J. *Flannery O'Connor and Robert Giroux: A Publishing Partnership.* University of Notre Dame Press, 2018.

Jesuit Fr. Patrick Samway takes us to a lost world—New York City publishing in the 1950s and '60s—and, almost by accident, shows us the beginning of a new world, the early years of the Iowa Writers' Workshop, the mothership for the hundreds of creative writing graduate programs that now exist in American universities.

Iowa became and remains the most famous now—not in the 1940s, as Samway claims. It began in a modest way in the 1930s, but only was put on the map under the directorship of Paul Engle, which began in 1941 and ended in the mid-1960s. What secured its place in history were its post–World War II graduates—a stellar list—and one of the most well-known, the subject or half-subject of the book at hand, being Flannery O'Connor.

The publishing world part is described through the person of Robert Giroux, who had the great good luck to encounter O'Connor early in his career through the intervention of the poet Robert Lowell, who had met O'Connor at Yaddo, the writers' colony. Lowell was a convert to Catholicism, as are any number of literary folk who were in O'Connor's orbit, circling around the real thing, cradle Catholic as she was. Indeed, converts were often first attracted to the writing of O'Connor, even if they knew her only as readers. And there was always something convert-like about her fiction since she wrote so much about Protestants.

For a Catholic of my generation, being introduced to O'Connor's work as a teenager by the literary mother of boyhood friends, a woman who was a neighbor and also a convert, was not an unusual occurrence, given that Catholics in the early 1960s were not, as they are now, so high up in the "college educated" statistic sweepstakes. Back then, they often needed or found former Protestants who were educated sufficiently to respond to O'Connor's work.

On the publishing front, Giroux, according to Samway, left Harcourt, Brace (O'Connor's first publisher), because of Giroux's perceived notion of its anti-Catholic bias. Upper management had not entirely been swept off their feet by all the upstart Catholics beginning to join what was once the restricted gentlemen's club of publishing. The paperback revolution, the changes yet to come, had only barely begun to disrupt the old order in the 1950s.

The O'Connor/Giroux "publishing partnership" results in an essential and pleasing volume. Readers not necessarily steeped in O'Connor lore will learn a lot about her and her remarkable work as we follow her dealings with the publishing world. She was no wallflower there, though not without some usual naiveté at the start. It has always been a paradox to me, the bespoke portrait of O'Connor being some sort of Southern recluse living on a farm stuffed with peacocks, as contrasted with her blatant worldly side easily seen in her fiction, given its sophistication. She went off to Iowa as a young woman—to study journalism at first, not "creative writing"—without much hesitation. O'Connor traveled not often but widely, lecturing and touring. Samway manages to correct the reigning stereotype throughout his book, detailing her interactions with the cosmopolitan types she encountered in New York publishing and elsewhere, beginning at Iowa.

Much of his book is steeped in Old World gentility. In a discussion of Giroux's short-lived 1952 marriage (its brief cohabitation, but no divorce till 1962) "to the daughter of a Cuban aristocrat," Samway writes, "Giroux was grateful for the love and support of his lifelong friend and companion [Charles] Reilly, who subsequently lived with him." Samway's account echoes the time when closeted homosexuality was only discussed sotto voce and in Giroux's milieu was seen as unique and special. Giroux's own Catholicism, a bond he shared with O'Connor, went through "a process of serious discernment," according to Samway, who is quite good at capturing the period and its mores in amber.

Given the slander and invective often aimed at today's creative writing programs, it is enlightening to learn how well O'Connor took to hers in the late 1940s, and that she continued throughout her short life to take suggestions and criticism on seemingly all her manuscripts from a small circle of accomplished writers and critics. Giroux's editorial style is another disappearing creature. His taste and attention are hard to locate these days, and his primary assistant when he was at Harcourt, Brace, Catherine "Katy" Carver, assisted O'Connor till her end. That she had a handful of steady literary confidantes and attachments to those she met (both fellow students and teachers) at Iowa throughout her life is the primary gift of attending a graduate creative writing program.

Giroux's career flourished after he left Harcourt, landing at Farrar, Straus and Cudahy, eventually to become Farrar, Straus and Giroux. Its high-end literary list was enhanced by O'Connor's work, and though Samway implies it was a personal favor to O'Connor for Giroux to reissue *Wise Blood* after it was out of print for nearly ten years, it was actually a mark of his business acumen to have his publishing firm gain permanent rights to the novel. Incidentally, *Wise Blood*, though not a success when it was first published in 1952, is one of the classic books burned at the beginning in HBO's 2018 film remake of *Fahrenheit 451*.

Again, you don't have to have read deeply in O'Connor's oeuvre to enjoy Samway's part-biography, part-memoir, part-literary analysis. It is full of interesting tidbits, often from unpublished letters such as O'Connor's view of *To Kill a Mockingbird*, "summarily dismissed as a child's book."

O'Connor's death in 1964 comes as a shock in Samway's telling because it is so offhandedly mentioned. Her omnipresent mother had her buried the next day. After spending so much intimate time with O'Connor, to vault over her demise seems to leave a reader shortchanged. Giroux lived till 2008. The genteel publishing world he had inhabited was long gone by then. What remains, though, are the immortal stories and novels of Flannery O'Connor.

National Catholic Reporter, October 5–18, 2018

PART II

■

RANTS

The following pieces are largely from the Huffington Post, *where I was one of the legion of unpaid writers toiling away for "exposure." A good many of them were older writers, often moonlighting professors, who had fallen into the paradoxical position affecting their young students, that is, working for no pay, as aged interns. Recall your Samuel Johnson: "No man but a blockhead ever wrote, except for money." For five years I was a paid weekly columnist for the* Chicago Sun-Times *(2001–2005) and when that ended—I being the canary in the coal mine for the collapse of print journalism—habituated to having access to a public, I continued to write weekly for* NUVO, *the "alternative" newspaper in Indianapolis, Indiana. Most everything there appeared online only—and for "free." After writing over two hundred columns for that publication, my time there ended, as it had at the* Sun-Times, *abruptly. Still not being able to shake my addiction, I climbed aboard the* Huffington Post, *again for no remuneration, though they were also free of copyright restrictions, till that ended in 2018, when they cut loose nearly all their "contributors." The now newly named* HuffPost *has come full circle, wanting to ape older venues, with a smaller staff and only a few outside freelancers. The Babel flophouse is no longer rent-free. Writers have to resort to their own blogs, hands out, tin cups rattling for readers not coins. Mine is* The View from the Couch *(http://orourke-theviewfromthecouch.blogspot.com/).*

The Great Refudiator

President Obama, I hope, will become the Great Refudiator during the critical year of 2011. Meaning, borrowing Sarah Palin's wonderful coinage, that Obama will make most of what I have said during the last year wrong and superfluous. That he will hold the line, battle the Republicans, reverse the gains of the filthy rich and bring up the "middle class" and the working poor, which, come to think of it, is most of the middle class.

Sarah Palin, though, has been repudiating her coinage of *refudiate* as mere blunder (in her Alaska "reality" cable show), even though she gave a nod to Will Shakespeare as a coiner of words. Instead of sticking with that line, though, she said her new word was a lowly tweet typo. Quickly, film of her using the word on TV previous to the tweet surfaced. But it would be better for the culture at large if she accepted the mantle of one of her literary predecessors (not Shakespeare), but Mrs. Malaprop.

Mrs. Malaprop, of course, comes from Sheridan's eighteenth-century play, *The Rivals*. And she is a forerunner of Sarah Palin, interested in world events and the consequences of the same. One of her memorable lines from that play is, "If I reprehend anything in this world, it is the use of oracular tongues, and a nice derangement of epitaphs!" Mrs. Malaprop is obviously (or perhaps not) a comic character, an object of satire, rather than desire. And, unfortunately, Sarah Palin is an object of some desire, as well as satire. Whom among us can refudiate that?

So Palin should take pride in inventing *refudiate*, the coupling of *refute* and *repudiate*. An unnatural union, it well might be, but it produced a reasonable offspring, now finding its way into dictionaries. English is the most malleable of languages, which is why it is taking over so much of the globe. More Chinese are bilingual in English than we Americans are bilingual in anything.

Why I want Obama to be the Great Refudiator is to quell the discontent percolating in his base. The false hopeful dawn of his election and inauguration has given way to this dreary dusk of discontent, so much so the White House may not even have to chide the progressive base, since it won't much matter to the administration this year. Of course, it will matter in 2012.

Though I've written about this in the past, it bears repeating, the fact that close elections are aimed at "independents" and "swing voters" makes them desperate affairs. For swing voters and independents are, in the main, will-o'-the-wisp lunatics who do not know their own minds, much less their own self-interest. Mostly, they go with the popular winds, whichever way they happen to be blowing. In Obama's triumph in 2008, all the enthusiasm blew them in his direction and he won formerly red states, like our own Hoosierville, Indiana.

But what group caused all that excitement, enthusiasm? Obama's progressive base, those who were with him at the beginning, and those who joined after he beat Hillary in the primary. The so-called independents and swing voters, as they are wont to do, went with the likely winner. It made a big number. Yet where will the enthusiasm come from in 2012? Nowhere, that's where, unless Obama becomes the Great Refudiator.

Alas, one of the great mysteries of our time is why satire has no efficacy. Why Sarah Palin can be walking satire and still get 30 percent of the national vote. Why Jon Stewart isn't considered a satirist, but a person a lot of educated people get their news from. Why *The Onion* seems like a news magazine. Unfortunately, satire requires people to know what is being satirized. It's a cause-and-effect loop and if the larger public is unaware of what is being satirized the loop is never closed. One would think we live in an Age of Satire, but we really live in an Age of Postsatire. Or a postsatirical age. If you want to refudiate me, go right ahead and try.

NUVO, January 4, 2011

Reality-Based Shooter

Supposedly, it was an anonymous Bush II–era aide who told Ron Suskind in 2004 that the Bush White House wasn't operating in a "reality-based community"; that they, the Bush White House gang and co-conspirators, created their own reality. Well, it's clear that it isn't just George W. and friends who create their own reality, it's a lot of other folks, too. Like the Republicans who read a redacted Constitution on their first day of business in the new Republican-controlled House of Representatives, leaving out the bits about slavery and women not being allowed to vote. And then there is the new edition from an Auburn University professor (Auburn!) of *Huckleberry Finn*, which removes the word *nigger* 219 times (and Lord knows what else), since some "readers" find the word itself offensive. But it's mostly nonreaders who find it offensive.

At times, words alone alter reality. One example: *test-tube babies*. Now that cojoining of sperm and egg happens in a petri dish, not a test tube, but the phrase *petri-dish babies* just doesn't have the same ring to it. The censoring of books has happened over the centuries. *The Hardy Boys* syndicate has redone earlier titles, taking out and replacing various anti-Semitic slurs and racial insults. Updated versions emerged, but not advertised as such (or two decades ago, last time I looked). Famously, Thomas Bowdler brought out a cleansed edition of Shakespeare back in the nineteenth century, wiped of the salacious parts by his sister; hence, the term Bowdlerized, which goes to show once again that those women who actually do the work don't often get credited (see Dr. Spock's work, etc.).

But taking out the unpleasant parts of the original Constitution and removing one word over and over from a classic text smacks of other things than Victorian niceties. People want to live in one world, rather than another. Well, after the unprecedented reading of the Constitution we had, in Arizona, the unprecedented (in terms of number of dead and victims) attack on a Congress member and her fellow citizens, including a federal judge. The shooter fit the typical pattern (becoming typical) of the unhappy college-age male with easy access to twenty-first century weaponry. Jared Lee Loughner (and perhaps the government should make a database of anyone with the name Lee as one of three, as in Lee Harvey Oswald) reminds me of the Virginia Tech shooter, Seung-Hui Cho (Hui rimes with Lee), a young man with a number of the same problems who found the same solution, except that Cho killed himself. At Virginia Tech thirty-three died; that many might have in Arizona had not the killer been tackled and disarmed by concerned citizens. Cho was twenty-three; Loughner is, reportedly, twenty-two.

Dallas got blamed a lot in 1963 after the assassination of John F. Kennedy; Arizona will be taking heat for this attack, some of it, like Dallas, well earned. Even Timothy McVeigh, the Oklahoma City bomber, was steeped in the hot brew of Arizona, the city of Kingman, where he lived with an old army buddy. It was all fairly crazy back then in the Sun Belt, with the Branch Davidians in Waco, Texas, and the survivalist-minded in Arizona, in the mid-1990s. Now all the craziness has gone mainstream, given the high number of non-reality-based communities that have sprung up everywhere.

Only a few are blaming the Wild West arming of America, thanks to the NRA's diligent work. Most people surfacing on the media say that Loughner would have found another way to wreak havoc. But then there's havoc and there's havoc. When I lived in New York City long ago I always thought the city was a testament to civilization. That so many could live (in Manhattan) so tightly fit and still function spoke to human beings' best natures. The many provide a check on the few. It's the open spaces that allow for wildness to sprout so lethally. Malls in Arizona; big-box sports stores selling Glocks.

Before all this havoc we only had President Obama's change is no change, with the appointment of more Clinton retreads, William Daley and Gene Sperling, to high White House posts. And many journalists actually said that both appointments were a sign of change, showing that they too had abandoned the reality-based community. If anything, change for the worse, I suppose. But the only winner of this unhappy week is the NRA. Guns don't kill people, people kill people, I heard all weekend. Which is about as helpful as saying, Rhetoric doesn't kill people, people kill people. Yes, indeed, one person with a semiautomatic can kill six and injure a dozen, all in less than a half minute. And the NRA is so powerful in Washington, DC, few even bother to suggest some mild limitations to impose on access.

Well, that makes sense, because no one wants to talk about America's largest going concern in manufacturing, armaments and weapons of war. Products bigger and more lethal than a mere Glock. Our military-industrial complex is healthy. And how. And if we had no wars to fight, unemployment would probably be in the mid two digits. That's reality based. The NRA has nothing to worry about. We're all in the gun business.

NUVO, January 11, 2011

Mourning Becomes Them

Amid a week of various kinds of mourning and recriminations and calls for civility, one contest that stood out was who gave the best impersonation of "mourner-in-chief." On the *NewsHour* (where they used the locution *comforter-in-chief*) Jim Lehrer interviewed the historian Michael Beschloss, who brought up Ronald Reagan's speech from the Oval Office the evening of the *Challenger* explosion and praised his performance. Though Lehrer mentioned it in his opening remarks, that Reagan had been scheduled to give his State of the Union speech that night, a fact neither he nor Beschloss mentioned was that Reagan, himself, was one of the causes for the *Challenger* catastrophe.

Lehrer doesn't call himself a historian, but Beschloss does, so he should have pointed out Reagan's role in the *Challenger* disaster. Reagan had planned to refer that night to the first teacher in space, Christa McAuliffe, in his State of the Union speech and NASA knew that, and it was an additional bit of political pressure on the chief bureaucrat running the launch, one thing that made him go against the judgment of a number of his engineers and scientists' verdict that it was too cold to launch. He wanted to please the White House and had the candle lit and the whole world got to see it explode.

But Reagan got to give a speech anyway, supposedly written by Peggy Noonan, which ended with the lines from a piece of doggerel called "High Flight," "They slipped the surly bonds of earth to touch the face of God," which was part of a TV-sign-off tape provided by the military, which I saw a hundred times in my youth, back when TV signed off. Doubtless, Peggy Noonan saw it, too, or whoever wrote Reagan's speech. This is the speech Beschloss praised. But he didn't give the viewers any "history," though he is supposed to be a historian. Reagan came off smelling like a rose, and, since history is written by winners, I suppose you could say Reagan won and continues to win, since the real story of his role in the *Challenger* fiasco is considered only by a few. And, of course, it didn't, in any case, change history. History, for people like Beschloss, is only those things that change history, not just what happens and why.

But it was the same amnesia everywhere else President Obama's Tucson speech was discussed. The *Washington Post*'s Dan Balz wrote, "Ronald Reagan did it with a short and eloquent Oval Office address...." The only thing the press got exercised about was the irrepressible Sarah Palin, the narcissist-in-waiting, and her it's-all-about-me speech, delivered from her version of an oval office in Alaska on—what else?—Facebook. Blood libels all around.

In the states these days the bar is set so low that the fact that President Obama can deliver a few coherent, appropriate remarks to the nation makes him stand out head and shoulders above most of the folk in Congress and in Alaska, at least those Alaskans with TV studios in their homes.

But the Republicans are now back doing their good work on the Job-Killing Health Care Bill, talking their usual nonsense, unafraid any historian will actually point out their lies and shenanigans, since it only matters who has the power and who wins, and they and their friends, like Beschloss (his wife runs a hedge fund), are certainly the winners.

NUVO, January 18, 2011

Mommie Baddest

I feel like taking a break from politics today, at least a break from writing about politicians, since most everything becomes political once discussed. So, let's talk about Amy Chua's new book, *Battle Hymn of the Tiger Mother,* since so many other people are talking about it. First, I want to point out, like a lot of books of this sort, it is aimed principally at upper-middle-class women. Not that middle-class women don't buy books of this sort, but they make up the aspirational audience, those that wanna be. A lot of the same people buy books about Princess Di. And it's not just nonfiction.

Imagine Ernest Hemingway writing about work, slaughterhouses, etc. Hemingway's unending popularity owes a lot to his subject matter, the lives of the rich, running with bulls, drinking at Paris cafés, going to bullfights, a whole host of leisure-time activities. Ah, that's the life. You can divide up literature this way; at least some authors write about the rich and the poor. F. Scott Fitzgerald, for instance, the subplot in *The Great Gatsby*. But, back to the Tiger Mother.

Now, nothing is going to get me to buy this book, so I'm writing about it based on a number of reviews, excerpts, and hearing Ms. Chua on the radio. Let's start with the title. Boy, does that put together two disparate cultures, the Chinese and the Old South. I don't often put those two things together, since the Chinese "slaves" (aka coolies) built a lot of things in America, but not so much down South way back when, since there were real African slaves to use.

Amy Chua is second-generation Chinese American, so she's stretching the Chinese part, but she doesn't seem to be able to get a joke, why her husband (mentioned, evidently, very sparingly in the book) laughed when she asked him accusatively if he had any "goals" for the family dog, and that might be part of her cultural heritage. But the real part of her cultural heritage (and not discussed anywhere I have seen—not that I have seen everything) is that she has two girls, no boy child, and that alone might account for a lot of her behavior. There are a lot of Chinese girls given up (and worse) for adoption to Western couples.

A couple of decades ago a small focus group I was studying (since I was one of the studied) looked like China. Every couple of the group who had a boy ended up with only one child. Those whose first child was a girl had a second, and a third, if the second wasn't a boy, which was most likely the case, since statistically the sex of your second child will most likely be the same sex you already had. And, even for the couples who get a lucky girl/boy, there's the case of acquaintances of mine who had an actual Chinese (immigrant) nanny, one who lavished attention on the younger boy child and ignored almost entirely the older girl child.

So, the Chinese mother part of Amy Chua seems to be an inner anger that she had girls, not a boy or boys. Her whole child-rearing methods may well have changed if she were raising boys, and certainly the father would have been more central than he appears to be, since the same-sex parent is usually much more involved, both literally and figuratively.

And, of course, Amy Chua could call one of her girls "garbage" and get away with it, since she's an upper-middle-class law professor at Yale, as is her husband. Some parents call their children garbage and also treat them like garbage, unfortunately, since they are poor and ill equipped with the parenting resources of the upper-middle class. Amy Chua's daughters can take a little abuse, since they have so many other advantages showered down upon them. All of the rest of the children out there, not so privileged, have a much harder time growing up with tiger mothers of any sort, much less tiger fathers, absent or present.

But the popularity of her book among the chattering classes does stem from the high interest other writers with children have in the subject. But it also comes from an age where people are inclined to go backward, to some vanished era when sparing the rod spoiled the child, when lives seemed more under control than they do now, today, when everything tends to be rationed for the ninety percent, and only loosened up for the top ten. You don't have to be a child of immigrants to teach children how to excel, but, evidently, you need to not be a child of immigrants to learn how to laugh at yourself, or get a joke, or know why something you say might appear terribly funny to someone, even your husband.

The View from the Couch, January 24, 2011

An editor at NUVO *refused to run this piece, saying I couldn't write about the author without having read her book, and I told the editor (who had just been appointed to the position) it wasn't a book review, but commentary, but that did not persuade her. I stopped writing for* NUVO *at that point and put this column on my blog.*

Class Warfare

Class warfare? Here's the real deal: it's not the ninety-nine percent versus the one percent; it's the ninety percent against itself. Most of the people who talk about class warfare are missing the point. The class warfare that has the longest-running tradition in America is the railroad-robber-baron Jay Gould (1836–92) sort: "I can hire one-half of the working class to kill the other half." Today there is a lot of chatter about class warfare, most of it misdirected, since there is very little history of the working class or the middle class or the salaried class, the wage earner, the non-job creator, running wild through America's gated communities. Way back when you'll find an episode or two, but since World War II such episodes have been few and far between.

Rioters, in any case, tend to burn down their own neighborhoods, even when riots occur. Economic injustice is on display, but in the preponderance of cases it is not the cause. In the states, it's only the international organizations, the G8, etc., that inspire destruction by protestors, not just the USA's economic inequalities alone.

The kind of class warfare that has been promulgated by the rich has been the type that turns the middle class against the working class, the upper middle class against them both, internecine warfare encouraged and supported by plutocrats most everywhere.

So, during the Vietnam War era, you had hard hats beating up on antiwar protestors, and you continue to have race-based conflict between segments of the laboring classes, you have yuppie disdain for all those of bad taste, and you have private sector workers jaw-boning against public service workers.

This has been going on for a long time, but the instigators of these attacks are the rich, the millionaires who hover above them. They have deployed their troops most everywhere, in politics and the media. Today, via talk radio, you have fat plutocrats like Rush Limbaugh stirring up his salaried dittoheads, the road-weary traveling salesmen of his audience, to hate one another.

Neighbor against neighbor. Fox News is a propaganda arm of the GOP, but it also is there to keep internecine class warfare going at a fever pitch. Their gold-plated bloviators, like the buffoon Bill O'Reilly, who claim ordinary-guy credentials at the same time they pit the old versus the young, the complaining crowds of the Occupy Wall Street sort against all right-thinking Americans. The Republican Congress itself is a cauldron of class-warfare instigators.

One reason this sort of class warfare has been so successful is that, post the Vietnam War period, most all the baby boomers and succeeding generational heroes have been high-octane capitalists. Beginning with the Beatles, through Bill Gates, numerous athletes, up to and beyond Mark Zuckerberg. The death of Steve Jobs and the eulogies and tributes that have followed demonstrate this beyond reason. The beloved billionaire. Jay Gould can be heard laughing from his grave.

The View from the Couch, October 7, 2011

Keyes to the Caindom

With any luck, we are counting down to the precious few last days of Herman Cain. This huckster is coming to the end of his string of charm; the smiling salesman, non-politician-politician act will only get you so far in this world. You do need to know a thing or two. Cain, like Clarence Thomas, has profited from the affirmative action culture he decries. Justice Thomas never thought he was being accepted for his own wonderful self. Why would he have been? He needed all sorts of help to get to Holy Cross and the same sort of help to get into Yale's law school; and the help was there for his generation. But he's repaid that help with great helpings of scorn and derision. And what has Thomas done of note during his twenty years on the Court, besides being the fifth vote majority for its conservative, right-wing decisions? He is only thwarted when the Court won't go as far right as he wishes.

Cain's adoption of Thomas's troubles, his high-tech lynching rhetorical excuses (and who now thinks Thomas innocent of Anita Hill's charges?), and Cain's penchant for attracting serial sexual harassment complaints of employees and potential employees, links them both. When Gloria Allred is on the scene, standing next to some aggrieved bottle blonde, watch out. Her client's resemblance to Gennifer Flowers is fate's unique talent for irony on display yet again. But Cain's feigned ignorance and forgetfulness about what he did and when he didn't do it is more of his own particular brand of harassing the general public. There's so much Cain doesn't know and a lot of it is that he doesn't know what he doesn't know. It's a sort of Donald Rumsfeld problem; the unknown unknowns of Herman Cain are legion. He gives the equally empty-headed Rick Perry a run for his money.

The current Republican primary process has been a debacle for the entire GOP. This isn't the first time the primary period has played a critical role. A memorable one was the New York state senate primary in 1992 on the Democratic side, one that allowed Alfonse D'Amato to have one last term. But destructive primaries are usually carried out on the local level; this is the first one that has been such a disaster on the national scene.

Debates usually have open audiences, and those were often seeded with supporters of the various candidates, but these Republican primary debates appear to have only the most partisan of audiences, which brings about cheering for the death penalty, leaving the sick to die, and boos directed toward gay soldiers and even to the mere question to Cain about "character" at the most recent debate on CNBC. This is new, too, and contributes another actor (the audience) to the circus clown show atmosphere.

Alan Keyes used to be the GOP's carpetbagging candidate, traveling most anywhere (even to Illinois to run against Barack Obama for Senate), playing the same role as does Cain, to show the "big tent" (pup tent) aspect of the Republican Party. African Americans who pop up in the GOP know they are working the less busy side of the street, where the road to advancement is quicker. Keyes was strange in a creepy way; charm eluded him. His initial connection to the GOP seemed to be the fact that he had been the roommate of Bill Kristol at Harvard, but Keyes was always willing to be the black face in Republican campaigns. He has since devolved down to being an anti-abortion agitator.

Cain is the other side of that GOP coin: the glad-hander, salesman, man of the people. He does not exude the rather too rarified semi-intellectual aura of Keyes. Keyes, like Cain, ran for offices as a business proposition. It didn't cost him money; it increased his net worth. This duo is the comedy-tragedy face of the Republican Party, AA minority division. Keyes was always too weird to be comedy. I can't remember him ever cracking a joke, and I wrote a lot about him in my book on the 1996 presidential campaign. He's the tragic view of life. But Cain is comedy through and through (Princess Nancy!). I'm not sure Mitt Romney will be the last man standing after the GOP freak show primaries are done, but I'm pretty sure his veep pick won't be coming from the other men and the one woman on the debate stages he's been sharing.

And Barack Obama will be able to slide through to a second term, if those who voted for him the first time around manage to drag themselves to the voting booths in November 2012, or, at least, a sufficient percentage of them—except for Bobby Rush—Obama has been exceedingly lucky in his opponents the Republicans have dealt him. But that's a big if and remains to be seen.

The View from the Couch, November 11, 2011

Saving Social Security, Not

Pundits are celebrating President Obama's "victory" over the Republicans for forcing them to their knees and making them pass the two-month extension of the payroll tax reduction. Excuse me, but I'm not applauding. Among the many stories the media has misreported over recent decades, Social Security is one of the most egregious examples. Journalists don't seem to understand the program until they start collecting payments from it in their sixties. Even calling the monies going into the program a "payroll tax" is misleading. They are premiums, since Social Security is an insurance program.

It is actually called the Old-Age, Survivors, and Disability Insurance Program. So, you may call them taxes, but they are premiums. Do you want to stop paying your fire, car, life insurance premiums?

That has been one of the right-wing complaints that they have successfully inserted into the pubic "debate" about Social Security: that when you die you can't leave "what's left" to your heirs. Of course, even that is a lie, since the surviving spouse gets her/his benefits raised if the dead spouses were higher; and minor children receive benefits. Nonetheless, since Social Security is an insurance program those who benefit the most are those who live the longest. Indeed, if you live into your nineties, Social Security pays off big; it is, more or less, an annuity, and the longer you live the longer (and larger) is your benefit. Insurance is usually a bet, because no one knows how long they'll live.

The anti–Social Security privatizers have spread so much misinformation about the program over the last three decades that it is no surprise so many people are confused. And the press has been of little help. The GOP is, of course, the worst offender; George W. Bush called the bonds issued to cover the Social Security surplus over the years worthless. This is the crux of the problem for both sides.

On one hand, Social Security takes in more than it puts out; it has for years. Now the yearly surplus is less, but it remains (recently so many jobless have retired "early" that there was a small dip, but now there is a surplus again). And the trust fund is stuffed with money from all the years of large surpluses; one hears, correctly, that if nothing is done to grow Social Security, it will be able to pay 75 percent of benefits indefinitely, beyond 2035.

But politicians, especially Republicans, don't consider the Social Security trust fund, the larger accumulated surplus (over $20 trillion), a surplus; they consider it debt, because it has been spent: given to Wall Street and the military-industrial complex, mainly. We arrive at the sad irony that America's working stiffs have been paying the bonuses for all the investment bankers over the years, as well as for our wars in Iraq and Afghanistan that President Bush kept off the books.

And now, we have the sad, smaller irony that the American workers are funding the Obama administration's tiny stimulus program, the lowering of the "payroll tax" (and for employers, too!). We paycheck workers are giving ourselves the puny amounts each month that Obama takes credit for.

And this is what is worse. Everyone is used to the Republicans trying to damage Social Security. But it is the Democrats who need to be watched. They like this "tax" break because it is so "efficient." No need to cut checks, start a program. Just reduce the amount coming in, and, voilà, money in everyone's pocket. Of course, it is their own money, which is being taken out of their insurance system and will eventually have to be put back—but at what cost? More federal workers furloughed? More Medicaid cuts?

It was too tempting for the Democratic suits in Washington, all that efficiency. They consider it a version of domestic realpolitik. Their chipping away at the system allows other attacks to wiggle in. They've given Social Security one fatal attribute of the touted 401(k) "retirement" program. It can be raided, gotten to when "emergencies" arise, which is why, among other reasons, so many 401(k)s have such small amounts in them at retirement.

Once the Democrats decided to lower the Social Security payroll tax, a thing the Republicans proposed long ago in order to weaken it, they opened up Pandora's box to other changes. Watch President Obama, even when, as it is likely, he wins a second term, go along with raising the retirement age, without raising the cap on the richest Americans' contributions; he'll be applauded by his Wall Street backers.

But, again, the chief irony is that working Americans have been funding the bubble spending, the wars and the bonuses, as George W. Bush merrily spent the Social Security trust fund surplus. Now everyone bemoans the deficit and wants to have the people, the workers, who contributed the cash for the bubble, take the hit and change Social Security so they will be paid back less, take the haircut that the Wall Streeters have avoided, all the while giving themselves a Christmas tax break, while the rich continue to give nothing, nothing at all.

The View from the Couch, December 24, 2011

A shorter version of this article ran in the South Bend Tribune, *January 8, 2012, under the title "Pandora's Box Opened on Social Security."*

Not Saving Social Security, Again (an Update)

The Republicans, once again, have "caved" on allowing the extension of the payroll tax reduction—if you consider furthering their anti–Social Security strategy an act of caving. I have been writing about Social Security on and off for over twenty years, but the subject bears repeating.

Social Security, or the Old-Age, Survivors, and Disability Insurance Program, is just that, insurance, in which the American public pays premiums. The system works, since there are different outcomes for different people. It needs to be a pool of most everyone to insure a basic floor for everyone.

A curious shell game is being played by the anti–Social Security forces: they have convinced most journalists that Social Security is supposed to be a "pay-as-you-go" system. It is actually a transfer system, where one generation transfers wealth to the next. Social Security wasn't pay as you go at its beginning, nor has it been for the modern period, though it might have to be someday if Congress doesn't step up. There wouldn't be a trust fund surplus nearing $3 trillion if it was, or had been, a pay-as-you-go system. But the fact that Social Security has taken in for years more than it has put out has somehow been ignored, made meaningless. It's the new GOP mantra: keep saying it until people believe it.

Although the yearly surplus is less, it still remains—because of the interest paid on Social Security's total income, according to the Social Security Media Watch Project. If the unemployment rate were cut in half, one wouldn't even have to count the interest to see a yearly surplus.

But the shell game of now-you-see-the-surplus-now-you-don't in the media continues. Journalists at both the *Washington Post* and the *Kansas City Star* have swallowed the sugar water that it doesn't really exist. In the *Post*, Lori Montgomery wrote in October, "The 2.6 trillion Social Security trust fund will provide little relief," and E. Thomas McClanahan, on the *Star*'s editorial board, claimed recently, "The payroll tax holiday is also destroying the myth of the trust fund." Such remarks have now become the chief talking point of the anti–Social Security forces. Of course, they don't say what I've said: we've stolen the payroll "tax" surplus over the years to fund the one percent.

The View from the Couch, February 16, 2012

The Superfluity of Iowa

As I wrote in *Campaign America '96: The View from the Couch*, the quadrennial election cycle is a WPA project for the upper end of intellectual workers: TV in all its forms, along with printers, newspapers, and their attendant personnel, all profit from the cash that Super PACs, and the candidates, lavish on the local media of various primary states, as well as from the millions that will be spent on the national election itself. So who would want to put a stop to it? Certainly not the chattering classes, which gain so much from it. But Iowa does strain one's credulity as being necessary to the political process.

Who cares about what the hundred thousand or so Iowans think about the candidates in question: in the case of 2012, the sorry group of Republicans vying for the nomination?

I'm certainly not the first or last to raise that question; this year it has already been batted around quite a bit. But it has provided a lot of fodder for discussion during the dull period between Christmas, New Year's, and, what, Valentine's Day? Look at Romney, who gets the same number of votes as he did in 2008 when he lost to the formerly obese former governor of Arkansas, now Fox News commentator, Mike Huckabee. Romney, the twenty-five percenter. Same as Rick Santorum, more or less, the pol who will protect us all from bestiality, though he's the senator who lost his last race in the great state of Pennsylvania by over 15 percent. And Ron Paul, who is hardly a Republican, though he votes with its caucus, since he is so much a Libertarian, of the old school sort, crazy as a loon, who somehow still lures the most gullible young, with his promises of legal drugs and no war.

Thus far, Iowa has shown us nothing has changed; the only thing all the lavished attention accomplished was the jettisoning of Michele Bachmann, the native-born Iowan who now brings so much pride and honor to the state of Minnesota. Rick Perry (aka Governor Fairy in some circles) now pledges to continue to stumble on, providing low comedy and high jinks wherever he goes.

But, given the general uselessness of Iowa, a place where, when Chris Matthews asked where he was on his own MSNBC *Hardball* and was told Des Moines, he indicated what he had meant was where, actually, was Des Moines located in the state, and when he was told, "somewhat in the middle," he offered up the excuse that he had flown into an airport and who would know, etc.—the meaning of flyover states came, once again, sharply into focus. Yet Iowa did play a most critical role in recent American presidential history. I haven't heard anyone mention it, though, doubtless, someone, somewhere, has. Certainly, when it comes to the GOP, Iowa is an empty hole, sound and fury signifying not much at all. But, when it comes to Democrats, Iowa changed history in 2008.

Iowa proved one thing: white people (aka Iowa) would vote for Barack Obama. That was its signal service to the commonwealth in 2008. And after Obama won Iowa (amassing nearly one hundred thousand votes in the caucuses), the red sea of racism was temporarily separated and the chosen people rushed through and managed to elect Obama to the presidency. I guess that's enough reason for the East Coast media to continue to dump so much money on Iowa and Iowans every four years. They're owed.

The View from the Couch, January 4, 2012

The First Lady's Lack of Firsts

Because of a new book, called *The Obamas*, a volume mainly about Michelle, the First Lady, there will be a lot of attention paid to her role in the White House, and I've decided to write publicly what I have been saying privately for the last year or so, before all is lost in the deluge of print to come. The *New York Times* ran an excerpt from the book on Saturday—its author is one of its reporters, based in Washington (this is what is called being well placed), and reviews are just starting to appear.

One reason I haven't written about this before is that it is a sensitive subject, and I was waiting for some woman to write about it. Coincidentally, or not, the new book is by a woman, Jodi Kantor. Why be a critic, or critical of, the First Lady? I have enough problems. Well, in any case, what I was being critical of is the Obama administration, through the public persona it has created for Michelle Obama.

It is as if the ascendancy of a black American as president was enough of a breakthrough that anything else would be superfluous. And the last Democrat in the White House, Bill Clinton, had the experience of putting his wife front and center (better to keep her busy, doubtless) and that didn't work out too well (see Hillarycare). The times had changed; boy, have they.

Yet, in the White House, it's been the 1950s for the First Lady. Her first big splash was her garden; it began in March of 2009. For months they (the press and the image makers in the White House) turned Michelle into a field hand. If I saw one picture with her posing with a yam in her hand, I saw a thousand. Of course, she was a more fashionable gardener than Martha Stewart, when it came to what she wore. But her first public image was field hand, the second image was clotheshorse, and her third large public project was to scold fat people.

Now all of this has a purpose and isn't necessarily venal, but it is so retrograde I was waiting for some feminist to point it out. But I didn't see one do so. Not that that means no one did. But Michelle Obama, one must remember, was a corporate lawyer, one that was asked to show the new guy, Barack Obama, the ropes when he joined the firm she worked for; when Obama finally won election to the Illinois State Senate she began to get even more gainful employment in the upper corporate management world.

But for the U.S. Senate and the presidency she has been turned back into housewife, become a most traditional First Lady. Fine. But what it shows and highlights is all the other turnabouts for the Obama administration—its (and his) tendency toward living high on the hog, palling around with the upper ups. Barack Obama successfully hid a number of things before he was elected president; had I known he was so fond of golf I would have been even more skeptical at the time than I was.

As I have written elsewhere, Barack marrying Michelle was, for Obama, a political decision in the same way Bill Clinton marrying Hillary was. Clinton knew he couldn't marry one of the bimbos he frequented if he wanted to be taken seriously as a politician. He had to marry someone serious like Hillary. Barack Obama faced the same sort of political choice.

Miraculous as Obama's election was for a boy from a half-Kansas and half-Kenya background, the first modern president-to-be whose father hadn't been born in the "new world," he would never have been elected senator, much less president, if he had married a white wife. But nothing said that after he was elected president he had to make his wife into a field hand, clotheshorse, or scold of fat people. But, Obama, the great conciliator, evidently didn't want to make any more waves than necessary, and certainly neither did all those "progressive" Chicago pols he brought with him into the White House, some of whom are gone, some of whom are still there. Luckily for him, the Republicans he opposes are so puerile he doesn't have to be exactly pure. But, please, no more yams.

The View from the Couch, January 9, 2012

Dr. Gingrich and Mr. Chucky

Now, we're done with New Hampshire. The interesting development is the blowback criticism of Newt Gingrich toward the predatory capitalist, Mitt Romney, echoed momentarily by the national nonentity, Rick Perry. Newt made a mockery (and a web address) of Mitt's "pious baloney," describing how Romney has been a financial firm show horse candidate since the early 1990s, not the "job creator" he poses as. And, more pertinently, Newt went after Bain Capital, Romney's never-ending private equity piggy bank, via his Super PAC, Winning Our Future, funded by the usual and strange FON, a tax-exempt fundraising dodge, backed by a casino-owning big better. Newt talks about Bain Capital "looting" companies, adding a laundry list of the usual corporate malfeasance.

It's been effective. Too effective for the GOP and Gingrich is under considerable pressure to walk back all his criticism. I'll wait to see if the half-hour *60 Minute*–like take down of Bain actually runs anywhere. Thirty-second commercials have thus far, but, again, the question is, Will they continue?

Walking back will be nothing new to Newt. He did so shortly after, rightly, condemning Paul Ryan's gut Medicare program as "right-wing social engineering." Later, he said anyone using the film of him saying so would be uttering a "falsehood," since he was now unsaying so. But this larger change in rhetoric came before Newt's appearance on *Meet the Press* back in May charging right-wing social engineering. I suppose one must credit Frank Luntz, or one of his Republican clones. Beginning in 2011 (and perhaps earlier), Republicans started appropriating the language of progressives: so one heard Sarah Palin (remember her?) denouncing "crony capitalism"; and other Republicans were whining about the evils of "class warfare."

The logic seemed to be: if you use the other side's words often enough eventually you will make the words meaningless. Since the GOP has been making words meaningless for years, it seems to be a long-term strategy. I'm not sure Luntz got everyone in the Republican fold to switch out "the rich" for "job creators," but you won't find the phrase *job creators* used much before 2011.

But Gingrich, et al., took the word-appropriation business a bit too far, since he was making whole sentences of them, not just phrases and sound bites. Mitt Romney has been speaking nothing but sound bites, pious baloney, as Newt pointed out.

Only when Romney goes rogue, speaks for himself, as he did last weekend, saying, "I like being able to fire people..."—it didn't matter, as he claimed, the words were taken out of "context," because Romney said them with such obvious sincerity—does his true self shine through. Romney may well win the Republican nomination, though, given his background as the former head of a predatory investment firm (private equity), it remains as improbable, given recent history, as someone with the middle name Hussein becoming the nominee of the Democrats in 2008.

Gingrich, though, will continue his usual Jekyll and Hyde performance; but I'm hoping, to update the analogy, that he lets his Chucky side come blazing through, rather than his professorial Dr. Gingrich side, creating mayhem all the while he continues to debase our poor, battered, language pell-mell.

The View from the Couch, January 11, 2012

Our Postsatirical Primaries

One thing is clear: Newt Gingrich is not running as Ronald Reagan, but as Margaret Thatcher, at least the Thatcher caricatured by *Spitting Image*, the Brit satirical television show, circa 1984. Gingrich has often been lampooned as a puppet, one in particular, the malevolent horror-film character Chucky, but *Spitting Image*'s Thatcher seems the more pertinent choice.

Watching the new film, *The Iron Lady*, where Thatcher is portrayed magnificently by Meryl Streep, it was startling how many of Thatcher's speeches of the 1980s sounded like Gingrich's recent ones: get those children off their duffs and give them a broom! All that sort of bootstrap rhetoric Thatcher favored: let everyone pay the same tax, rich and poor alike, which will end the terrible graffiti in the council house neighborhoods, etc.

The two recent films about twentieth-century historic figures, the UK's Thatcher and our own J. Edgar Hoover, are, oddly, both love stories. That might not be strange for Hollywood films (though *The Iron Lady* has a lot of British support—even, evidently, money from the UK's public arts program. Thatcher would be spinning in her grave, if she were in a grave).

Both films have the star power of famous American actors in the namesake roles, and both Streep and Leonardo DiCaprio give more warm human interest to their subjects than either of the individuals possessed. They make both figures somewhat lovable, not a quality either had, or projected, in their public roles.

But love stories both films are: Thatcher and her husband, Dennis, and J. Edgar and Clyde Tolson, whatever Tolson could be called, husband, confidant, bromance boy. During the Harrisburg Seven trial in 1972, Hoover's visage kept reminding me of a line from a popular song of the period ("MacArthur Park"): "Someone left the cake out in the rain." That's what Hoover looked like back then. DiCaprio's makeup in *J. Edgar* isn't up to the quality of Streep's; indeed, DiCaprio, however he ages, still looks like a little boy in all his roles, and, for Hoover, it is a strange look indeed.

Back in 1972 Clyde Tolson and Hoover's relationship wasn't commonly known; journalists were more discreet then, at least nationally. You had to be in the know. Now everyone's in the know. When I watched *The Iron Lady* in a midwestern Cineplex only six people were in the theater; even if Streep wins an Oscar for her performance, the film will still be a hard sell for Americans. You really need to know a lot about the history of the period to keep anything straight (though that is true even for *J. Edgar*), and even if you know—and I do: my novel *Notts* is about the Thatcher-era NUM coal-mining strike—it remains confusing in the film.

But history is always confusing, I suppose. We'll have to ask our historian-in-chief candidate, Newt Gingrich. Less confusing if you say everything, as Newt does, with such conviction and bravado. The less conviction one has, the easier it is to sound absolutely certain. Like most serial adulterers, Newt shows signs of being a pathological liar, one well practiced.

One historical comparison that offers itself is that Newt is playing J. Edgar to Mitt Romney's Clyde Tolson. Gingrich is the huffer and puffer, a la Hoover, out front, hogging the limelight, while Romney remains the tall, handsome figure in the shadows, looking confused.

Because of the unprecedented number of debates and the compressed onslaught of caucuses and primaries, the Republican primary season has elevated all its participants to the realm of the grotesque. (Just name those who have dropped out and you can see what stalwarts in that regard even the B team was.) So, it is fitting that the most grotesque figure of them all, Newt Gingrich, is now the Republican frontrunner. Spitting Image, indeed. He's a Hogarth etching in the flesh, but, it doesn't much matter, since we are now all living in a postsatirical age.

Huffington Post, January 25, 2012

I had become a contributor for the Huffington Post, *still unable to curb my addiction, though I continued to also put the columns on my own blog. The* Huffington Post's *"blog team" told me that was "no problem."*

A Primary History Primer

Let me be blunt: when Republicans run against an incumbent Democrat president, they usually choose a damaged war veteran as their candidate. The 1996 election set the pattern: Bob Dole versus Bill Clinton. (A less caustic analysis is that they pick someone who has run before in primaries and lost. It was Dole's turn, given that logic.)

The secondary GOP default for picking a nominee is to hand it over to whichever suitable patrician is available, one preferably with strong political family connections. In 2000 that was George W. Bush, who, though absent of most of his father's abilities, had one large advantage his father lacked: his six-pack ordinariness, his common man touch. It proved to be the right cultural mix for the times, even though Al Gore won the popular vote and had the election stolen out from under him by the Supreme Court.

The Democrats in 2004 threw up their own patrician, John Kerry, also a war vet, perhaps damaged, at least by the Swift Boat forces. Then, in 2008, Barack Obama continued his run of electoral luck and the Republicans broke their pattern and nominated John McCain, yet another damaged war veteran, someone born to lose.

Among McCain's problems was that the conflict that damaged him was the Vietnam War. It was a war no one wanted to revisit. Indeed, when Dole ran in 1996, it was at the height of the Greatest Generation craze. Dole profited from that, but nothing else. The Vietnam War in the 2008 primaries was shouldered by Hillary Clinton and, finally, Democrats turned away from Hillary and it: it was the war her husband, Bill, had managed to avoid. One reason Barack Obama won the nomination is that the electorate was tired of both the Vietnam War and the Clintons.

Obama represented the future. Boy, the public was thirsting for the future, to put behind them the Bush family, the Iraq and Afghanistan wars, the Wall Street meltdown. They wanted to turn the page and no page was more different than Barack Obama. But when they finally read the page, it turned out to be the same old, same old.

Now, in 2012, we have a GOP with a unappetizing choice, devoid of damaged war vets; in fact, there are two chicken hawks available, with no more military service between them than Bill Clinton had: both Romney and Newt Gingrich had deferments from the draft, and when the lottery was inaugurated, Romney drew a high number. By that time, Gingrich had children from his marriage to his former history teacher.

Everyone, though, of the appropriate generation, has been damaged one way or another by the Vietnam War. Only Ron Paul, ancient as he is, brings up Romney's and Gingrich's lack of service, since he served in the air force from 1963 to 1968 as a medical officer. It is nothing short of amazing to listen to Ron Paul take on (in his "victory" speech after his fourth place finish in the Florida primary) the mantle of the only antiwar candidate in the field, both Democrat and Republican. Apparently, it is one of the major things that attracts the young to his candidacy.

After Florida, it appears to one and all to be a "two man" race. Romney, like George W., is assuming the role of the patrician candidate, son of George Romney, born in Mexico, but a future presidential wannabe (the birthers were a generation late; but John McCain had the same problem, since he was born in the Panama Canal Zone), a governor of Michigan, and a member of the Nixon cabinet.

Gingrich will continue to be a pest, though it is not out of the world of probability to imagine a Romney/Gingrich ticket, if only to "bind" the splintered party together.

But, and this is a large but, Mitt Romney has one positive precedent hidden in his history that may ultimately benefit him. Romney personifies everything associated with Wall Street and the beleaguered one percent. He is the person who represents the 2008 meltdown, the cause of wealth disappearing everywhere (except into Swiss accounts and banks in the Cayman Islands), the reason the Troubled Asset Relief Program (TARP) and both the Bush and Obama administration spent the people's money to bail out the too-big-to-fail financial industry.

One would think someone who represents to a tee everything the majority of Americans finds reprehensible in recent history could not win the presidency a mere four years after the crash and the start of the Great Recession.

Yes, one might think that. But here is the counter example: What would be the odds that seven years after 9/11 a man with the middle name Hussein would be elected president of the United States? A trillion to one? That is the precedent that Romney may be counting on. That the voters of America will do something totally unexpected and then suffer their bitter disappointment later, silently or not so silently, given their past precedents.

Huffington Post, February 1, 2012

Halftime in Pink America

The Super Bowl was, well, super. The game had its moments: the first "free" touchdown in the big game that was, supposedly, not meant to happen (but once a running back turns around in a sitting position on the goal line, he's only gonna fall in backward, pushed by all the momentum he already generated) and Tom Brady's last-second Hail Mary pass that was almost caught by a Patriot, but not quite. (The Giants won, 21-17.)

But there were other Hail Marys thrown that night. First there was Madonna, the original Hail Mary, her namesake that is. The present earth-bound Madonna, all fifty-three years of her, did the cougar world proud. All those hours working out over the years paying off big. Now there was a production! Those folk know how to put on a show. I kept wondering how many of its participants were in the Actors Equity union, but it was abundantly clear this sort of spectacle has replaced the Broadway musical in the hearts of the younger generation, used to these sorts of extravaganzas at the concerts of pop singers for at least two decades now.

Madonna's performance might have been aimed at her faux protégé, Lady Gaga, showing Gaga who's who and what's what. But there were also echoes of other, older grand dames, for instance, Elizabeth Taylor in *Cleopatra*, given all the beefcake "slaves" supposedly hauling Madonna onto the Lucas Oil field's fifty yard line. After the Material Girl's exhortation of capitalism unbound, she signed off with World Peace. Ho, ho, ho.

But it was another halftime performance that seems to have more legs: Clint Eastwood and his Chrysler commercial. It was instantaneously clear that it would be taken as an Obama endorsement. From Chrysler, which we, the people, more or less, still own. But, what struck me was that this commercial may be the first time the word *halftime* was used, or understood, politically to stand for a second term presidential election.

While writing *Campaign America '96*, which covered how the campaign was covered, I don't recall any of the hundreds of commentators I heard ever use the term *halftime* that way, meaning the pause between a possible two terms for a sitting president. But its usage was unmistakable in the Eastwood commercial.

Which is why Republicans are complaining. But, it's been another bad week for the GOP, because of yet more Hail Marys: the Susan G. Komen for the Cure pink ribbon flap, defunding Planned Parenthood and, consequently, the women of

America reacting and Komen's decision eventually reversed. This, too, was a commercial of sorts, but one aimed at Mitt Romney, not Barack Obama. The Komen "charity" had managed all these years to avoid scrutiny the way anyone not running for president avoids scrutiny.

But defunding Planned Parenthood put Komen in the election season spotlight and what was seen was not very pleasant. It was like seeing Mitt Romney's 2010 and the "summary" of his 2011 taxes: all those Swiss and Cayman accounts. In Komen's case, it was the ratio of what was raised yearly and what was given to breast cancer research, roughly 20 percent, while around 80 percent went into the fundraising itself. It was the same, it appeared, as the salaries and bonuses of the one percent, because the Komen foundation was run like any Wall Street hedge fund. The lion's share in expenses, a pittance for the disease in question. Komen is certainly a job creator, since it does employ a lot of lawyers suing people who want to use the word *cure* in their fundraising.

Those who were paying attention learned more about the Komen foundation in the last ten days than they ever knew the last ten years, and what they had known was next to nothing: how Republican it was, how its new, and now resigned vice president, Karen Handel, was a GOP-losing candidate running for governor in Georgia, like Romney is currently doing, on the I hate Planned Parenthood GOP platform.

Karen Handel carries on the GOP tradition of calling black white when she said, in her resignation letter, "no one's political beliefs" were involved in Komen's decision to defund Planned Parenthood. This is all an election period neurosis, an emperor's new clothes phenomenon. The naked truth is clothed. What everyone can see is false I will claim as true.

But back to the Super Bowl: Madonna said there would be no "wardrobe malfunction" in her show. Maybe not, though that malfunction had to do with a breast, and, thanks to the Komen foundation and Karen Handel, the malfunctions have been many and frequent, and now the Komen world stands as naked and exposed as poor Mitt Romney.

Huffington Post, February 8, 2012

Contraception Wars and Woes

I share at least one attribute of the U.S. Conference of Catholic Bishops, now at war with the Obama administration: I don't want to talk about contraception, either.

I've taught for over three decades at the university that some characterize as the place where the American Catholic Church "does its thinking." Well, here are some thoughts on the matter. The first is the one above: the Catholic bishops are really put out, miffed, because they don't want to talk about contraception, but the Obama administration, allegedly, has forced their hands.

The bishops don't mind talking about abortion. They find some purchase on that topic, some sympathy with the larger American public, along with a good many of the "faithful." Indeed, most everyone wants the number of abortions decreased to as close to zero as possible. But a debate over contraception puts the bishops in another place altogether.

Had the Obama administration announced their "compromise" first, rather than second, after a bit of clerical harrumphing, the issue may have left the public square and gone away. Indeed, more than half the states, as it has been pointed out, already have similar mandates, and Catholic universities and hospitals have been dispensing "birth control" for a variety of reasons for many years.

It's not clear whether the Obama administration took this strategy—getting the bishops all exercised—deliberately, or accidentally, by mishandling the policy rollout. Regardless, it's out there now. The bishops don't want to talk about contraception, because it puts a spotlight on one of the Church's least defensible, and most paradoxical, strictures.

Oh, it can be defended alright: as a matter of faith. A show of loyalty demanded of the flock, an act of hazing and abnegation, aka sacrifice. My generation wasn't to eat meat on Fridays, though this dietary no-no eventually just went away. But religions require this sort of thing on the part of their co-religionists; the secular version pops up in the news now and then when fraternity members die because their hazing rituals become too intense.

And speaking against contraception in the twenty-first century makes the bishops look anti-science. Catholics are not anti-science, though a number of their evangelical supporters certainly are. It puts Catholics in a crowd that they don't necessarily want to be in: all those anti-evolutionary troglodytes scraping their knuckles on the ground, the we-don't-descend-from-apes crowd.

Whenever the word *abortifacient* is uttered, the attack-on-science banner is raised. We're down to molecules and biochemistry at that point. But it is an attempt to drag contraception onto safer ground, or, at least, ground they have captured, the well-tilled anti-abortion fields.

But another important, but hardly mentioned, reason the bishops don't want to talk about contraception is it makes them talk about themselves, which highlights, in the starkest ways, the all-male hierarchy of the Catholic Church and its women problem. The control of women. And the bishops don't want to get into any of that, since it is obvious to all that a totally male clergy, burdened with a vow of celibacy, wants its parishioners to be like them, mostly celibate, however preposterous that sounds today. Abortion, however, lets the bishops talk about two people, one of whom might be male.

The pro-abortion movement has been saddled with an all-too-focused name. It's actually a pro-woman movement, insofar as it was always women who took the lead to change the laws of the land. The pro-"life" anti-abortion movement began as a male-dominated movement, and male figures are featured most prominently still. You should have seen the odious figures who showed up at Notre Dame when President Obama's commencement speech was announced: Alan Keyes and Randall Terry, grubbing for attention (which they got).

Since the early 1970s and the passage of *Roe v. Wade* the term Catholic Right has been more or less coined. Back when I originally published *The Harrisburg 7 and the New Catholic Left* what was new was the Catholic Left. There had been the old Dorothy Day Catholic Left, but the antiwar priests and nuns of the Vietnam period were the new Left.

They were in opposition to the bishops back then, too; but the Catholic Church wasn't thought of as "the Right" back then. The bishops were, of course, that, but then there was no need for labels. But over the decades a Catholic Right was created, or, rather, more pertinently, a religious right was hatched, to try to ecumenically turn back the progressive impulses that reared their multiple heads throughout the period. The Catholic bishops being the repository of authority does not go unchallenged, as Gary Gutting effectively points out ("Birth Control, Bishops and Religious Authority," *New York Times*, February 15, 2012).

Natural law, of course, is full of contraception. Garry Wills goes into the theological background of "natural law" ("Contraception's Con Men," *New York Review of Books*, February 15, 2012), but I prefer a more pragmatic approach:

fertilized eggs are lost in the thousands, if not millions, worldwide by couples trying to get pregnant. (There is always a poignancy in the case of couples trying to get pregnant and the majority who are trying to avoid it, or those who become pregnant at the drop of a hat.) And natural law also includes the ever-present, it seems, tried-and-true, centuries old, methods of birth control that include famine, pestilence, natural disasters; and, in place of abortion, we have infanticide. You see where all this sort of logic can lead.

Catholics have wrestled with contraception and the Church's teachings on it over the decades, generation by generation. The younger generation seems to be wrestling less, given the advances in the methods of contraception now available. Forbidding contraception kept the pews and classrooms full; the self-serving aspect of the prohibition is hard to deny. One of my sisters (I'm from a family of eight children) got birth control pills back in the 1960s when the doses involved would choke a horse (or, at least, make a horse infertile), because of her "irregular" periods, before she went off to a nunnery for a couple of years.

My mother, at the same time, had three painful, late miscarriages in a row, after having her eighth child, when a friendly priest finally permitted her to use birth control, saying she had brought enough Catholic children into the world. Such stories of my mother's generation are legion—and often heartrending.

But, enough. Religion may no longer be the opiate of the people, but it is certainly the father—not the mother—of all political wedge issues.

Huffington Post, February 24, 2012

Barney Rosset U.

Upon his recent death, I realized I had matriculated in the Barney Rosset School of Literature, or, more correctly (since I didn't know who Barney Rosset was when I started), the Grove Press University of the Arts. I also went on to graduate school at New Directions U., founded by James Laughlin. I didn't know him, either, back then, in my teens and early twenties.

There's been a lot of bemoaning over the decades of how badly students are being educated, how little they know. Leave Most Everybody Behind, etc., has been the general rule. Since I came along at the predawn of the baby boomers, in 1945, my generation benefitted enormously from the paperback revolution that was underway. Why? Not just because of the cheapness of paperbacks, which took hold via the military, since they were distributed to World War II soldiers, but because of the authors they published. It wasn't altruism, even in the case of Barney Rosset; it was because the great authors, or Dead White Males of yore, were out of print, not afflicted by copyright, and the publishers didn't have to deal with even the minimum problem of royalties.

So, who did my generation get to read? What were the mass paperback books filling up newsstand racks (not the snooty "trade" paperbacks of today)? Oh, Tolstoy, Dostoevsky, Shakespeare, Homer, Balzac, Victor Hugo, those guys. And cheap. Less than a buck. The first book Barney Rosset published at Grove Press was Henry James's *The Golden Bowl*. That cost more than a dollar.

Try to find any of the above at an airport bookstore these days. And people wonder why everyone has gotten more stupid over the years. Take a look at the dates when the SAT scores turned downward. By 1972 the shelves began to be full of other sorts of books.

Publishers played a unique role for the 1960s decade—and some of the '70s. They set the curriculum for a generation of curious and avaricious readers such as myself. It might all be called pornography now, but Rosset brought me D. H. Lawrence's *Lady Chatterley's Lover* in the midsixties, which, of course, led me to other Lawrence titles. Rosset made available to my cohort almost the entire reading list of modernism, even as it swerved toward postmodernism. And it wasn't just international. He championed Henry Miller, became the publisher of the sexual revolution of the time, literary division, and made a lot of young people eager readers. Now they have, alas, Harry Potter.

Grove Press led me to New Directions, which carried on the same tradition, though more thoroughly continental, Sartre, etc., but also the new expatriate American generation, Paul Bowles and his crowd, along with Tennessee Williams, authors who filled the list of doctoral dissertations to come and come.

When I got older and more established, I met an early Grove Press author, the world-class translator Anthony Kerrigan, who introduced Borges to the English-speaking world, or, certainly, to Americans, with the publication by Grove Press of *Ficciones* in 1962. Tony told me Barney Rosset had asked him whether he wanted royalties or cash now, a "for hire" contract, for his translations. Kerrigan, being of the older generation of writer/bohemian, took the cash up-front. If he had waited for royalties, instead, he would have had an annuity for life—and he sorely needed one, which he didn't have.

Of course, this super tutorial that two publishing houses carried out for so many students and writers-to-be didn't last forever. But, it certainly helped fuel a good bit of what has become to be known as "the sixties." Yet when you're filling a void, it sooner or later is no longer a void. Now it's a matter of oversupply. Publishers today are no longer playing that guiding role.

Now, with Amazon and other outlets, any book ever published is available for purchase. But when you can have everything, there is often no way to choose anything. Or too many ways. It was limitation, back in the sixties, that had power. Grove Press and New Directions opened the literary world's doors for me and many others. Now there are nothing but doors open and, alas, very little (or far too much) awaits beyond them.

Huffington Post, March 5, 2012

Oh, Rush, Poor Rush

Rush Limbaugh, as far back as 1989, named his fans "dittoheads," though he is the chief dittohead himself. I've been listening to Limbaugh since 1996, when he played a role in a book I was writing, *Campaign America '96*. Happily, when I finished the book, I didn't have to listen to him anymore and I stopped, except, occasionally over the years, when I turned him on while driving through NPR-deprived areas of the country, where the only thing you could find were evangelical programs or Rush. None of my cars had the new satellite connections, where all stations are possible.

I am an absolute free-speech advocate for a variety of reasons. Though there are many people I would like to be able to shut up, let them all blather on is my attitude and that includes Rush. The transactions here are complicated. I grew up with George Carlin's "Seven Dirty Words" you couldn't say on the radio, much less on TV. In 1978 the Supreme Court decided *FCC v. Pacifica Foundation* in favor of censorship (aka regulation) in a 5-4 decision. Sound familiar? Five-four is the current far-right censoring vote on the Roberts Court.

Now it's Erectile Dysfunction ads on all the channels and what is on cable is anyone's delight or cause for dismay. OK, back to Rush. After my campaign book appeared I was on the Michael Feldman show, *Whad'Ya Know?* Feldman, a funny guy, was miffed I seemed sympathetic at times to Rush (and not to him, a misreading), and I replied, "I have a soft spot for overweight overachievers." Feldman shot back, "Oh, and not underweight underachievers?" Feldman is skinny. Rush, of course, is a big fat pig.

The young Rush had been the underachiever of a substantial mid-Missouri family, the almost ne'er-do-well son with successful siblings. Rush's biggest job back then was working PR for the Kansas City Royals. He was one bloated bumpkin. Then he got on the radio and found his fortune and his shtick: finally an overachiever! When I caught up with him in 1996 he was close to the zenith of his influence. Bill Clinton had energized him, along with Newt Gingrich, the Contract with America, etc., the first rising of the New Republican Party, the one that has now reached its apotheosis in 2012.

By the time I was on the Feldman show in 2000 Rush had gone into eclipse and, as I told my host, that was cyclical: Rush would wax and wane. The waning included his drug scandal in 2003. A number of media figures have survived these lifestyle scandals (such as Bill O'Reilly), and Rush did too. His subsequent hearing problems seemed punishment enough to the general public. Now he's been waxing again, during these crackpot months of the Republican primaries. But once again he's gone too far.

Or so many think. I'm not for silencing people. Let Rush say what he wants. Let the people see it, hear it—judge it. Rush is listened to, mainly, by white guys who drive a lot, salesmen, truck drivers, God knows who? (And God and the ratings people *do* know.) Dittoheads. When Rush's current victim, Sandra Fluke, expressed surprise that it seemed "acceptable in today's society to say these things about women," one wonders where she's been the last twenty years.

Rush was doing his best to be clever, lecturing the "feminazis" (one of his earliest coinages which he employed during his current remarks) on the notion that free contraception was payment for having sex and he used the words *slut* and *prostitute* to insult Ms. Fluke. (Then he continued, really letting his id out, imagining videos on YouTube.) What struck me, hearing reports on what he said (I, thankfully, was not listening to Rush) was that was just what many others were calling sexually active women lately, given the debate over contraception waged by the Conference of Catholic Bishops, Virginia lawmakers, and the Republican candidates, especially Rick Santorum. Or, at least, what was implied, the unspoken words that traveled under the conversation, not above, except in the case of Limbaugh. Again, let free speech reign, let us hear what they really think.

The last First Amendment case I wrote about (in *The Nation* and elsewhere) was *Barnes v. Glen Theatre*, which was about go-go dancers in strip bars claiming that their dancing should be granted protection as speech. I agreed, but not the Rehnquist Court, which, in 1991, decided 5-4 (again!) in favor of police power, rather than artistic expression. Rehnquist wrote the majority opinion, but the swing vote then was Justice Souter, who held that Indiana's (the case started in South Bend, of all places) statute helped prevent secondary effects, such as prostitution. Souter was more or less calling the dancers prostitutes, not to say sluts. That was the implication. Since Ms. Fluke is a law student at Georgetown she should look up the case. If only one of the dancers had ended her routine making the Black Power fist, the Court would have been stymied.

Just as the public has profited from seeing the slapstick show of the Republican primary candidates, it actually helps to see what men like Rush Limbaugh actually think—when he can be said to think. Sunlight is still the best disinfectant.

Huffington Post, March 9, 2012

The Oak Ridge Three

Last year, in April, 2012, there was a weekend event in Harrisburg, Pennsylvania, commemorating the fortieth anniversary of the trial of the Harrisburg Seven, which had ended in 1972, with a hung jury on the major counts—conspiring to kidnap Henry Kissinger and blow up heating tunnels in Washington, DC—and convictions on minor contraband counts, smuggling letters in and out of a federal prison in Lewisburg, Pennsylvania. The Harrisburg trial became the capstone of a number of antiwar trials that had begun in the 1960s, some involving the Berrigan brothers, Daniel and Philip, most notably the case of the Catonsville Nine; these trials had marked the new Catholic Left's ascendancy in the public eye as symbols of "nonviolent" resistance to the Vietnam War. Though the government lost the Harrisburg Seven trial, its fomenters, J. Edgar Hoover and his FBI, won what they were after: to besmirch the reputations of the Berrigans and the larger Catholic Left resistance movement and to knock them from the high moral pillar they occupied.

A reissue of my 1972 book, *The Harrisburg 7 and the New Catholic Left*, had appeared a month before, so I gave the keynote address following a panel on the case, held at the Midtown Scholar Bookstore in Harrisburg. One of the original defendants, the former nun Elizabeth McAlister and spouse, now widow, of Philip Berrigan, had been on the panel and was in attendance. It was a large crowd of some two hundred filling the bookstore, the size of a warehouse, where we all convened, the average age sixty plus. (A podcast of the event might be found here: http://famousreadingcafe.podomatic.com/). I began my remarks saying that when I had written the new afterword for the Harrisburg book I had never imagined that I would be reciting parts of it aloud to Elizabeth McAlister.

Three months after that event, another nun, Sister Megan G. Rice, along with two men some decades younger—she was eighty-two in July 2012, the men in their fifties and early sixties—were arrested after breaking into Y-12, our nuclear storage facility of storied history in Oak Ridge, Tennessee. They came with the usual Plowshares movement equipment: hammers, spray paint, human blood, but also a hefty bolt cutter. The Oak Ridge Three. They were tried in Knoxville, Tennessee, in early May, and, after a two-day trial, were convicted on two counts, one of obstructing the national defense and the second of "depredation" of a government facility. The former, the sabotage count, carries a potential penalty of twenty years.

There was very little coverage of the trial itself, nothing like the Harrisburg case received four decades ago, and the Knoxville local news and the Associated Press, in their reporting, kept referring to the defendants as the Y-12 trespassers, not the Oak Ridge Three, thereby de-nationalizing the case. Sentencing for the Oak Ridge Three, who currently remain in jail, is scheduled for September. The *Washington Post* did run a mini–book report on the case before the trial on April 29, in its Style section, complete with fourteen "chapters" (all very short, Dan Brown–like), written by Dan Zak, with many web-friendly photos and extras (http://www.washingtonpost.com/sf/style/2013/04/29/the-prophets-of-oak-ridge/). The *Post* is fly-fishing for a Pulitzer.

In 2012 the Nuns on the Bus had received more coverage than the Oak Ridge Three (many things get more publicity), but beating swords into plowshares doesn't get a lot of traction these days. It's hard, in the Age of Obama, when the "antiwar" former presidential candidate continues to oversee the two wars his predecessor began, and Gitmo remains open (though the president really, really wants to close it), to push through all the noise with this type of antinuclear protest. The Plowshares movement rose from the ashes of the Harrisburg trial, nurtured and populated by both Berrigans, Philip and Dan, along with Elizabeth McAlister. Its protests began, more or less, in 1980, with the King of Prussia, Pennsylvania, action at the GE Missile Re-entry Division. More hammers and blood. Eventually, after a number of protests, the Berrigans and Elizabeth spent time in jail, some shorter, some longer, as did others.

These days activists have taken to calling such events as the Y-12 prophetic acts, rather than protests, thereby sidestepping the endemic futility found in this sort of protesting. The participants have been mainly the remnants of the Catholic Left, carrying out their never-ending mission. Protest movements in the secular protest world, and their general fecklessness, were demonstrated most starkly by the Occupy movement, the marathon sitting-in sort in a park near the heart of the beast on Wall Street in 2011. Other moments of occupation have occurred elsewhere in the country with little effect, as well as the more anarchistic protests at G8 meetings (held infrequently in the United States). One secular protest movement with teeth, though, has been the Tea Party, a largely Astroturf creation, though anchored in the small hardcore anti-tax groups of long standing, but was hatched into its current form by high-end Republican organizations with the bright idea of creating a "third" party within a party—the GOP—avoiding all the shortcomings of traditional third parties.

Coincidentally, a new documentary, *Hit & Stay: A History of Faith and Resistance*, which premiered at the Chicago Underground Film Festival last March, focuses on the Catholic antiwar movement, largely the draft-board raiding contingent, of the 1960s and '70s. (Its website: http://www.hitandstay.com/). At a panel after the premiere, the usual question was asked: Why weren't more young people out in the streets protesting? My answer was that they were saddled with so much educational debt they don't dare. And, there is the continuing influence of the Democrat antiwar president whose earnest rhetoric tamps down youthful fervor to protest the government he represents.

One often-overlooked reason of why the late 1960s and early '70s became the golden age of protest was the state of the economy back then. There was both an excess of surplus capital and, briefly, recession, which allowed a lot of youth the time to be both fancy free and willing to take a stand. Reagan economics and the transfer of most of the wealth to the top had yet to take place. Today's economics perversely put a choke hold on large-scale protests. The current volunteer army was not forced upon the government by the antiwar protestors of the time; the war makers longed for it, and got it in 1973. 1973! The one statistic that has changed in the wars we now fight is the average age of the dead. It has risen. We're no longer killing the footloose teenage males we had such an oversupply of in the Vietnam period. Those who die now have marriages, families, some experience of real life, however truncated.

When the Plowshares people turned to antinuclear protests, going from draft board raids to nuclear annihilation, they chose to go from the limited and symbolic to the purely symbolic and sorely limited. Prophetic actions, indeed. The history of protest has many rooms, but these symbolic acts are demonstrations of resistance, idealized pleas for actual magic, as if spray paint and human blood and the marks of hammers could actually turn an article of war (a nuclear sword) into a helpful tool of humanity (a plow). Prest-O Change-O.

The general public might not have much reaction or exposure to octogenarian nuns spray-painting a building filled with enriched bomb-grade uranium, but Congress certainly did, and hearings on the Oak Ridge incident quickly were held. A number of representatives thanked Sister Rice for pointing out the deficiencies in its security systems. The thorough Lax account, courtesy of the *Washington Post*, points out the usual laughable lapses, the sort you get when you privatize the military. One of the horrors of nuclear weapons is how they wedded the greatest intellectual minds to the greatest amount of destruction. Our cultural DNA since the 1940s has been tainted, given this arranged marriage of science and war. It can be argued, though, it has always been so.

The Nobel prizes, the awards for the highest rarefied sort of thinking, were founded atop a pile of dynamite, or rather, Alfred Nobel's patented dynamite and detonator. The first Nobel prizes were awarded at the start of the twentieth century, in 1901. So many symbols speak for us, there is no quiet on the earth. The events of 9/11 are both symbols and facts. Though, in war, the presumption that you might die is a given, there is a stark difference when to die is the participants' desire. The way our country and government have reacted to what we call suicide bombers is to redefine what war is and what we are willing to do in such a war. President Obama's speech on counter-terrorism to the National Defense University on May 23 tried to acknowledge that he, if nothing else, is aware that the not-so-brave new world we are now in cannot go on forever. But he may be wrong, for as he pointed out the contradictions between what we say and what we do, he also demonstrated neither the will nor the power to change it.

The Oak Ridge Three may have carried out a profound prophetic action, certainly it was courageous, but it is our own government's symbols and actions that contain the most alarming prophecies.

The View from the Couch, July 19, 2013 and *The Nation's Greg Mitchell* (blog)

The Nation's Greg Mitchell *blog ended and the URL is now defunct, a problem with the electronic age, where things can disappear, or, at least, not appear. Mitchell had put the piece up on his own blog,* Pressing Issues *(https://gregmitchellwriter.blogspot.com/search?q=William+O%27Rourke). Good luck to us all.*

Torture? What Torture?

Americans have a rather baroque view of what constitutes torture. That is easily seen in the 2-1 endorsement of the conduct that went down under the Bush II administration at various CIA black sites during the first two wars Bush and Company ran. So many fellow Americans are ready to agree with Dick Cheney, and a small segment of the legal community, that all of that was merely "enhanced interrogation." All societies, it seems, define torture with some specificity, based on their own ideas of cultural norms, what the general public thinks is cruel and unusual punishment. And our country's moderate and modulated response to the early December release of the Senate CIA torture program report bears this out.

When I was a very young man, hardly a teenager, some decades ago, I used to look at so-called men's magazines that some older boys and fathers had left around. These were not girlie magazines, but men's magazines, full of manly subjects. One of the most compelling was the often-used spread on "Arab" crime management, the cutting off of hands and sometimes heads for minor infractions, or what I thought of at eleven as minor. Now that was what I would have classified as torture.

What the Saudis may think of such acts I do not know, though they apparently continue to this day.

No, what Americans think of when they think of torture usually involves chain saws, or sledgehammers, or the like. Walk though any of the mega-hardware stores of the modern period, as Hollywood producers often do looking for new ways to kill people in movies, and you can gather what constitutes torture to most of the population.

It usually entails cutting, smashing, gouging, body parts lost, whatever carnage that has appeared over the last couple of decades at the local cineplex.

I have always thought it curious that waterboarding has taken pride of place in the torture sweepstakes that have been roundly condemned of late. Americans have very conflicted views about water and it has been seldom looked at as outright torture. True, it has been seen as a vehicle of catastrophe, of peril, but not necessarily as an instrument of torture: hurricanes Sandy and Katrina, for instance. But that of course, is weather. Various myths about water have taken hold in the American psyche: parents, particularly fathers, throwing children into pools as a means of instruction to either sink or swim. Sharks in the ocean are scarier than the ocean itself. Backyard pools were always a luxury to aspire to. Everyone, or a lot of people, have found themselves at one time or another choking on too much water, either learning how to swim, or because of some other mishap when at play. Water water everywhere.

Former vice president Cheney on *Meet the Press* made one odd concession to our country's most recent form of waterboarding. In order to differentiate it from the World War II Japanese sort, for which perpetrators were hung by the neck till dead, Cheney said that we "elevated" the feet of the waterboarded, so they wouldn't actually drown. I had never heard that before, the elevated feet business, and I've paid attention over the years to the placating statements that the overly involved have made.

And all the business of slamming people into walls, and other sorts of rough treatment. Americans seem to give that a pass too, as official torture, given that NFL stars are knocking out their wives in casino hotels' elevators and beating their children with switches, to say nothing of all the nonstars' bad treatment of wives and children we all see about us. Torture? Almost usual behavior of some alarmingly high percentage of our fellow Americans.

But it is the waterboarding that people keep coming back to. Somehow water's properties are too conflicted, so many good, so few bad, for Americans to see water as real torture. It is something: EIT. Enhanced Interrogation Techniques. George Orwell is spinning in his grave. Hanging from ceilings, sleep deprivation, so much of that sounds too familiar to too many people, something they have put up with. Rectal feeding? Apparently some folks have enemas for fun.

It does seem that Americans, at least 2-1, roughly 70 percent, are ready to give the CIA and the Bush II administration a pass on the torture question, as long as they don't turn up at their doors someday with chain saws and sledgehammers, or gardening scissors and red hot pokers.

The View from the Couch, January 12, 2015

An earlier version of this article ran in the South Bend Tribune, *January 10, 2015.*

To Kill a "Second" Novel

Most of what has been written about the *To Kill a Mockingbird/Go Set a Watchman* controversy has been wrong—at least in one important way. Harper Lee's second novel, just published, *Go Set a Watchman*, keeps being referred to as an early draft of *To Kill a Mockingbird*. It obviously isn't a "draft," as almost any published writer could tell you.

It's clearly a first novel, a first book. And it was sent in 1957 to an editor who, though not wanting to buy it, suggested Lee write another book. A draft is an earlier version of the same novel, one eventually published. It may often have a different title. Authors are not always the best title-ers.

But the editor wanted a different book. Most editors, strange as it may sound, want books that sell. Tay Hohoff, Lee's editor, thought *Go Set a Watchman* wouldn't. Why? Even from the reviews, it is quite clear why: Who in the late 1950s wanted to read about a young woman who fled to New York City from a dreary Southern town with a racist father and unpleasant friends? But Hohoff saw a way out. There was this character Scout, the book's protagonist when she was a young girl. A novel in her voice might do the trick.

Back in the 1950s and '60s, Southern racism was in the news and wasn't news to many. Large numbers of Americans do not like to read realistic fiction about the unpleasant here and now. I should know, since I published one of the earliest anti–Vietnam War novels in 1974. There were a number of advantages Lee's editor saw in a novel told with a child's precocious voice. The events recounted moved back in time, whereas *Go Set a Watchman* was too contemporary, too much of the times in the late 1950s.

Lee's editor functioned as some modern editors do today. Writers I know have, occasionally, succumbed to them. When a manuscript is offered up and these (mainly) young editors see talent and possibility, they will ask for "revisions." But what the editor really wants is a different work: a novel that will sell. In extreme cases, like Lee's, that creates an entirely new book. New last chapters. New first chapters. New characters. New protagonists.

Hack authors of the past have been accused of writing to formula: westerns, police procedurals, etc. Today, it is the editors who want to impose a formula: likable characters, happy endings, general uplift, rather than dour downers.

They think they know what sells. Look at the tables of trade paperback novels at the bookstores. Do their covers all look alike? They do. There's a reason.

Lee's editor was ahead of her time. She wanted Lee to write then what today is one of the few flourishing fiction genres left. A Young Adult novel, a YA. One with uplift. Uplift is important. The Pulitzer Prize in fiction historically is given only to uplifting works. Novels thought to be leading candidates for the prize, even when presented to the board, have been denied the prize for supposed lack of uplift. Thomas Pynchon's *Gravity's Rainbow*, for instance.

Nonetheless, quite a few second books published by young authors don't achieve the same success as the first. That is because the second book published is often the first book written, published because of the success of the first book. It happened to me. My first book (*The Harrisburg 7 and the New Catholic Left*) was successful enough to cause my second (*The Meekness of Isaac*), which I had written before the Harrisburg book, to be published. It happens enough to be noticed as a second-book letdown. It's because the second book was actually the first.

But that didn't happen to Harper Lee. In her case, her (unedited!) second novel, actually her first, is a flabbergasting success, over a million copies sold. But that is only because she waited—if that's the word—over fifty years to let it be published. She got that right.

The View from the Couch, July 28, 2015

An earlier version of this article ran in the South Bend Tribune, *July 26, 2015.*

My Hillary Problem—and Yours

For close to a year I have expected Bernie Sanders to embarrass Hillary Clinton in the Iowa and New Hampshire primaries. It now looks as if he well may injure her.

Most Democrats, I assume, thought Bernie would be a salubrious tonic for Hillary, keeping her honest, more or less, during the primary season, and, then, after sufficient chastisement, Bernie having made his points, she would walk off with the nomination, and, given the chaos of the Republican field, win the presidency, if not easily, at least convincingly.

Well, so much for conventional wisdom.

If Sanders wins both Iowa and New Hampshire, the gloom and doom now percolating in the pundit class about Clinton's second presidential campaign will only increase, and, as most history proves, battering primaries injure the eventual nominee, given that they serve as a period of free oppo research for the other party. Indeed, the Republicans have mostly aimed their ire at Hillary, considering Sanders superfluous, evidently, too easy a target.

Eight years ago Iowa signaled Clinton's likely electoral downfall. It showed white folks would vote for the African American candidate.

It's at this point difficult not to consider what a Clinton 2 presidency would have looked like back then. Certainly, Hillary would have not shown the naiveté that Obama displayed his first term. I have always been surprised that no one took him aside after he won the election and told him, "You know, the last Democrat who won the presidency for two terms was a white good old boy, called Bubba by many, from Arkansas, and you know what the Republicans did to him? They impeached him. What do you think they will do to you?"

Hillary, doubtless, would have been more combative from the get-go, not being as easily hoodwinked by the Big Pharma medical-industry complex, perhaps even not caving in to the no-tax GOP zealots by letting all the Bush tax cuts expire, reverting to her husband's not-so-oppressive era of taxation. Why those tax cuts were set to expire was that even the Republican bought-and-paid-for economists couldn't claim the deficit wouldn't balloon if they stayed.

Didn't happen, obviously. Obama persisted in his Rodney King why-can't-we-all-get-along presidency for too many years. The deficit went down a few times, but only at the price of the country's infrastructure collapsing, corroding, imperiling many here, there, and everywhere. What may have remained the same in a Clinton 2 presidency is Obama's handling of the Middle East maelstrom. Hard to imagine Hillary doing anything much different.

But now she is haunted by Bill's two terms, thanks mainly to Donald Trump, everyone's naughty Puck in his own gaudy production of his extended Midsummer Night's Dream (or nightmare), abetted by the other players in the Republican crowded cast. The various scandals of Clinton 1 parade around, the sex imbroglios, the Defense of Marriage Act, the end of Glass-Steagall, the deregulation of the big banks, etc.

And the internet serves up cheap reproductions of all this history as fast as McDonald's puts out french fries.

Not that I don't think Hillary still could win it all. Bernie does make her appear younger. She is well qualified, though that doesn't appear to be currently part of the job description.

The presidency, as we have seen for the last seven-plus years, has limited powers. Neither Hillary, nor the long-shot Bernie, will have that much weight to throw around, especially if the Supreme Court gelds the office as the conservative justices on the court seem to want to do this coming June. And the reason most staunch Democrats put up with their flawed candidates is that the president still nominates Supreme Court members.

The coming months of the election cycle may be painful, but they won't lack for morbid entertainment. To turn a well-known Orwell remark around, we all get the presidential campaign we deserve.

Huffington Post, January 29, 2016

A version of this article ran in the South Bend Tribune, *February 2, 2016. I had stopped writing for the* Huffington Post *in 2012, doubtless because they didn't run something I sent them, but the 2016 presidential campaign was too much of a lure, and I resumed with the above column.*

Accidental Presidencies

Donald Trump isn't the surprise frontrunner he's made out to be. He is the result of a long trend line, heading downward, in American politics. Clinton, himself, is an example of the accidental president, insofar as he wouldn't have been elected in 1992 without the wacky intervention of the slightly be-crazed third-party campaign of Ross Perot. Perot dropped out of campaigning and dropped back in at the end. And we think Trump is unstable? Perot, evidently, hated George H. W. Bush and effectively did him in.

George H. W. Bush, Reagan's veep, ran as Ronald's running mate to heal divisions their primary race had caused within the GOP. Bush won his own presidential race in 1988 against the accident of Michael Dukakis, an unfortunate campaigner (tank photo, Willie Horton).

Bush picked Dan Quayle as his veep, a strategic choice, given that it was made to help his sons down the road, since Bush knew the Vietnam War cohort had to be vetted and Quayle would serve as the lightning rod for that debate. Unfortunately for Bush, in 1992 he ran against Bill Clinton, the draft dodging, etc., but Quayle had already made all that history less toxic for the Vietnam generation. George W., though, eventually profited from his father's foresight. W was an accidental president, too, since he lost the popular vote and had to be elevated to the office by the Supreme Court.

Elections aren't necessarily always a roll of the dice, but the vagaries of pure chance are often quite spectacular. President Obama's election history demonstrates this: his 2004 Senate race was aided by a sex scandal that knocked out his white Republican opponent, Jack Ryan, and the local Republicans came up with a last-minute replacement, the carpetbagger Alan Keyes, who had a bit too much beamed-down-from-the-mothership in his makeup. Recall that Obama had lost his previous primary election bid to Congress in 2000.

Keyes had been Bill Kristol's roommate at Harvard. Kristol, of course, played a similar role when Obama ran for president. The default candidate of the Republicans in 1996 and 2008 had been an older maimed war veteran, Bob Dole and then John McCain. McCain's fate was sealed when Kristol, among others, recommended the irrepressible Sarah Palin for vice president.

A lot of slips between cups and lips in presidential races. Now, for 2016, we have the new Trump-istan brewing, his chance of being the Republican nominee growing, but The Donald, setting aside his appeal to the angry and alienated, has been, and continues to be, aided by the strange coincidence of two Cuban Americans (or one Cuban American and one Cuban Canadian) making it possible for his dedicated followers to win battles and state primaries no one thought he would win. Who can make this stuff up? Yet very few horse races have seventeen animals in the starting gates.

Vulgarity in presidential politics, unfortunately for Hillary Clinton, began with Bill Clinton and his Oval Office trysts. Consult the *Starr Report* paperback for all the graphic details. It's a doozy.

Ceci n'est pas une cigar, as Magritte might have said. Now that Trump's pictorial similarities to Il Duce have been widely noticed, The Donald, our own Herr Mousse-olini, has his followers doing stiff-arm Sieg Heil pledges. It is a little much. Trump is certainly leaning in. But look who he is running against, the two die-hard gusanos, and the placid Ohio governor, splitting the vote disastrously.

The GOP deep bench is laughable. Not that the Democrats have any sort of bench to speak of. Beyond the short-lived campaign of the former white mayor of Baltimore, Governor Martin O'Malley, Democrats have two septuagenarians running. One reason Bernie Sanders won't be Hillary Clinton's veep is that he is too old. What has happened to both the major parties? I do have a clue. In *Campaign America '96*, I quote an acquaintance saying that the presidency is now middle management and that is why you don't get the best people running for the job.

Back in the Bill Clinton days, Beltway types would refer to "President Rubin," the former secretary of the treasury. Now, Rubin had some power. President Obama, after holding office for a while, was quoted as saying one thing he was allowed to do had made him "really good at killing people."

Of course, there are a few other things a president can hope to do. And the American people have seven more months to decide just who that president might be.

Huffington Post, March 10, 2016

Revenge of the Sixties

Ted Cruz, the Dump Trump movement's great white hope, is the kind of guy who gave high school debate teams a bad name. A hectoring know-it-all who favors Chautauqua—not Hillary Clinton's Chappaqua—stage gestures and oratory. Ineffably smug. But the oddity is that the Democratic number two, U.S. Senator Bernie Sanders, shares some of these same qualities, the hectoring know-it-all side at least, though he seems, unlike Cruz, lovable and grandfatherly.

I recently gave a talk at Lone Star College in Houston on the humanities and income inequality (see "Making Poverty More Bearable," in part 3). Lone Star is part of the state's junior college system and the students know firsthand a lot about income inequality. I brought up the nineteenth-century bohemian tradition, which meant to make poverty bearable and discussed beatniks, hippies, and the short period during the sixties and beginning seventies when antimaterialism was afoot. Back then there was enough surplus capital around, and higher education, at least in state schools, was not very pricey. Students actually had time on their hands to join movements and protest and organize.

Of course, that period ended with a bang and hardly a whimper. Reverence for the rich came in full bore with Ronald Reagan. Education policy changed, resulting in the for-profit college explosion over the last three decades, a form of privatizing, which was going on everywhere, even, and most stealthily, in the military itself. First end the draft, second begin to privatize around the edges. In modern history one result of that could be seen in Benghazi, an event more about contractors than enlisted soldiers.

During the same timeline Wall Street average salaries in the NYC securities industry went from about $50,000 a year in 1981, double that of all other private sector jobs, to $400,000 a year by 2008. The Wall Street bonus economy bloomed in the 1980s. Salaries skyrocketed from double to more than six times everyone else's.

That rise didn't just affect people working on Wall Street. CEOs across the land, top executives at most every corporation, including academia, felt deep in their souls that they were being underpaid. If those twenty-somethings at Goldman Sachs were making a half million, why weren't they? Salary inflation at the top was contagious. During the 1970s the ratio of CEO pay to the company's workers was around 20 to 1. By 2012 it went to 350 to 1. And that figure is the average.

These three developments, privatization, Wall Street profligacy, CEO salaries, were not disconnected. It was an imperfect storm, but well thought out. One example of this forward thinking is the so-called Powell Memo, the "Confidential Memorandum: Attack of American Free Enterprise System," written by the future Supreme Court justice Lewis Powell in 1971.

The right-wing think tanks were created, thanks to Powell, and the changes to universities he predicted certainly came to fruition, though even Powell didn't foresee the wholesale privatization, or the creation of the one percent, resulting in the current state of income inequality. The *one percent/ninety-nine percent* phrase was more or less coined in 2011, during the Occupy Wall Street eruption—though a movement largely feckless, the Occupy label has continued, stuck on all sorts of demonstrations.

Bernie Sanders has two or three things to say and he's been saying them since the 1970s. What is amazing is that it has taken nearly five decades for his message to be heard. He is the revenge of the sixties. The older folk who are solidly in Bernie's camp tend to be remnants of Ralph Naderites; Nader, in his youthful incarnation, was one of Powell's chief villains in his mordant memo.

And though Bernie is running for the Democratic nomination, his campaign does have the atmospherics of a third party contest. As does Donald Trump's. There is a divide being created that may turn into a chasm, and it is still unknown if it can be healed, if Hillary Clinton ends up the nominee. As Bernie would remember, back in 1968 a lot of the titular Democratic young did not vote for Hubert Humphrey, allowing Nixon's win, because, as was often said back then, progressives wanted to "heighten the contradictions." Humphrey lost by less than 1 percent of the vote. Alas, over the decades, thanks to the Republican right, the contradictions have certainly been heightened.

Huffington Post, April 7, 2016

The Haunting of Hillary

One thing that made the Clintons so mad about the 2008 presidential election is that Hillary would have won in a walk. That knowledge alone can account for Bill Clinton's anger back in that campaign over the realization that Barack Obama would be getting the nomination. Bill had lashed out at Obama in January 2008 over his superior "antiwar" stand, in opposition to Hillary's vote for the war in Iraq: "Give me a break. This whole thing is the biggest fairytale I've ever seen."

The same sort of anger by the former president was displayed some ten days before the New York primary when Clinton again lashed out, this time at Black Lives Matter protesters in Philadelphia who yelled that black youth weren't "super-predators" and Bill shouted back, "You are defending the people who killed the lives you say matter." That both incidents eight years apart fell into a shadow caused by race may not be coincidental.

Back in 2008, John McCain was a weak candidate made even weaker by his selection of Sarah Palin as half the ticket. Who profited? Of course, Barack Obama, who may have not become the first African American president without running against such a vulnerable pairing. It was six of one, half dozen of the other. It would have been either the first woman president or the first black president. How easy an election did it turn out to be for Democrats? Americans elected a black man to the highest office in the land, that's how easy. This is not hindsight. It was obvious at the time.

Previous to the recent New York primary, which Hillary Clinton won handily, the same 2008 dynamic was at play. And that is why she showed anger against the Sanders campaign, its mucking up of her march to history. Whatever the final act of the Republican implosion theater turns out to be, it will present the American people with an even more damaged alternative than McCain/Palin.

As Donald Trump tries to clean up his act, now cross-dressing as presidential, rational, and contemplative, both Clintons, thanks to their domination of the New York State political apparatus, may step back from and lessen their irrational fears of losing the nomination again. It remains to be seen if Senator Sanders plays along and stems his straightforward attacks against many of Hillary Clinton's obvious shortcomings. He has saved Republican Super PACs millions of dollars in advertising expense by doing their work for them. But once she is the nominee they will unload their millions in the same sort, and worse, of vilification.

I happened to be in Israel when the news of the Monica Lewinsky scandal first broke in 1998, standing atop the infamous Masada plateau looking out at the Dead Sea. Some Israelis were joking that it was a Mossad plot, inserting Lewinsky into the White House. When Trump's campaign first gained steam, I heard from fellow Americans that he must be a Democratic agent, so successfully was he crashing the Republican house of cards.

Both surmises are doubtless equally true, being not true at all, except in effect. If Trump is the GOP nominee and Hillary Clinton the Democratic, she should walk into the office easier than Barack Obama did.

In 2008 sufficient Americans placed their hope in a young, relatively untested first-term senator from Illinois, while the Republicans presented their dysfunctional odd couple, McCain/Palin, for the country's approval. This time around who will they select? Trump/Kasich? Trump/Haley? It is conventional wisdom that vice presidents don't matter, but this coming election may prove that wrong, for a lot of obvious reasons, balance, gravitas, etc. Nonetheless, the Democrats, barring the fatal unknown, should win, furthering the mixed legacy of the Obama presidency.

Obama, as it turned out, wasn't too good to be true. That he was—at least he was true to himself. He just turned out to be too good to be as effective as his voters had hoped.

Huffington Post, April 22, 2016

Ted's Excellent Mansplaining

I was exercising at my university's faculty gym when Ted Cruz was laboriously mansplaining on TV why he was choosing Carly Fiorina as his virtual veep for his holographic future presidency. It was a classic case: I, Ted Cruz, a man, will now tell you why I have the good judgment to select Carly, a woman, the glass-ceiling shatterer. Fiorina may or may not have the potty mouth of Julia Louis-Dreyfus's character in *Veep*, which seems to be the chief qualification of our modern era, but, at this point, who cares? While exercising away, I kept wondering when Cruz was going to bring on Fiorina, since I had been on the elliptical machine beyond my usual allotment of time, and Cruz, who had appeared around 4:15 p.m., was still blabbering on after 4:30 p.m.

Cruz grins inappropriately during his speeches and his unhappy slice of smile signifies the pleasure he takes hearing his own voice. I left the exercise room fifteen minutes later and Cruz was still there yapping. No Carly. I don't tweet much, but had I a smartphone, as a number of other fellow exercisers did, staring transfixed at their small screens, I might have tweeted: #WhereIsShe?

I saw later in the day from various news outlets that Fiorina finally made it to the podium, to little effect. God knows Carly understands losing, having done it so often both in the private and public sector. From the clips I saw, she evidently sang a song and seems to have a pleasant voice while singing.

Indiana is now hot. Cruz and Carly came to South Bend yesterday and clogged up the downtown when I tried to get to the road show version of *The Book of Mormon* (I'm trying for contrast here) playing at the Morris Performing Arts Center. A lot of Cruz supporters in his crowd at the nearby Century Center were obese (less so at the Mormon musical, which was wonderful theatrically, but reprehensible in every other way), though I don't think, unlike the First Lady, Cruz considers obesity a national health issue. I am not body shaming, I'm just reporting. In any case, the Cruz rally was in one of the Century Center's smaller venues, a room I last was in when a friend took me to a cat show held there. Lots of cats in cages.

Trump is coming to the Century Center on Monday night and Bernie Sanders is booked there Sunday, May Day. Hillary Clinton appeared at a more or less private setting, the AM General plant outside of the city that now makes Mercedes-Benzes for the China market, a couple of days ago.

Some commentators out there in mediaworld are saying that Indiana may be someone's Alamo, Cruz's, Trump's, it's hard to tell. The connection is very thin. Maybe it's because Cruz is a senator from Texas. Is he Jim Bowie, Santa Anna, Davy Crockett, the Mexicans, the fort? It doesn't make much sense. Who is running over whom? I guess it's the last-stand business.

Truth might be the first casualty in war, but language seems to be the first in campaigns. Now, the self-presumptive Republican nominee, Donald Trump, wants to sloganize once again "America First!" Not that many voters are going to think of Charles Lindbergh and his various enthusiasms pre–World War II that were attached to the slogan when first coined. Lindbergh loved the Luftwaffe. Poor Lindbergh. He flew planes. The Donald owns many. Perhaps Pat Buchanan is Trump's unacknowledged campaign model.

Locally, there are contested races down ticket going on throughout Indiana, which may or may not affect the upcoming election. A Senate seat is open, thanks to the happy retirement of Dan Coats. He returned to Indiana in 2010 to assume the seat vacated by Evan Bayh. Coats is the only recidivist senator, once retired, active lobbyist, then elected once again.

But the Democrats are still hoping for a win eventually against Mike Pence, the current governor, former right-wing radio talker (*The Mike Pence Show*), who even moderate Republicans have difficulty putting up with, especially after the costly fiasco of his Religious Freedom Restoration Act of late March 2015. Pence was pictured with what looked like a high school production cast of *Nunsense*, after he signed the bill. Yes, let us restore all those lost religious freedoms! Pence has half-heatedly "endorsed" Ted Cruz, "I will be voting for Ted Cruz..." this coming Tuesday. Democrats have John Gregg running for governor, who has run and lost before, but this time is changing his image, becoming a bit less rustic.

But it is the Republican primary for Senate that is interesting. Two contenders, Marlin Stutzman and Todd Young, both GOP Indiana district U.S. representatives, are lashing out at each other for the position, given Coats' departure and longing for the hard work of lobbying. No love lost there, just like most of the Republican presidential primary cohort. Both candidates are really unappetizing, so there's a slim chance for the potential Democratic candidate. Baron Hill, who lost to Coats a long time ago, in 1990, is serving as the warm-body sacrifice.

But what really goes on here in Indiana won't be covered much in our week in the sun. It'll be more drive-by journalism, the ninety-plus percent hoping for good visuals, the desired seen and heard reportage. On the bright side, if Trump gets the nomination Pence may well lose his reelection. I am not much into predictions—I was wrong about waterbeds way back when—but in the presidential primary race here I will predict wins for Bernie and The Donald. In any case, it will be close.

Huffington Post, May 2, 2016

Transforming The Donald

Transformations within the Trump candidacy are ongoing. Unfortunately, the one that is the most worrisome is how the national press is treating him. With respect, that is. This first turned up with the photograph MSNBC uses of Trump on primary nights, the headshot that goes up beside his many state victories. It's the most complimentary picture of Trump that I have seen, even if he doesn't currently look like the photo. In it, he has darkish hair, brown, brunette, thicker on the sides with a touch of gray, neatly combed, a winning smile. It is Mitt Romney hair.

There are a lot of photos of Trump, but why this one? So friendly and, I hate to say the word, presidential.

The same photo continued to be used the night Trump won the Indiana primary. And this week's West Virginia and Nebraska primary triumphs, more or less uncontested. Of course, the audience could see Trump himself after the Indiana win in the lobby of the Trump Tower, giving his victory speech. That night his remarks were subdued, full of love. His hair was the usual blend of orange and copper and brass, yellow, and, from the back, a color favored on birthday cakes, lemony, pound cake–like. Or bad teeth, old piano keys.

My contention is that there is no upside for the network/cable conglomerate, any of them, for not treating Trump with deference. If not immediately The Donald himself, his new staff is praised. See, they are serious guys! The media now seems to understand Trump might actually win. At least, he has a shot, even if one very long, much longer than his fingers.

The same thing occurred in 1980. Until the summer of 1980, the time of the Mariel boatlift, a lot of the establishment press treated Ronald Reagan as a clown, his candidacy as an amusing sideshow. But that all stopped in the summer. By then it was clear that Reagan might actually win, become president. Carter's administration was falling apart. Castro was sending over all those Trump-like rapists and criminals from Cuban prisons, the mentally disturbed, and, by far, the largest and darkest group of refugees Americans had ever seen coming across the ninety miles to Key West. The proportion of criminals and the disturbed has been estimated at between 2 and 3 percent, doubtless the same figure for Trump's marauding Mexicans.

By 1980 the Iran hostage crisis was in its second year, lines had formed at gas stations, we had boycotted the summer Olympics, given away the Panama Canal, and, in April, had helicopters burn in the desert during a botched rescue attempt, etc. So, Ronald Reagan went from being a lightweight Hollywood figure with odd ideas to a remarkable statesman. I was in Key West in the summer of 1980 watching dilapidated school buses being filled with Cubans heading to the underpasses of Miami highways, Arkansas, wherever. But what I read in the daily papers was more shocking, this bestowing of new seriousness on candidate Reagan.

The national press needed to elevate the eventual winner, because Carter had loser written all over him. The titans of the press diminish their own importance if they have to cover a buffoon. Their impulse is to raise him up in their estimation. The Carter-Reagan race is not unlike the current one—Hillary Clinton, of course, being Jimmy Carter and The Donald being Ronald Reagan. Carter was president, but Hillary has been senator and secretary of state. Trump, of course, has some fractured Hollywood allure, but has never been governor of anywhere, so we've actually, as a country, lowered basic requirements for eligibility to run for the highest office in the land.

President Obama may well be Hillary's last bulwark, if no crisis beyond the usual turns up pre-November. Carter was beset by biblical plagues his last year in office and, in contrast, Obama is having what can pass for a good year.

But you now see it everywhere, the nascent elevation of Trump, the begrudging self-censorship of the pedantry (or punditry), though one can still read demurrals here and there. The press corps, too, along with the flummoxed Republican establishment, is trying to come to grips with the new nominee of the Grand Old Party. I've been saying "President Trump" to friends for months, much to their expected horror.

But now people are beginning to say it without irony, because, after the summer, when there are only two candidates to choose between, the odds become, alas, 50-50. No sure bet there.

Huffington Post, May 12, 2016

Clinton Exhaustion

Many recall "Clinton fatigue," one of the reasons Hillary Clinton's 2008 presidential campaign faltered and fell. Now people are tired of even bringing up that old fatigue excuse, though, of course, it still pertains. I am not a fan of counterfactual examples, but one that seems pertinent is what this primary season would look like if Bernie Sanders didn't exist, or, almost as fantastical, if he played the role most people expected before the primaries started. That is, he appeared and then quietly disappeared, like that other fellow, what's his name? O'Malley?

Without Bernie I wonder if Hillary would be getting any daily coverage whatsoever from the networks and cable. Imagine her campaign coverage if the Democratic primary season had been seen as a coronation? With no real opposition. Donald Trump, as many have observed, has been getting the lion's share of coverage as it is. If Hillary had no real competition, Trump would be gathering not just the lion's share, but the whole pride's share, the entire veldt's share. Hillary would be an afterthought.

The social circle of the press would doubtless have to nod in her direction (emails!), but Clinton fatigue would generate a general soporific. Trump's attempts to slime Bill Clinton, and by inference, Hillary, actually serves to create history lessons for all those young Bernie supporters, most barely born in the 1990s.

Without Bernie giving Hillary a real run, who would be taking any interest in the Democrat primaries? Bernie has served as an engine of interest for the Hillary campaign. And now Bernie wants to debate The Donald. And, who knows, it might happen, since Trump loves spectacle. Now, there's some virtual counterfactual television to come. But don't hold your breath.

Donald Trump running for president fits his business model, especially his model used the last couple of decades. He's now leasing his brand to the GOP and is willing, it appears, to lease it to the country at large: THE TRUMP PRESIDENCY! We already have Trump Tower and, in Chicago, a once quite compelling-looking skyscraper perched on the site of the old *Chicago Sun-Times* building, recently defaced with just the name TRUMP in garish letters.

We'll have to wait and see if we eventually get to see the 18th green below the North Face of Yosemite's Half Dome, the future final hole of the Trump Presidential Course. And why not? There's already an airport at the Grand Tetons National Park, so the rich of Jackson Hole can fly in private jets.

See, it's hard to stay on the subject of Hillary, since she has been so much a part of our country's national lassitude, brought on by and bringing to mind all the things that have been haunting us for decades. Do I need to name them? Starting with the largely created story of Whitewater, the sorriest low-rent land deal of the last century.

Remember the name of the guy who was at the center of it? Poor Jim McDougal. What would he have done back in the day when he tried to rope the Clintons into buying some bug-infested lots along Arkansas's White River if someone had said to him, "Jim, you know your friend Bill Clinton, the governor, will be president of the United States and you will die of a heart attack in solitary confinement because of him." Hard to believe. But The Donald is bringing up yet another sacrifice to journalists with nothing better to do, Vince Foster.

Fishy, indeed, Foster's suicide. There are arguably more books about Bill and Hillary Clinton published during (and before and after) Bill Clinton's two terms than any other president in American history. Of course, 90 percent of them were attack books. There was a vast right-wing conspiracy, except, despite Hillary's popularizing of the term, it wasn't a conspiracy—it was quite out in the open.

Bernie claims over and over that he trounces Trump in the polls. I doubt if Hillary's right-wing-conspiracy crowd has spent a dime on Sanders, but, if the unexpected happened and Sanders became the nominee, they would drop more than a dime on him.

Regarding the Republican right's focused attention, as Madonna would say, Bernie's like a virgin. So far, he's gotten more or less a free ride from the vast attack machine so critical and instrumental to the country's quarter century of Clinton fatigue. So, Hillary owes Bernie a thank you for succeeding as well as he has. He keeps both the spotlight on her and, more importantly, off of her.

Huffington Post, May 30, 2016

Bye Bye Bernie

In the early 1960s I was a big Ann-Margret fan, first associating her with the film version of *Bye Bye Birdie*. Before that I was a Brenda Lee fan, who came to town to star in a road show production of the musical at Kansas City's Starlight Theatre.

I knew, slightly, a local dancer who helped fill out the chorus line. She was invited to a party at Brenda's hotel room after a performance, and I tagged along, hoping to get to meet Ms. Lee. We went up in the hotel's elevator with what looked like two bodyguards and my friend was admitted to the party, but not I.

I didn't yell that the system was rigged, nor rail against the bodyguards (superdelegates!), I just went off quietly into the night. It doesn't yet seem that Bernie Sanders is going off quietly into the night, but he did, it was reported, spend nearly ninety minutes in a hotel room with the presumptive Democratic nominee, Hillary Clinton, who is, I think, taller than Brenda Lee.

I don't know if it was a "One Last Kiss" moment, or a first kiss moment, but Bernie qualifies as just a "Normal American Boy," a tune whose chorus went something like this:

> We love you Bernie
> Oh yes we do
> We love you Bernie
> And will be true!
> When you're not near us
> We're blue!
> Oh, Bernie, we love you...

Young women sang a variation of this in *Bye Bye Birdie*, not a bunch of tone-deaf Bernie Bros, but you get the point. The musical, as a teenager, seemed political to me, based, as it was, on Elvis Presley being drafted. The Vietnam War had not yet captured the country's attention, and Elvis, I believe, went off peacefully to Germany.

Where will Bernie go? Not back permanently to sleepy Vermont, but to Philadelphia, city of brotherly love, where he intends, so he says, to get rid of, as Donald Trump calls her, Deborah Wasserman Schultz, ram through the most progressive platform ever passed (ha!), achieve real electoral reform in the Democratic Party, and get rid of those glowering superdelegates blocking the party door of the promised land.

Meanwhile, The Donald, who appears not to want the job (the presidency), continues trying to lose, but, however he attempts to self-destruct, his people stand by him. Nonetheless, Bernie now wants "open primaries," because, evidently, they stood in the way—their absence that is—to his winning the nomination. All those New York independents deprived of voting in the Democratic primary! Bernie feels the bern—it burns him up.

As large as my disappointment was in not meeting Brenda Lee, I'm sure Bernie's disappointment is even greater. Far greater. I was just a green kid, starstruck, while Bernie finally turned himself into a star, even to the picky Green crowd. No longer a callow youth, Bernie's hair, toward the end of the primaries, began to be styled Julius Caesar–like, at least the usual Hollywood version. Caesar was a great orator, but a lousy dictator. *Et tu*, Wasserman Schultz?

I have always thought Bernie Sanders was likable enough, though he didn't turn out to be quite the overachiever that Donald Trump has come to be. Close, but no cigar. Though I do expect to hear, especially from Sanders's #NeverHillary supporters, this wan, persistent chorus being sung all the way to November:

> We love you Bernie
> Oh yes we do
> We love you Bernie
> And will be true!

Huffington Post, June 20, 2016

The Birther Business

A number of publications have been running President Obama assessment articles, given that he is nearing the end of his second term. And the campaign of Donald Trump is also fomenting retrospectives on the Obama administration, given The Donald's role in the "birther" controversy during the president's second-term contest.

During Obama's initial campaign in 2008 there was not that much mention of birth certificates, more of Hawaii, though—the media seemingly needing to acquaint the mainland with its existence back then. No birther blather rose all the way to the top, since John McCain had been born somewhere in Panama, so that fact made Obama's place of birth rather moot.

It always struck me as funny that so many people wanted to believe that Obama had been born in a hut in Kenya. The contemporaneous birth notice in a Hawaiian newspaper would have been, by itself, far beyond the heroics of the most *Manchurian Candidate*–esque conspirators.

What the birther controversy was about, however, was Obama's blackness, his alleged foreignness, his presumed shadow religion—linked to that unfortunate picture of him with the cloth head wrap—the not American-ness of our president, running for his second term. What might be hard to remember is that the country's native latent racism had been fairly suppressed, muted, during Obama's first run for the office.

One odd reason for that was the charges made, at first, by Hillary Clinton's original African American supporters claiming that Obama wasn't black enough, that he hadn't grown up with the usual African American experience back on the mainland. There was too much Hawaii and Indonesia, only turning up in the contiguous states permanently when he went to college. Like his father, the Kenyan.

None of the Obama-isn't-black-enough critics made that last charge back in 2008, to my knowledge. In fact, during that campaign year there was much more made of Obama's mother and his white Kansan grandparents who played such a role in raising him when he was young. The not-black-enough campaign, however short lived, had unexpected positive results.

The birther business coming again before the second-term election was the tip of the spear of all the finally released accumulated racism that had built up during Obama's first four years. And Donald Trump's antic search for Obama's birth certificate let all that simmering racism be focused.

But what has always struck me as strange was the singular fact that of all the American presidents, Obama was, is, the only one whose father wasn't born himself in America, or in Ireland—three presidents (Jackson, Buchanan, Arthur) had fathers born there. Even George Washington's father, Augustine, was born on American soil, in the Colony of Virginia, in 1694.

When Obama was/is referred to as African American, it is truly literal. He is first generation. His father was an African. Obama is half Kenyan. I always thought that was remarkable in and of itself. Forget birth certificates. The only birth certificate I ever wanted to see back in 2008 was LeBron James's. He looked like he was in his midtwenties when he played basketball in high school. I would have been interested in seeing proof of his date of birth.

Early in Obama's presidency I was also struck by the fact that the last two Democratic presidents, both ending up with two terms, grew up without their birth father. What were the odds for that? In Bill Clinton's case, his father died and was unknown to the future president; only his stepfather, whose name he eventually took, figured in his life. In Obama's case, the father was there, largely invisible, in the world, until he wasn't, certainly inspiring all those dreams from his father that resulted in Obama's first book.

Both of these fatherless boys married women suitable for their nascent political careers. Bill Clinton seemed in his youth to favor bimbos, but he knew he would have to have a serious wife if he wanted to rise in politics. Obama's calculations were a bit different, but no less obvious and political. Both men, it is clear, lucked out in their choices.

Yet the Republicans have taken it upon themselves to stress Obama's blackness, even in the current election of 2016. They may, or may not, given their liking of archaic terms, favor the word *mulatto* to speak of our half-white, half-black president, but they have made it clear that such a person only gets a seven-year term as president, not an eight-year term. Mulattoes, according to the GOP leadership, Mitch McConnell principally, are only entitled to seven-eighths of a presidency. Hence, no movement at all on President Obama's nominee for the Supreme Court, the last and most blatant example of Republican obstructionism.

And, of course, the presumptive Republican nominee, The Donald, keeps denouncing immigrants of whatever sort, along with claiming right of ownership of various races ("Oh, look at my African American over here"). But President Obama's father wasn't even an immigrant, illegal or otherwise. Yet Trump's current wife is an immigrant, filling, as she did, that important immigration fast-track category of supermodel.

I haven't thoroughly checked, but if her husband gains the office, unlikely as that now seems, she might well be the first foreign-born First Lady. It's not that I am a raging jingoist, but I am trying once again to make the obvious more clear: the world is getting smaller and smaller. That changes most everything, but, unfortunately, it doesn't make the people who want to run it any larger.

Huffington Post, July 4, 2016

Pensive Pence

On July 7 I tweeted this: My pick for GOP veep is Newt, since he's the only one whose career won't be ruined, since it's already ruined. A lot of commentators were picking Newt, right up to a few days before The Donald picked Mike Pence, my governor. I have been living in Indiana for over three decades and have seen a number of governors come and go. A couple of times I have even been down in the Governor's Mansion in Indianapolis, back when Evan Bayh was governor. Never met him, but I did speak with his wife. It was an arts in Indiana gathering.

Now Bayh is running for the open Senate seat, vacated soon by Dan Coats, who won it when Evan skedaddled for the greener pastures of lobbying. Now he wants back in. I'm all for him, given the Republican competition.

But it was Mitch Daniels's two terms as governor that most upset me. Mitch sold ("leased") the Indiana Toll Road, I-80, America's Main Street, thereby reaping monies for him to lavish on his cronies and favorite projects, however ill advised. I wrote about all this in 2006. I drove the length of the Toll Road in early June this year and admired, a decade later, its ruins, the closed highway travel plazas, now looking like sets from *Mad Max* movies, the road itself so pockmarked that repairs can no longer be put off.

Daniels is a lot like Paul Ryan, elevated as a Republican intellectual regardless of all the evidence to the contrary. Currently, Daniels now heads Purdue University, hoping to privatize as much of public education as he is able, repeating there his experience as governor. Daniels led Indiana to be one of the first Right to Work states while championing school vouchers. The only luck for the population is that he won't be returning to national politics anytime soon, given the controversies surrounding his marriage have left Mitch in a matrimonial ditch.

Now we have Mike Pence, who is Mitch Daniels with fewer brains. The litany of Pence's many missteps as governor (the Religious Freedom Restoration Act, anyone?) has been covered by the media, more or less, since he was selected as Trump's veep. Since looks, appearances, are important to Trump, I presume he thought Pence passed muster—Trump evidently didn't want to be paired with either Newt or Christie, two overweight court jesters. Pence has always seemed to me as if he was beamed down from the mothership, someone who could easily be cast in *Star Trek*, a few strands of DNA away from an android.

But Pence does fit the double-mask Janus candidacy that Trump wants to run, though, in fairness to Janus, this campaign is more a comedy/tragedy masquerade: pick which one applies to Pence. Whichever, Pence is on the ticket to "shore up" the GOP base, all those rabid evangelicals and anti-abortion zealots. Pence is nothing but a Republican talking-points machine, now augmented by lines about how great Donald Trump is and how he hears the heartbeat of the American public.

So, who is Hillary going to pick? Her choices aren't much more appetizing than Trump's. I had always favored Sherrod Brown, but no one wants to lose a Senate seat from Ohio, where the convention no-show GOP governor would name a replacement. Tim Kaine, though, is also a senator, but Virginia has a Democratic governor. Kaine is a favorite of many, though, in the Trump mode, lookism being supreme, Kaine is too much of a feminized male, soft in aspect, not the sort of masculine image Hillary Clinton may need at her side. He's definite second-husband material. She's doubtless tired of alpha-type males, but who she picks will matter. She needs younger, but experienced, though Pence has certainly lowered the veep-debate-ready bar.

And speaking of Indiana vice presidents, Dan Quayle has taken too much blame for his sorry service to George H. W. Bush. Quayle contributed to H. W.'s second-term loss to Bill Clinton. Recall that Bush was having health problems toward the end of his first term, which brought on fears of Quayle being able to ascend during Bush's second term, if he secured one.

But I have always held that Quayle all along was a brainchild of 41. George senior wanted to prepare the way for his sons, one or the other, George or Jeb, neither of whom went off to Vietnam. He went with Quayle, knowing that someone of the Vietnam generation had to go through the crucible of public opinion about that issue. And Quayle did survive the fire of that debate. But, of course, what Bush did not foresee was that the presidential ambitions he ironically protected was that of the draft-dodger Bill Clinton, though Bush had no idea he would be running against the guy when he ran in 1988.

When George W. finally came along he did escape the Vietnam–service gauntlet, barely. He "beat" a man who actually served in Vietnam, Al Gore. I don't think Hillary will play the veteran card for her veep pick, since the most likely veterans available would have served in a war she supported and her base abhors.

Huffington Post, July 22, 2016

Hillary's Voice

Hillary Clinton's speaking voice when addressing large crowds is something of a disaster. I know I am not alone in this opinion. Early on in the primaries there were a number of articles. Just last weekend on MSNBC both Chuck Todd and Jonathan Alter referred to her troubles, yelling at crowds as if she wasn't holding a microphone in her hand. No "modulation," etc. I've wondered about this particular voice she uses and how it plays into the ears of even the micro-misogynists who hear it, much less the full-bore sexists. They, doubtless, as I do, associate it with the voice she used in the past to yell at Bill.

Voices get a lot of play in presidential campaigns, especially this one, where Donald Trump declared at the GOP convention, "I am your voice." Though superficial, voice problems have crippled careers. The once-rising great nonwhite hope of the Republican Party, Bobby Jindal, for instance: his Waterloo took place at the site of his great triumph, selected to give the GOP reply following the first Barack Obama State of the Union address in 2009. It was universally panned.

But I had always presumed, since some of the criticism focused on the speech's "delivery," that the problem was that Jindal was likely having some cosmetic work done on his voice, in an attempt to rid himself of the traces of his pronounced ethnic accent. In other words, I speculated he was undergoing some voice lessons that hadn't yet concluded. He was in a mid-voice-change moment and, boy, did it seem odd. Now, Jindal speaks with the American equivalent of BBC English. You can hear the difference over the years on YouTube, not that it matters anymore.

Part of the problem is the continuing degradation of journalism, especially television's version. Take the more or less universal praise of the Trump children, each shilling for their father at the GOP convention. Many commentators were handing out participation trophies to them, since it was all about public speaking. We've gone from a literate world to an oral one. No reporting about the kids' histories marred the surface presentation. And, as Joe Biden would say, they were all certainly "clean."

In Hillary's case it seems to be a matter of audience. Also on the web you can listen to her speech at Wellesley in 1969. That voice she used then, though not to a crowd in the thousands, only in the low three figures, is certainly modulated. Wellesley put out an edited recording of that speech, often referred to in biographies, leaving out her mild criticism of Edward Brooke, the first black senator, a Republican, to be elected by popular vote, who was on stage with her. Hillary Rodham knew her audience, took them as equals, her fellow students and their parents.

When she talks to large crowds, the masses more or less, I don't think she sees them as equals. They are not intimates, folk she necessarily respects. They are the ones she shouts at. Bill Clinton, of course, as a public speaker, has intimacy in his voice in spades. It's his philanderer voice, as if each person in the crowd is important, because he is trolling the audience for a conquest. All that biting of his lip business. Rodham Clinton doesn't have such remarked-upon mannerisms. Hillary isn't looking for conquests. But she should.

To throngs at rallies her high-pitched delivery is a louder version of her exasperation voice, highlighted during the Benghazi hearings, when she exclaimed, "What difference does it make?" now a favorite attack line employed by the Republican-right smear machine.

Unfortunately, when it comes to making history as the first woman major-party nominee to the presidency, it's not quite pure, unadulterated history. It's in the Lurleen Wallace mode, George Wallace's wife, who became the governor of Alabama in 1967, after George was term-limited out. Other American political wives have gained office in this manner. We'll all have to wait for a woman to become president whose husband hasn't been there before.

Nonetheless, it surprises me, even at this point, that Hillary's speaking voice hasn't been addressed by anyone in her circle. She, too, could have used some voice lessons. But a chilling fact is that it is possible no one around her is brave enough to tell the candidate she should do something about it.

The View from the Couch, August 4, 2016

The Huffington Post, *still then screening posts editorially, declined to publish this article, since it didn't seem sufficiently Hillary friendly to them. Unlike my experience with* NUVO, *where I quit, and despite my earlier balking in 2012 at the* Huffington Post, *I continued this time to do the columns, beginning after the election (February 15, 2017), when they changed their format once again and "contributors" could post willy-nilly without much supervision.*

It's the Voter Suppression, Stupid!

Voter suppression is the big, somewhat neglected story of the 2016 election, insofar as that phenomenon is what caused Hillary Clinton to lose and Donald Trump to win. And it wasn't just the well-planned and rigorous voter suppression being carried out by Republican-controlled states throughout the nation, photo-IDs, exaggerated myths of the fraudulent individual voters, fewer places and days to vote, etc., but a more insidious sort, a by-product of negative ads and the atmospherics of disenfranchisement.

What the Republicans succeeded in doing was to trumpet Hillary Clinton's shortcomings and, more cunningly, they helped raise Donald Trump's negative ratings, too.

Indiana was a test case for this, given all the attack television advertising aimed at the Senate and governor race. Hard to count all the faults of both the Republican and Democrat candidates that viewers were exposed to: whoever was to be elected was already branded a crook, a criminal, or worse. Unfortunately, most of these ads were accurate, though less so the NRA's.

In the presidential race, the statistic that the media most often repeated, either wittingly or unwittingly becoming co-conspirators to suppress the vote, was both Trump's and Clinton's "unfavorable" ratings, higher than any other candidates in history, commentators crowed.

The general distaste for both Trump and Clinton was promoted relentlessly over the course of the campaign and had its effects, both intended and accidental. Hillary Clinton's own weaknesses played into this version of events, as did the outstanding boorishness of Donald Trump. Weirdly, the "high-road" behavior of President Obama and the First Lady drove up the contrast between themselves and those vying for the office.

The result of the 2016 election had a variety of causes, but voter suppression proved crucial. The distribution of the votes echoed the 2000 contested election: it's cities versus country, college towns versus rural towns. Hillary Clinton, like Al Gore, won the popular vote. The enthusiasm gap between the contenders reared its head. A lot of people tried to deny it existed. This election may, or may not, be the last hurrah for a couple of generations of white folk. What do I think? As Jesus purportedly said on the cross while soldiers cast lots and divided up his garments: "Father, forgive them; for they know not what they do."

Yes, we live in a divided America. But, as Bernie Sanders showed in the primaries, dividing garments and casting lots was in vogue. But, unlike the Bush versus Gore contest, the 2016 campaign itself suppressed the vote. The statistics are now just starting to come out that prove the point. Donald Trump barely received more votes winning than Mitt Romney received losing. That could only happen in an election where the chief attribute was voter suppression.

Americans tend to suppress the vote in any case, since barely half even bother to vote. But, in addition to those tendencies, this time there was a certain sort of not voting that led to the outcome. In Michigan, Michael Moore pointed out on MSNBC after the election, some twenty thousand voters who *did* vote skipped voting for any candidate for president.

This sort of thing has happened before, and I wrote about it in *Campaign America '96*. In the race for the Senate in New York State in Bill Clinton's first win in 1992, tens of thousands of voters did not vote for anyone for senator in that election. The reason was the Democratic primary had been so cantankerous and ugly that voters, mainly women—that primary was full of women candidates (Geraldine Ferraro, Liz Holtzman) and the eventual winner, Robert Abrams, was wounded by winning—voted for neither candidate. Alfonse D'Amato, the Republican incumbent, won narrowly. Republicans retained the seat because some Democrats felt aggrieved. Sound familiar? See Bernie's boosters.

After that contest, in an autobiography, D'Amato wrote, "A significant number of liberals were so turned off by Abrams that they voted for Clinton and then did not vote in the Senate race at all. I may not have won liberal Ferraro voters, but Abrams lost many of them. As I learned... in a close election every vote and every non-vote counts."

I am sure the nonvote count in the 2016 presidential category will be the largest in modern history. Voter suppression takes all forms and we have just witnessed the pernicious result of its success.

Huffington Post, November 18, 2016

A version of this article ran in the South Bend Tribune, *November 23, 2016.*

Similarities

A small number of commentators have pointed out some similarities between Ronald Reagan and Donald Trump. The actor, Chuck Norris, provided "Top 8 Similarities between Trump and Reagan," and, at the other end of the pundit perspective, Josh Zeitz attempted to answer the question, "Is Donald Trump Like Ronald Reagan?" Zeitz has taught at Cambridge University and Princeton, and Chuck Norris is, well, Chuck Norris. Both published their pieces during the past campaign, Zeitz in March and Norris in July.

One similarity that Norris leaves out is all the race-baiting, dog-whistle tactics that both successful candidates employed, the fact that Reagan held one of his first large campaign events at the Neshoba County Fair, some seven miles from Philadelphia, Mississippi, a town notorious for the killing of three civil rights workers. But race-baiting long has been a staple in American elections, and both Trump and Reagan weren't pioneers in that muddy field.

But what interests me is the flip-side similarities between Reagan and Trump, the 180-degree comparisons. Similar but different. Reagan the optimist, Trump the pessimist, Reagan the civilized, Trump the barbarian, that sort of thing. Ronald Reagan strove to be a picture of decorum, the modest superstar, humble with his successes as well as his failures. His televised apology for lying to Americans during the Iran-Contra scandal is a model of the latter.

Indeed, when Reagan began his campaign in 1980, as I have written before, most of the coverage treated him, if not as a clown, as an amusement. It was only during the summer of that year that reporters realized that he might actually win, given all of Jimmy Carter's accumulating troubles. Ditto Trump. It wasn't necessarily Obama's troubles, but Hillary Clinton's, that were piling up, thanks to the usual suspects, the Russians, the head of the FBI, etc. But, earlier on, it was the fecklessness of Trump's primary competitors that let him emerge, and then Hillary became the likely villain and victim. Crooked Hillary.

I had heard from a reliable source in early 2016 that the CIA would not let Trump become president. I wasn't necessarily picturing drones over the Trump Tower (which, ironically, may now happen, military drones that is), and didn't take the prediction seriously till the former head of the KGB entered the fray. Putin must have heard the same thing, and it became a stimulus, a challenge, to his institutional pride. Hence, all the email hacks.

Some observers wonder why the emails interested journalists so much, whereas all of the Trump scandals—Trump University, charities, foreign entanglements, etc.—didn't seem to hold the same allure, or promote the same daily coverage. Well, unfortunately, journalists read and send emails all the time, whereas very few, almost none, attend bogus universities or fly around the world to luxurious hotels and golf resorts. They write what they know.

But, as the old Ted Kennedy joke goes, they'll drive off that bridge when they come to it.

Two other presidents have the same, numerically, assortment of similarities: Bill Clinton and Barack Obama. The last two Democratic presidents who served two terms didn't have their biological fathers in their lives. Grandparents played a role in their early upbringing. Both are left handed and both made very strategic marriage choices, breaking their earlier—and in Bill Clinton's case, continuous—dating patterns and history.

And, of course, both saw their two terms as president almost go for naught. Clinton being replaced by his opposite, George W. Bush, the scion of an entitled family, a man reckless and oblivious to the responsibilities of the job. And now Obama, leaving everything at risk to another heir, a ludicrous choice foisted on the American public by less than a hundred thousand disgruntled voters distributed in three states, a man who seems more devoted to his twitter account than the presidency.

Both Clinton and Obama were children of the meritocracy. Bush and Trump not so much. But both Democrats failed, leaving office with their annulled presidencies, insofar as they had eight years to encourage successors and neither seemed to find that important, crucial, to everything they stood for. And it's small comfort that in both elections that followed their terms the popular vote went to the losers. Another bothersome similarity that could have been predicted.

Huffington Post, January 2, 2017

Trump, Trumped, Trumpery

Trump's executive orders are most assuredly public relations stunts first and foremost. Secondarily, they echo his campaign promises and that is the point, wanting to claim at a later date he fulfilled all his promises pronto. How else to explain the haste, shoddiness, and their language, a mixture of simple-mindedness and obscurity?

I can't recall previous presidents holding up such signed documents to the assembled cameras, as if they were large glossies of Miss Universe candidates. All that was visible was Trump's EKG-inspired signature, an alarming sight. The executive orders haven't been coordinated with the applicable agencies, and one reason floated for that is Trump's fear that bad guys in the bureaucracy would bollix up his good intentions. The travel ban has become the most notorious, but the others are future poison pills.

It's government by spectacle, not a surprise, given the previous campaign. Trump continues to tweet his semiliterate bon mots, contradicting himself anytime he feels like it, subletting his responsibilities as quickly as possible to his underlings, such as giving over the decision on "torture" to his defense secretary.

Trump continues to say he believes in the efficacy of torture and that doubtless comes from his self-knowledge that if he were pinched on the arm he would give up all his secrets. It's been clear for decades that those who are deterred from wrongdoing by the thought of going to prison are only those who never imagined themselves in one.

It appears Trump himself finds it hard to believe he's actually president. Why else go on so long about the size of the crowd at his inauguration? And claiming he would have won the popular vote except for the three-to-five-million illegals who voted, thereby showing more civic engagement than regular Americans who couldn't be bothered. Unfortunately, such complaints are catnip to television news, which loves to compare pictures. No visuals, no story, in our age of looking, caught in a culture of seeing. This was especially true during the campaign, so many fixated on the size of his fingers, the size of his whatever.

Worse, of course, is to come. The Gorsuch selection for the high court is a Trojan horse for the second pick Trump expects to get. The Republican-controlled Congress won't be a rubber stamp for Trump, Trump will be a rubber stamp for Congress. Former Indiana governor Mike Pence, who thought he would lose his reelection and hitched his wagon to the Trump campaign, is all over the early policy changes, and the Breitbart creature, Steve Bannon, who seems as aggrieved by the so-called elites—actually people who are culture celebrities—as his master Trump. Regardless of both Bannon's and Trump's own Ivy League credentials, they look at the world as an internal, eternal, high school Darwinian experiment, jousting with the in-crowd and the out.

They want to beat what they can't join, and they have. Thanks to the disgruntled blue-state voters who put Trump over the top, individuals that Trump and Bannon would be appalled to spend any real time with, they now have the power to beat and pulverize all the adherents of the former in-crowd, especially the arugula-loving Obama followers.

Where will it end? I have no faith Democrats will rise up in less than two years and capture either the Senate or the House. The Republicans have gerrymandered their way to semipermanence in state houses and in Congress. Trump's America will be gaudy and crazy on the outside, but mean and punishing on the inside, thanks to the Pence/Bannon/McConnell/McCarthy/Ryan view of America.

Huffington Post, February 2, 2017

Trump Monkeys

The Trump administration puts to the test the "infinite monkey theorem," since so many journalists are typing away, chronicling the daily saga of the new president. Very little Shakespearean prose has yet resulted, but we have to consider the source. Trump's address to the "joint session" of Congress produced amazement at the new Trumpian focus, his ability to read—and stick to—the teleprompter for an hour or so. Two times, though, he did deviate, letting the inner Trump ooze out: claiming some sort of record for applause had been reached and the soul-churning idea that the deceased Navy Seal, William "Ryan" Owens, was looking down at the assembly and smiling. Perhaps Trump was channeling the apostate Mike Pence sitting, smiling, behind him.

This brings me to the chief spectacle of that night, the sight of the Seal's widow, sitting, standing, crying, mumbling, suffering. It is cheering that the earliest critics of that display were other military people calling this for what it was: exploitation. Trump, understanding television if nothing else, along with his obsession with ratings, knew he had a winner: Who cannot be riveted by the sight of a good-looking woman in extremis?

I tried to imagine which American actress (or British, French, etc.) could have done what the widow was doing so convincingly. What the viewer got to witness was, seemingly, minutes of high-quality grief porn. Always a big draw, though only if the woman involved is attractive. In this case, a willowy blonde in a black dress.

Why did she consent to be used this way? Evidently, she has a military background herself, and when the commander in chief asks, she responds. She was obviously still traumatized by the recent death of her husband, but Trump knew she would be a good show.

Trump's treatment of women was already well broadcast during his campaign, but since he assumed the presidency he still is treating women badly. On his inauguration day, pictures showed him neglecting his wife repeatedly, and the largely absent First Lady was hauled out finally in Florida on February 18, ten days post the news of her libel lawsuit against the British tabloid the *Daily Mail* broke, detailing how it would cut into her future income, to give her brief I-am-not-a-hooker speech. Her remarks began with a recitation of the Lord's Prayer (aka, the Our Father), the Protestant version, which no one could accuse her of plagiarizing. Yet another weird spectacle.

(Though it needs to be said that Michelle Obama took awhile to get her footing. Back during her first year as FLOTUS, she was stuck hoeing that godforsaken garden built at great cost on the White House lawn. Even I wrote a column back then claiming I would lose my mind if I saw another picture of her holding a yam in her fist.)

But the prize this past week goes to Trump's tweets on Saturday morning, calling President Obama "sick," a bad guy, for "tapp"-ing his phone in Trump Tower. As they say, these tweets dominated the news over the weekend and into this week (below is the last):

> How low has President Obama gone to tapp my phones during the very sacred election process. This is Nixon/Watergate. Bad (or sick) guy! 7:02 AM - 4 Mar 2017.

How low can he go? Good question. We're now back to Trump the unhinged, rather than Trump the presidential, according to the rounded-up usual suspects among commentators. I did like the continuation of Trump's new evangelical rhetorical streak, given his "very sacred election process" characterization. In the same vein as the dead Seal smiling down at us. See, Mike Pence is exerting influence.

Speaking, as did Trump, of the former president, contrary to the gushing coverage, Obama's "last" speech as president in Chicago was completely delusional—it can be summed up in this paraphrase: we're doing swell and the rest of you are screwed. And given his vacation photos and the family's alleged $65 million book deal, it appears that he is. Obama, ironically, is enjoying the traditional honeymoon period, not Trump the nut.

One reason Trump was apparently comfortable during his speech to Congress was that he was speaking largely to an audience of millionaires. Consult the statistics of the average wealth of the typical senator or congressperson. It's somewhat like the crowd at Mar-a-Lago.

But as the news cycle speeds up, the attention span of the audience slows down. Trump monkeys have to keep feeding the beast and can barely stick to a story beyond twenty-four hours. (On to the American Health Care Act!—Trump, I expect, will want to tweet that Obamacare should be renamed the Kenyan Health Care Act.)

We have all lived with "false equivalency" for a few years now. Trump's "Obama bad" tweets seem to have worked their dark magic, and Republicans are all ready to drag Trump's wiretapping accusations into their investigations into the Russian campaign hacks. False equivalency rises in committee hearings, costing money, time, and attention. The Swamp needs more muddy waters. It wasn't enough for Trump's drained swamp to end up in his cabinet.

Huffington Post, March 9, 2017

Trump Rising

It's hard to keep up with The Donald's buffoonery, so I haven't been trying, but it was hard to miss that he finally got a chance to play Zeus hurling thunderbolts, in Trump's case, 59 Tomahawks, getting rid of inventory, lobbing them at the Syrian airfield. Not Iraq, as he told Maria Bartiromo on Fox. Thankfully, he lets his generals decide where to drop the bombs, like the MOAB, supposedly never used since created in 2003, that they let loose over Afghanistan. More inventory reduction.

Trump's popularity went up, though only a point or two, not a surprise, though there does appear to be a gold-plated ceiling where The Donald is concerned. The Trump method, doctrine, if you will, is distraction, and it is quite successful. Trump himself is the chief distraction, while the House and Senate Republicans knit away, Madame Defarge–like, only backward, undoing the fabric of the Obama state, canceling protections right and right.

Neil Gorsuch sits on the high court. Gorsuch, like Mike Pence, was raised Catholic, but now seems to be a fashionable Episcopalian, thereby finally adding a Protestant to the court. Paul Ryan, the Speaker, remains busy dreaming his apocalyptic dreams—no taxes! No entitlements!—Mitch McConnell continues his haughty hypocrisies, do not as I have done, but do as I say.

Democrats are resisting, though it would have been better if they had been voting in 2016. Those shouting "You lie!" to Joe Wilson at his South Carolina town hall should have been yelling it back in 2009 when he shouted out in Congress to President Obama.

I have written quite a bit on elections since 1996, and it still seems credible that outcomes rely on the so-called low-information, late-deciding undecideds. In Trump's case, he had direct access to the same crowd that George W. Bush profited from, those voters who most identified with him.

Not the self-identification of bogus billionaires, but which person they wanted to be next to, have a beer with, etc.; W. had more than a leg up on that constituency, compared with Al Gore. Even though Gore won the popular vote—England has its royals and we have the Electoral College—Gore would have won even that, had the whole state of Florida been counted correctly, yet not many voters wanted to have a beer with him. Trump, of course, doesn't drink alcohol, but his coarse bonhomie, similar to the younger Bush's, struck a chord with the common voter.

Hillary, poor Hillary, had more in common with Al Gore than her titular husband. And, though the usual suspects—email server, Ruskies, Wikileaks, Comey, etc.—did their dark work, Hillary's losing ground was well prepared by Bernie Sanders. Sanders's largest success in public office likely will turn out to be his assistance in helping Donald Trump become the forty-fifth president of the United States.

Nonetheless, Trump is rising, given the begrudged acknowledgment by most of the media that he is the president. No one with a sense of self-importance wants to believe a dangerous nitwit is presiding over the Oval Office. Oh, no, it flies in the face of self-regard. So, Trump may not be presidential himself, but he is being treated as the president. With respect, of a sort.

And, if the presumed shake-up in Trump's administration is coming and The Donald is throwing the more picturesque clown car occupants under the bigger bus, more of this incipient fawning will continue. Trump may not be acting more presidential, but the people around him are, and that will likely be enough for the permanent establishment, in both the media and Washington.

Steve Bannon does stick out as a sore thumb. Even when he wears a suit and tie he just doesn't look the part. He looks like the alt-right zealot he is, disheveled, unhealthy, and though he might have millions he doesn't look well cared for. Compare him to the typical senator. Those folks know how to look the part. They all look like a million dollars.

And poor Sean Spicer. How can he stay? His latest pratfall about Hitler doesn't *gas his people* (other Austrians?) contained the priceless coinage, "Holocaust centers," a phrase that can only be the product of a Cuisinart brain, chopping into tiny bits vocabulary and ideas that are swirling around the plastic bowl of his mind.

If Ivanka and Jared are really running things Sean will be gone soon. It is alarming to look at the people Trump has been discarding: Paul Manafort, Carter Page, Roger Stone, General Flynn, and, possibly Bannon and Spicer, all true believers, each helping in their own twisted way Trump become leader of the free world.

Huffington Post, April 17, 2017

Richie Rich, Baby Boomers, and, Look Out, 2018 Looming

The baby boom generation has suffered a number of ignominies, especially in the fellow boomer presidents who have been elected as the cohort has grown and matured. The first of the generation to take office, Bill Clinton, ended the meritocracy those born post-1945 had enjoyed. After his total lack of common sense, given the settings of his interactions with Monica Lewinsky (the Oval Office), he was impeached, which prevented the other baby boomer, Al Gore, from advancing, handing over the election, barely, to George W. Bush. Clinton's legacy is the Bush II administration and all the calamities it wrought, most of which are still ongoing in 2017.

The Bubba cost his wife the recent election because even Democrats were tired of both Clintons in 2008, and Clinton fatigue had barely dissipated by 2016. The less said about George W. the better, as he wiles away his late years doing old-age-home arts and crafts. But, one presumes, the greatest affront to boomers is Donald Trump, currently president of the United States. We have gone from the smartest guy in the room—Bill Clinton—to the incarnation of baby boom–era comic-character Richie Rich, minus Rich's purported kindness and impulse to charity. This final insult is hard for the generation to absorb.

Presidential elections have been swinging the last couple of decades from the bootstrap candidates, Clinton and Barack Obama, to the entitled, George W. Bush and now, The Donald. Seemingly, the American public is riding on a pendulum, favoring the self-made office seeker and then the rich. Political success in the country now appears to be the real estate of the very wealthy, those who buy their offices outright.

The next national election of consequence is the one where the presidency is not involved. The year 2018 rises in importance, given the chaos of the Trump administration and the GOP's lock on governing the party now holds. Here in Indiana, Senator Joe Donnelly's prospects for reelection in 2018 are seen by many political observers as a test case of the strength of the Democratic Party. The year 2018 will reveal whether or not the Democrats are actually the basket case they seem.

Donnelly may have profited in the 2012 Senate race in Indiana from two things: an astoundingly inept Republican opponent (Richard Mourdock of the "gift from God" fertilization by a rapist) and a presidential election year that helped boost turnout. Donnelly had chosen not to run for his congressional seat, given the state's GOP gerrymandering of the second district. Donnelly, unfortunately, left us with the elusive Jackie Walorski, a state-level politician, one of the many Republicans who finds open town halls toxic. Donnelly opted for the high-risk-high-reward Senate contest and it paid off.

Donnelly is one of the most vulnerable Democratic senators of a red state. Indiana went for Donald Trump by seventeen points, showing more Hoosier pride—Mike! Pence!—than enthusiasm for Trump, helped by a woeful overall turnout—Indiana ranked fortieth out of fifty states. Hillary Clinton won St. Joseph County, a Democratic stronghold, by less than a point.

Unfortunately, it doesn't look like our wunderkind South Bend mayor Pete Buttigieg will be a candidate for Congress in 2018. Given his sterling performance running for chair of the Democratic National Committee, the fundraising window for him would be wide open and, certainly, he would have helped improve turnout in the second district, thereby aiding Donnelly statewide.

Walorski is ripe for defeat. The all-male leadership of the DC Republicans have kept her on a very tight leash. They may have improved her visual presentation since 2013, restricted her to a few sentences to say, over and over, and put her in any number of photo-ops, even with Donald Trump, since there are so few GOP women (sixty-two Dems, twenty-one GOP), but she continues to be the same old lovable "Wackie Jackie" of yore, applauding the president's one-page-joke tax plan and swooning over the Senate and the House's reverse–Robin Hood decimation of Obamacare, and whatever other craziness Donald Trump indulges in.

Donnelly has been, and will be, attacked by both the right and the left. Various purity tests have been engaged by some Democrats, including Donnelly's vote for Supreme Court justice Neil Gorsuch. The three non-Republican votes for Gorsuch came from red-state Democrats. Their reelection contests will be mudfests, especially Donnelly's.

That the Democratic leadership took the hardest line against Gorsuch, knowing that the Republicans would invoke the misnamed and hyperbolic "nuclear option," was ill advised. Gorsuch was laureled with what are considered the most reputable credentials, though, at heart, he seems to be just another Republican Party hack. Democrat opposition turned out to be yet another futile political gesture.

An all-out fight against the second Supreme Court nominee—if Trump gets one, which is likely—would have been more useful. Since only a bare majority vote is now needed in the Senate to confirm, Trump can serve up even a Liberty

University zealot and the Democrats will be hamstrung. Better they had contested a less-credentialed person than Gorsuch, one that even some sensible Republicans would balk at.

In addition, the anti-abortion lobby is second only to the NRA in its focused, single-issue, get-out-the-vote capabilities. Democrats are now sparring over making a pro-choice stance for candidates mandatory, which is absurd, given the party's ethnic and religious history, though what most Democrats would agree on is that prolife Democratic officeholders resist limiting the reproductive rights women already possess.

Some diehards these days think Bernie Sanders could have won the presidency if he had been the nominee. Isn't it pretty to think so? as Hemingway would have said. The Republican Money Machine didn't bother to lay a glove on Bernie during the primary season. Picture the garbage that would have been heaped on him had he been the nominee. Recall that along with Trump it was Sanders who didn't release his most current taxes during the primaries—it was Jane who was doing them, he'd cry. What were they hiding? Now Jane and Bernie are under investigation for the usual kind of money shenanigans. Yet Democrats remain divided today because Sanders was essentially a third-party candidate. And he is too old to be a baby boomer.

What motivates Democrat voters who sat out the election, or voted for Jill Stein, or the fairly crazy Libertarian candidate, in 2016 was well put by David Hoppe in the Indianapolis weekly *NUVO*. They were folks "who think of voting not in terms of collective self-interest, but as a hermetically personal form of self-expression."

If Joe Donnelly loses in 2018, self-expression—and Trump and the Republicans—again will have won the day, to say nothing of the House, the Senate.

Huffington Post, June 28, 2017

"What a Dump!" the Presidency, That Is

During the last two or three presidencies (starting with Bill Clinton) there has been talk of the "permanent campaign," campaigns that never end. Continuous fundraising, etc. Usually, this sort of talk dies down, especially when it comes to the presidency itself. But, lately, we have crossed over into so many new, unsuspected realms it is clear that the presidency itself is leading the way without any surcease of campaigning.

The Donald has not stopped his campaigning, because it is the only political experience he has. Never elected to nothing was his calling card, and the other suspect preceding presidents (principally Ronald Reagan) had some electoral success in their pasts, besides their celebrity. One needs to go back to the generals to find a novice, Dwight David Eisenhower. Trump has surrounded himself with generals, though that displays his authoritarian impulses, more like the typical Banana Republic administration, where military power props up despots.

As any number of folk have noticed, Trump is, was, more or less, an open book. He hid practically nothing of his inner self during the campaign. The only truth Trump consorts with is Truth in Advertising, meaning most everyone, except for the deluded (not that a large number—see Michigan, Pennsylvania, and Wisconsin election margins), knew who they were voting for.

When Trump and Melania first visited the White House, before the inauguration, hosted by the Obamas, I told anyone who would listen at the time that Trump's first thought during the tour would have been "What a dump!" I doubt that Melania would have known of Bette Davis's famous coinage, so she was likely just mildly appalled. No spa! Old plumbing! Even a cursory understanding of The Donald would have prompted this insight. And, recently, not to my dismay, he even said it aloud ("a real dump"), to his golfing buddies. Trump is not a complex personality.

What is surprising to me is that Trump manages to best himself week after week, meaning that he finds a way to be freshly outrageous and inappropriate. (See yesterday's "impromptu" presser, revealing yet again his shallow understanding of history, much less his racist inclinations.) I was in Cuba at the end of the Obama presidency and the start of the Trump era, so I did not get to hear his inaugural address. Sitting on the patio of the Hotel Nacional I couldn't imagine what that speech would be, because Trump seemingly is incapable of eloquence or sincerity. After I returned and heard bits of the "American Carnage" diatribe, I realized his speechwriters went the only place they could, to a dark, dangerous place, full of invective and doom.

David Brooks, who has gone on his own strange journey since being hired on by the *New York Times*, from an early comedic conservative writer to his pompous new-agey book-report fetish columns (Look what I read last week!), wants to wash The Donald out of his hair, but, unfortunately, none of us will be able to do that for another three years. I've always held Trump will be a one-term president, given that the job, the actual work of the presidency, won't be much fun for him. And, decidedly, it doesn't look like he's having much fun.

Yet behind the gaudy scrim of The Donald himself truly terrible things are happening. Look at his Cabinet of Deplorables, what they are doing to their bailiwicks. Justice, EPA, Education, etc. And Republicans in Congress are getting to play out their repressed economic and social fantasies of the last half of the twentieth century, attempting to dismantle all that the Democratic Century (the twentieth) had managed to create.

In a review I once wrote of a book (*Tip O'Neill and the Democratic Century*) that covered the period, I dejectedly prophesied that if progressive people didn't look out, the twenty-first would become the Republican Century, and that appears to be the case. At this point, it seems unlikely Democrats will win back the House of Representatives and add to their count in the Senate. What Mitch McConnell did to Obama, making him a seven-year president, rather than an eight-year president, was an act of racism just as blatant as any that was seen recently in Charlottesville.

And, in permanent-campaign-mode epitome, President Trump has continued to be the president of only his base, all the rest of the country be damned. And it is apparent he will get away with it, given that barely 50 percent of the country bothers to vote in presidential election years and less in off years. And that circumstance continues to be promoted by state Republicans everywhere, making it more difficult, rather than easier, to vote. The notion of false equivalency has become popular in the last few years, but one false equivalency is that this country is run by a two-party system. Democrats and Republicans are not equal. Trump's win was proof of that, given the third-party candidacies (including Bernie's) doomed Hillary Clinton.

Looking back on the history of presidential campaigns, Trump's victory, though shocking, is only the culmination of a trend line that has been trending for a long time. And if he is the nadir, which he may well not be, what will come next? Of the many frightening things to contemplate, add that one to the list.

Huffington Post, August 17, 2017

Ken Burns, Boy Capitalist, and *The Vietnam War* (Part I)

Given my age (seventy-one), I have had a long history with the Vietnam War. Ken Burns, a little less so. He was born in 1953 and is a different sort of baby boomer, blessed with a self-reported high draft lottery number. I ran into my own fate a few months before the lottery was put in place. Those experiences resulted in my first novel, *The Meekness of Isaac*, which appeared in 1974. It was reviewed fairly well for its time, a long, supportive review in the *New York Times Book Review* by C. D. B. Bryan, who died recently.

Not many in 1974 wanted to read about the Vietnam War while it was still raging. It was similar to the fact that no one wants to discuss fire in the middle of a conflagration. No paperback, no audience to speak of. Around that time (1975) Tim O'Brien's nonfiction book, *If I Die in a Combat Zone*, did have a paperback, but his hit novel, *Going after Cacciato*, didn't appear till 1978.

Now we have Ken Burns and Lynn Novick's eighteen hours of the war. I have only seen four episodes thus far. Unfortunately, for me, the project's first few minutes were its worst. Two things occurred. First, we see a Missouri vet saying that, though he and his wife were good friends with another couple, they didn't know both of the men had fought in Vietnam for twelve years. This either questions the notion of what good friends are or is a distortion of history. The vet claims no one spoke about the war. He was in Vietnam in 1969. In his case, this seems to be a personal problem, not a public one. In my circles, the war never vanished as a subject of conversation.

Back in the late 1960s and early '70s, I was in the midst of the antiwar movement, insofar as my first book, *The Harrisburg 7 and the New Catholic Left*, which came out two years before my first novel, was about relatively famous protesters of the Vietnam War. Not many read that book either, though it was on the *New York Times Book Review*'s New and Recommended list for six weeks. Even then, television was supreme and I wasn't on TV.

Ken Burns has always been on TV. He knew, knows, which way the culture was/is blowing. Yet Burns most resembles some fellow 1950s births of renown: both Bill Gates and Steve Jobs were born in 1955, two years after Burns. What Burns shares with those two (and others) is that at heart he is a satisfied capitalist. Not all of his baby boom predecessors found in the antiwar movement were cut from that cloth. And, like Gates and Jobs, he likes lawyers and doesn't hesitate to threaten and sue his critics. A friend of mine, now dead, wrote a book about documentary filmmakers some years back and managed a few mild criticisms of Burns, and Burns and his hirelings harassed her publisher in order to suppress the book. Gates, too, was always a big suer, Jobs, also. You have to protect your interests.

And that, doubtless, accounts for the other problem with the *The Vietnam War*'s beginning, practically the first thing Peter Coyote says is that the war was started in "good" faith by "decent" men. No they weren't, one or another, or both. Burns is solidly in the "both sides" camp, like another capitalist, Donald Trump. Nice white supremacists and bad protestors, blame on both sides, now as then.

I can understand. If you need to be funded by huge corporations, including David H. Koch and Bank of America, you have to be nice to rich people and not offend them. It was one of Barack Obama's problems. You don't become president of the *Harvard Law Review*, much less of the United States, and not be nice to rich people.

But, beyond the first few minutes, thus far, the episodes have been great, if by great I mean truthful, hard hitting, more than appalling in their revelations. The early few mentions of the antiwar protestors have problems. Like most television, the series, in so many ways, is superficial. No analysis of Political Economy, no Follow the Money, no War is the Health of the State.

I fear Burns is on the way to endorsing the "spitting on soldiers" narrative that has been a right-wing favorite for decades. That is what is now called fake news, trumped up by the government then and now, attempting to create animosity between soldiers and citizens. (Here are pro and con spitting stories: http://www.startribune.com/disrespect-for-vietnam-vets-is-fact-not-fiction/160444095/ and https://slate.com/news-and-politics/2000/05/drooling-on-the-vietnam-vets.html.) Would the most successful (and last) antiwar group, the Vietnam Veterans Against the War, have become so honored if that were true?

What did occur back then I recount in my 1974 novel. Before its veteran character, based on a good friend of mine, left Nam for the World, as it was called, the planeloads of departees were treated to a lecture saying they would be harassed by their fellow citizens when they returned and they should be on alert. That warning causes a scene of semiviolence in the novel. Again, this was back in the early 1970s. The government had a settled policy to enhance friction between soldiers and the rest of their countrymen. Hence the spitting stories. None of this has gotten better, other than the hollow "thank-you-for-your-service" mantra handed out to the one percent by the ninety-nine percent. The military always wanted a volunteer army—easier to privatize wars that way, fewer people in the streets.

And, boy, did we get that, along with all the continuing wars we have. I'll wait for Burns's documentary on the good and decent folk who brought us all the Middle East wars that, if they have their way, will never end.

Huffington Post, September 25, 2017

Ken Burns, Boy Capitalist, and *The Vietnam War* (Part II)

What the eighteen hours of Ken Burns and Lynn Novick's *The Vietnam War* were was exhausting. I kept wondering about the demographics of the viewers. How many young people were watching this? Was the audience only aging baby boomers? Somebody must know. As usual in Ken Burns's projects it was as much human interest as history. Indeed, if you didn't already know a lot about the history of the Vietnam War, you wouldn't be able to fill in the roughshod way Burns and Novick raced through those years. But, unfortunately, their project will become history, since it will be watched by a generation that prefers watching over most anything else.

Here are some odd things it would be helpful for watchers to know: the friction college students felt when they were "ranked," grade point averages implied, in order to retain student deferments. Ranking drew protests, but, unmentioned, it was the Selective Service Qualification Test that was administered widely and was given preference. I took it in the spring of 1966. If you scored high enough you didn't lose your 2-S deferment.

Social scientists, then as now, worked with the military to arrange their own Darwinian methods for selecting soldiers-to-be. Now, it is torture that occupies them, then the draft.

The narration mentions that "banks" were bombed. It didn't mention the radicals' favorite targets were branches of Bank of America, since it is one of the film's major backers. The Weatherman were said to have blown up a statue of "six policeman." It would be helpful to know that statue commemorated the Haymarket Riot, where seven, not six, policeman were killed, and the statue itself only featured one policeman, with his arm raised in an unfortunate position, presaging the Nazi salute some three decades down the road. The gathering at the Haymarket Square in Chicago was supporting the forty-hour week back in May 1886. It eventually became the rallying point for May Day celebrations around the world, honoring workers, but not in the United States.

In an early episode, Benjamin Spock was mentioned writing about children injured by napalm, but no mention of the Boston Five trial in Boston in 1968 where he was a defendant because of antidraft activity. There is, I suppose, a reason the series is called *The Vietnam War.* The war predominated and there was very little of the antiwar movement and its offshoots. There are other documentaries on the antiwar movement, but none got, or get, the play Burns and Novick's has enjoyed.

There were other lapses. The documentary's talking heads were barely identified. One of the most egregious was John Negroponte, notorious for his work in Central America. Wherever Negroponte went, death squads sprang up. To say the least, no one speaking was saddled with a full biographical notation. Most just were ID-ed by their affiliation: "Army," "Air Force," etc.

As was Tim O'Brien, who gets the documentary's last word, which was "endured." He was reading from his short story, "The Things They Carried." Given all the horror that was covered, Burns and Novick seem to privilege endurance over all, the humanity of the ordinary person, despite all the evidence to the contrary. What was interesting was the coverage and the unstated linkage of that war with the present day. Especially the foreign involvement presidents partook in: Nixon, primarily, getting the South Vietnamese to delay peace initiatives until after his election. Reagan running against Carter did the same thing with the hostages in Iran, not released till after Reagan's inauguration, through back channels, arranged by his old OSS and CIA buddy, Bill Casey. And, of course, The Donald and the Russians.

And it was illuminating, the difference between the Oval Office tapes of LBJ and Nixon. LBJ's did seem to be used in the service of history, whereas Nixon's were in the service of the prosecution and his removal. There was a lot that was illuminating. Such as the numbers. Over three hundred thousand Chinese going to Hanoi to free up a like number of Vietnamese to carry on the war. The amount of war material supplied by the Soviets and the Chinese. Higher-up North Vietnamese sending their children to Europe for education during the war, avoiding their own sort of draft. Burns and Novick are after, it seems, all sorts of equivalencies. The Americans were heroes, the North Vietnamese were heroes. It's their kind of history, remaining sunny even during the slaughter.

Almost no one seems to think the war was a good idea, though there are some who seem to think we could have done it better. When we cut and ran out of Saigon is portrayed as a stain of sorts, how the South Vietnamese were better allies than we were and there is a tinge of regret, as if we somehow should have found a way to "win." There was no winning, though it is implied the hope was always for some sort of South Korea solution. Yes, we should have remained in South Vietnam forever, as we seem to be heading to remain in Iraq and Afghanistan forever, is the import. The plea heard occasionally in the series was that they—the South Vietnamese—would tell us to leave. And that would have been peace with honor. Ah, yes, it is pretty to think so.

Back in the day, I thought the war was fought for all the usual reasons, natural resources, strategic location, Cold War ideology, etc. But it is most ironic, and not covered by the filmmakers, that nearly sixty thousand Americans were killed, and hundreds of thousands of Vietnamese, so Ralph Lauren and Nike and other apparel and shoe manufacturers could have access to cheap labor. No one in the antiwar movement, no matter how cynical, ever offered that as a reason for the war. The only other thing, the only positive thing, it seems to have created was the growth of Vietnamese immigrants, and the younger generation of Vietnamese Americans. But it is still impossible to be thankful for that war for any reason.

Huffington Post, October 18, 2017

Cuba and Carnage

I went to Cuba last January and I've had a long, sketchy history with the place. In the 1970s I hung out at the Center for Cuban Studies down in the Village, being interested in the woman who ran it. I managed to avoid being blown up by anti-Castro Cubans when they put a bomb outside its door one night I didn't visit. And I had lunch with a Cuban UN representative at Jean and Leonard Boudin's home on St. Luke's Place, complete with armed bodyguards. Leonard was Cuba's lawyer for a time back then. And, some years later, Cuba played a role in a novel I wrote called *Criminal Tendencies*.

But, like most Americans, I had never been there, till the Obama administration made travel less onerous, or legal, and a number of publications began running "People to People" tours. I had never gone on a tour, fully escorted as they say, but I decided, Why not? I booked one sponsored by *The Nation*, a magazine I had written for over the years, but not lately. I could imagine the demographics: old lefties wandering among the ruins. I wasn't disappointed.

A picture was taken of most all of us in front of the U.S. Embassy, which is close by the esplanade, the Malecón, the picturesque road next to the water with a view of Old Havana. Barack Obama was still president, but just barely. Donald Trump was to be inaugurated in a couple of days, right before our departure home. Out with old, in with the new. I couldn't imagine Trump's speech for the ceremony (and I didn't hear it), since it seemed impossible for him to sound articulate or heartfelt. I heard soundbites after my return. "American Carnage," indeed.

Now, it appears, the embassy was the scene of unseen carnage, some sort of sci-fi attack, as it is described, rendering personnel there with hearing loss and other disturbing brain and behavior problems. I seem to have escaped unscathed. But visiting Cuba was both sad and dispiriting. Our group stayed at a hotel near the Hotel Nacional, the Capri, allegedly the first hotel in Havana built by the Mob in the 1950s, newly reopened after it, too, was blown up by anti-Castro Cubans in the 1990s. One section, with bright red doors, was not in use, the large casino attached to the high rise. There was a pool and a nice bar on the roof, convivial with happy vacationers. It was all very Las Vegas in the fifties, if that's your taste.

Our days were full of lectures and encounters with the "people," a number taking place at the Hotel Nacional, just down the street. It is an impressive place, still capturing its aural of bygone wealth and status, though in the same way as a number of England's lesser castles display. It, like the rest of the country, has fallen on hard times. Our embargo and sanctions have been very successful, and the Cubans have suffered the blows of the fall of the Soviet Union and the cratering of Venezuela, both implicated mightily in the failing economics of the island. Tourism has taken over as a replacement and we spent a lot of time in new Chinese buses being taken here and there.

Many Cubans announced they want to expand the tourism sector. Given the crowded streets and roaming hordes, I couldn't see how they could fit any more Chinese buses and ambulating foreigners anywhere. Havana seemed overstuffed. And it appeared to be falling down. A shocking number of buildings do collapse each week, either thirty or three hundred, I can't recall, though either figure is alarming. I wasn't taking notes. Havana doesn't resemble Key West, or the American Southwest, or anywhere else I've been. It looks, I imagine, like Spain, since Spaniards were its colonizers for centuries. And Old Havana seems to be a calendar of those years, ancient buildings, some semirestored by those who get remittances from American relatives, others just in the process of falling down, though still occupied. The Lower East Side, where I lived in the late 1960s, was in far better shape back then, long before gentrification. Gentrification is a forlorn dream for Cuba's glorious old city.

It was all very sad. The Cubans I met all seemed to be pleased with the Americans wandering around. We took a side trip to Viñales, a tobacco-growing region's small village busily building B&Bs. On the way we stopped at a teaching hospital (Latin American Medical School) and listened to a talk by a physician who was the dean of students. They send their graduates to underserved countries around the globe. She was a compelling figure, most likely in her fifties, and Fidel Castro, who had died a few months earlier, almost inadvertently was mentioned, and she momentarily choked up, a show of emotion that surprised me. When we reached Viñales, after a tour of a tobacco farm, sitting at a very makeshift cantina, the local guide, responding to a question, also became emotional speaking of Fidel. So, high and low, they really seemed to love the man.

Unlike Vietnam, which, after our barbarous and useless war, has been brought into the American orbit, their former peasant economy being a source of cheap labor for U.S. clothing manufacturers, Cuba remains an outlier and it shows. That's what happens, I suppose, when you educate a whole population, make them literate and informed. They don't want to become cheap labor. Though, in Cuba, professors and doctors seem willing to be taxi drivers and bartenders in order to work in the tourist world, where they can get their hands on the more lucrative cash side of the country's idiotic two-currency system.

It's sad in Cuba, and doubtless more so, since Hurricane Irma raked the countryside and flooded parts of Havana. More buildings will crumble. And America's vengeance for losing the country and never killing the Castros (see the recent JFK assassination semidump) continues unabated and, post-Obama, redoubled.

Huffington Post, November 13, 2017

This was my last column for the Huffington Post, *appearing right before it became the* HuffPost *and cut loose their legion of free content providers.*

Brett Kavanaugh, a Suit, and the Bro Culture

I

The SCOTUS nominee, Brett Kavanaugh, is a creature of Washington, DC, and the problems he is going through now are also a large part of his success. Kavanaugh is first and foremost a Suit, a guy who has credentialed himself as a GOP operative, and he shares a number of attributes with other past DC scandal figures. His roots go back further than Anita Hill; they reach into history, at least, to the Nixon administration, the Watergate episode, complete with eager young Washington GOP lawyers, especially the group that was adept at "ratfucking."

Kavanaugh reminds me of Donald Segretti, memorialized in the film of Woodward and Bernstein's *All the President's Men*. Kavanaugh is not as smarmy as portrayed by the actor in the film, his sad monologue full of self-pity—though about the same amount Kavanaugh showed in his Fox News interview. Indeed, Kavanaugh is a few steps above Segretti in the career-advancement sweepstakes. He's a federal judge, after all, another lifetime appointment.

Kavanaugh has an odd connection to Donald Trump. Being nominated to the Supreme Court might be the same sort of catastrophe for him as being elected president has been for Donald Trump. Everything was going along swimmingly until Trump reached the top. Trump and his circle were shocked and awed when he won. It's been downhill for them since, though the Republicans in Congress have had a field day. The supposed runner-up for the Supreme Court, Amy Coney Barrett, should take note and be happy she has a good permanent job and decline any further offers.

Over the last few decades I have watched with some alarm while the bro culture has produced so many successful Republican male lawyers and financiers, Wall Street types riding Harleys: heavy drinkers, most athletes of a sort, womanizers, hale, hearty and well met. Capitalists all, they seemed; with rare exception they favored the GOP. They did produce the ubiquitous use of the modern phrase *toxic masculinity*, which first entered common usage in the early 2000s. Previously, the rise of Microsoft, Apple, Facebook, etc., seemed to cement the hegemony of single-minded men, though that tech crowd was softened somewhat by their West Coast geographies. The East Coast made the men meaner; Washington, DC, or as J. Edgar Hoover and the FBI used to refer to it, SOG—seat of government.

Given what we know now about Kavanaugh, it looks like Yale finally managed to civilize young Brett, or, at least, teach him that being drunk all the time didn't lead to success. He seems to have changed his vices to excessive NBA basketball tickets, or, it is suspected, gambling. I, too, went to a Jesuit all-boys high school, one that shares the "Men for Others" motto, though I did tweet recently that Brett should adjust the motto to Men Atop Others. I went to my high school in the early 1960s and, to say the least, the social mores were far different than those of the '80s. God knows what the Jesuits were thinking at Georgetown Prep, but supervision didn't seem to be a priority. Though alcohol consumption has always been the most approved Catholic failing. And most Jesuit high schools remain all boys to this day, the last bastion of single-sex exclusivity.

Given his background working for Bush II and Ken Starr, both tainted figures, Kavanaugh does seem to play fast and loose with the truth; he employs a sort of pragmatic lying, well sanctioned by politicians and their staffs in DC. When it came to his clerkship with his "mentor," Judge Alex Kozinski, who resigned after decades of sexual harassment, Brett took the former wrestling coach Rep. Jim Jordan's ignorance defense: seeing nothing, hearing nothing, saying nothing.

I am writing and posting this the day before the scheduled public hearing, which appears to be mismanaged by both sides. Christine Blasey Ford doesn't appear to realize that a smaller room and one camera will truncate the spectacle and make it less Anita Hill–like than she might want. But, unfortunately, we will all see—or not. In our present culture everything can change in a day. Take this as part I; part II will follow.

II

Starting with his nomination I was taken with Kavanaugh's first pitch: that he was a great family man, a friend of women everywhere, a coach to his girls, practically a feminist, though he didn't claim that, just let it be implied.

It reminded me of the political tactic that had been used successfully by Republicans against Democrats for decades. Attack the strength of your opponent. This was crystallized during John Kerry's campaign for president, though used before. The Swift Boat attacks. Kerry was known as a Vietnam vet, a plus against the stay-at-home George W., as he went in and out of the National Guard, depending on his whims, it appeared.

It's always been overlooked, except by me, that when W's father picked Dan Quayle for his veep, H. W. was playing a long game. He knew someone of that generation had to soften up the hard ground of the Vietnam War conflict and Quayle was his sacrificial Hoosier. He took the heat for his guarding the golf courses of Indiana during that war; that generational battle was fought during the campaign. Bush I was preparing the road for a future presidential run by his son. Little did Bush know that he was actually helping future candidate Bill Clinton. Had Quayle not preceded him, Clinton would have had even a harder time dealing with his lack of service, his credited draft dodging, his letter of thanks to the draft board.

In any case, what Brett was doing by trumpeting his women-friendly credentials was a variation on the Swift Boat strategy. He and his handlers obviously knew that his history in high school and college might come up and this was their preemption of the issue. It almost worked.

Dr. Ford's "letter," its existence, must have entered the rumor mill, or Kavanaugh might have been forthcoming about possible youthful minefields. Why else parade his women bona fides so flagrantly?

It turned out the scorpion stung itself. And it all came crashing down when his first accuser and he himself testified. The only rational reason I could find for Kavanaugh carrying on the way he did is that he already assumed he would never get on the court. The only thing that counters that is that he is already on a court, a not unimportant one. Obviously Trump wanted his pick to fight back, but what transpired had flop sweat and desperation all over it. Anger, rage, because he had already lost. He wasn't out to persuade.

One less (never?) quoted remark in his "unhinged" (the commonest description) testimony needs some attention: when he claimed he had already picked four clerks, all women, to serve him on the Supreme Court. I'd like to see their pictures. Who wouldn't want to be surrounded by smart, lovely women? Kavanaugh favors harem professions, my term for men who are the boss of many women at once. Male dentists are the most obvious examples. One man and a cadre of women "assistants."

[The above was written before Justice Kavanaugh was sworn in, before the 50-48 vote, but I will just leave that be and carry on.]

The Tiger Mom, Amy Chua, of Yale, is credited with saying that the new justice likes a certain type of female clerk. I have yet to find a group picture, but someday one will doubtless appear. Nevertheless, I'm sure it's a harem well worth spending time with.

Obviously, even in the Trump era, I can still be surprised, since I thought Kavanaugh wouldn't, in the end, make it onto the court. But I was once again wrong. Susan Collins fulfilled all the predictions that she was a creature of the Republican leadership, not an independent thinker. Her confirming speech will doubtless be preserved as a lesson in self-delusion, but her squawking voice seems to be a curse that long ago had been visited upon her. Her transformation into an owl may, or may not, be final by 2020.

I tweeted during the final days that if Kavanaugh got on the court it would be a new, indelible definition of White Male Privilege. As if we need more definitions... Also, he and Clarence Thomas doubtless high-fived each other when they first met. At least George H. W. Bush didn't publicly apologize on behalf of the nation to Thomas.

What Justice Kavanaugh chiefly represents is just the most public signpost of what the Republicans are getting away with in Congress and legislation as Trump continues with his carnival sideshow, taking up so much space in the public's (and media's) consciousness. This was always the dread, that The Donald would distract and they would act. And now the dread has increased and, given that surprises still happen, I can't imagine what the world will look like if the Democrats don't win the House in less than thirty days.

The View from the Couch, September 28, 2018 and October 9, 2018

PART III

■

COMMENTARY

This section stretches the meaning of the word commentary; *if you get toward the bottom of its various meanings in dictionaries you will find "a historical narrative or memoir," though its usual definitions do not often promise length. What follows are pieces of different scope, not exactly a jumble, but they do make up a compendium of forms. I am not a traditional essayist, insofar as I am often commenting on things, events and don't seem to be a writer who wanders in nature, only human nature, as so many typical essayists do. Birdwatching, anyone? The first long piece here began as the afterword to the 2012 edition of my 1972 book,* The Harrisburg 7 and the New Catholic Left. *Not everyone who might profit from it encountered that volume, nor did its slightly truncated appearance in the* Notre Dame Review *solve that problem. But, once again, I hope to enlarge its audience, as is true with the other pieces that follow, ending with the letters of Edward Dahlberg and my commentaries on them.*

Whither the New Catholic Left?

Though the government "lost" the 1972 trial of the Harrisburg Seven—achieving only a hung jury on the major conspiracy counts (10-2 for acquittal) and convictions only on minor "contraband" counts, the smuggling of letters in and out of prison, for just two defendants (Philip Berrigan and Elizabeth McAlister)—the government actually won the trial, accomplishing what it wanted to do, by toppling the Catholic Left from its pillar of moral superiority.

Public opinion—whatever small part of the public that was paying attention—certainly noted that the trial had ended ambiguously, without vindication for either side, but the public also absorbed the message that the priests and nuns involved no longer seemed exactly like saints and had, if not abandoned their commitment to nonviolence, at least flirted with it, coming closer to the other protest movements of the time that had taken on violence as a tactic, such as the Weatherman group.

The paradox made visible was this: by the end of the Vietnam War the most successful antiwar protest group still standing was the Vietnam Veterans Against the War. It is a long, strange war that puts up the men who had fought it as the most effective protesters against it.

Originally, the Catholic Left had scored a substantial victory with the trial of the Catonsville Nine, the protest action itself, and the play and movie that resulted from it. There had been a number of draft board raids in the late 1960s, a clot of them that alarmed the government, but the ones that garnered the most publicity involved the Berrigan brothers, Phil and Dan. (The Boston Five draft card burning case of 1968 set the stage for further prosecutions, since it established a precedent for going after leaders rather than followers.) But even then, the seed of violence was planted in the draft board raids at Catonsville (and even earlier in the case of the Baltimore Four, another less-covered draft board action). In order for the Catonsville draft files to be burned, they had to be procured, and instead of breaking in at night and getting them, the group took them in the daylight (for better press coverage) and had to push aside the women who worked at the draft board. It was a puny amount of violence, but since the Catholic Church is tied to so much symbolism, doing symbolic protest almost always requires artifacts, something to work with. In Baltimore, blood had been poured on the files, but inside the draft board office itself. Blood, paper, fire. Catholics are used to having one thing turn into another. It's the basis for much of the Church's rituals.

So it seemed like a leap, but not that much of a leap, for Philip Berrigan and a couple of other defendants to contemplate more complicated actions, scaling up to violence against property, not people. Though people are hardly absent from property. So heating tunnels in Washington were investigated, kidnapping Kissinger was discussed. One successful action prompted dreams of other, larger ones; it was hard to retain stasis. They wanted to "up the ante," as Daniel Berrigan has said more than once.

The civil rights movement already had a track record of nonviolent protest. The Reverend Martin Luther King Jr. was the legitimate American heir to Gandhi; the example of the Freedom Riders bestirred the country in the early 1960s, and King and other groups who fought for civil rights, fought nonviolently, and, ultimately, effectively. Their vein of Protestantism eschewed a lot of the redolent symbolism of the Catholic Church. No Mass, only services. No adoration of the Eucharist, no conversion of bread and wine into the body and blood. This led to a critical difference in behavior; it actually made embracing nonviolence easier. But Catholics revered their symbols, and the Catholic Left wasn't any different. Pouring blood, burning draft files, were all rituals they couldn't avoid or abandon.

Such actions all had their camel-nose-under-the-tent aspect when it came to violence. A little something physical was required to get things going. The Catholic Left wasn't necessarily in competition with the civil rights protest movement, but it took King a while to turn his attention away from his cause to the Vietnam War. And he began to address it publicly only the year before his death in 1968. But the Catholic Left was, like King's movement, religious at its core, with priests as prominent figures, as King and others in the civil rights movement were ministers. Again, they all gained moral authority from their professions, which often brought along skills at leadership. But the Catholic Left quickly became identified with the Berrigan brothers, and the mixture of the two brothers' temperaments made a powerful brew. Philip was forever the man of action, champing at the bit, whereas Daniel was more contemplative, though not chary of acting—his period underground post-Catonsville was proof enough of that—but in combination, they did set up, if not polar opposites, at least a demonstration of the tensions within the movement. Nonviolence or escalation? Symbolic acts or bold acts?

The civil rights movement, too, had its contending sides, including those who wanted more than nonviolent protests, such as the Black Panthers, who took another stance. And, of course, there was Malcolm X, another religiously oriented figure, who had moved from violence toward nonviolence, but was killed before any actual transformation showed itself. It is difficult to do a thumbnail sketch of the evolution of the protest groups of the 1960s and 1970s, but not impossible—it is even harder to condense forty years into a few pages, but here goes.

The civil rights movement coincidentally shadowed the history of the Vietnam War, starting slowly in the mid-1950s and developing throughout the 1960s, ending with the fall of Saigon in 1975 and the fading of the Black Power movement. And that pivotal decade of the sixties was marked with individual and group violence, beginning with the assassination of a president, John F. Kennedy, by a former Marine, Lee Harvey Oswald. President Kennedy had to be dragged into the civil rights fight by the earliest protestors at the start of the sixties, culminating in the violence wrought upon the Freedom Riders of 1961. King, though not an instigator of the Freedom Riders (that was the Congress of Racial Equality [CORE]), lent his presence to them, since they professed his nonviolent tactics.

Though the Vietnam War, in the early 1960s, still involved a mere handful of American advisers, Kennedy was already dealing with the botched CIA invasion of Cuba and the creation of the Berlin Wall and the Cuban Missile Crisis that followed. Before Kennedy's assassination, Vietnam was on the back burner of the American consciousness, but there was plenty of violence to go around.

But the combining of the two movements, civil rights and anti–Vietnam War, came about with the coincidence of the two later assassinations, those of Martin Luther King Jr. and Robert Kennedy in 1968. Lyndon Baines Johnson had undertaken both causes: civil rights legislation was passed in 1964, and the escalation of the number of troops in the Vietnam War began (thanks to the Gulf of Tonkin resolution) the same year.

It is hard to minimize the military atmosphere of the late sixties. The collapse of the Soviet Union had not yet occurred and the Cold War atmosphere was acute. As for the Berrigan brothers, I assume they thought that nonviolence, ultimately, would not necessarily end a war, though they must have seen it had resulted in victories for civil rights. Civil rights, unfortunately, seemed an easier sell to the American people. But war—as many have noticed (beginning with Randolph Bourne in 1918)—is the health of the state. It keeps the armaments industry humming and imposes a certain military discipline on the citizenry. It is difficult to remove that dark engine from any nation, or, at least, our nation, begun with armed revolution and the suppression of native peoples, and in its entire bloody history, now revered by our present-day Tea Party advocates. The idea of demilitarizing our country is one of the most laughable tasks on the face of the earth. Imagine what the current unemployment rate would be if the United States got out of the arms business?

The Cold War did a lot for education in our country, the space-race part especially: the Sputnik moment made it seem we were behind the Soviet Union in technological know-how, and so generous amounts of money flowed into higher education. Kennedy wanted to go to the moon and back by the end of the decade, but his space-race challenge had more effects on earth than on the moon. And though the demographics may have forced the fact in any case, the 1960s saw the number of people in institutions of higher learning triple. (In the decades before it had never even doubled.) And the country got to see what you get when you educate so many of your young so quickly.

You get protest movements, you get a high enough percentage of young people who will be altruistic and involved, courageous and stubborn. Off they went, to the civil rights movement, the antiwar movement, so men like King and the Berrigans had recruits for their causes, followers for their talents at leadership.

For a while, the rise of protest groups of the young mystified and then angered the powers that be. Demographics may be destiny, but those in authority certainly wanted to put a stop to the rebellious, activist youth. The Cold War ideology still alive then in the FBI and the CIA let them think of the protesters as spies in the heart of the country and they were dealt with as such, with wiretaps, surveillance, informers, agents, provocateurs—the whole nine yards of Cold War techniques.

While a small proportion of America's youth went a'protesting, another portion (with some overlap) headed off in the direction of the Summer of Love and/or Woodstock. (This part of the youth culture did spawn some of its own trials, but of the Charlie Manson sort, when hippies began to haunt the imagination of the middle class, with youth cast as vagabond killers, as the members of the Manson family actually were in 1969.) All of this "rebellion" did not happen without notice. Members of the power elite decided they couldn't have succeeding generations get too much smarter, and have so much free time and life choices, so they set out slowly but surely to make education more expensive; they underfunded it and did their best to saddle college graduates with so much debt that they needed to get jobs immediately, if they could find one, to pay off their debts. It took nearly four decades, but they have more than succeeded. The question is asked, Where are the young protestors? The Tea Partiers had to be invented to fill the vacuum in the streets, as geezers displaced the young. Two exceptions have only recently occurred: pro-union protests in Wisconsin and Ohio and the Occupy Wall Street movement.

A melancholy gathering took place shortly after the Harrisburg trial verdicts, when Elizabeth McAlister came to talk to some of the defense committee kids who had worked so hard during the trial, getting the word out, organizing events, and the like. I was the only journalist in the room. Elizabeth looked distracted, worried (she had been convicted on minor contraband counts), but she said a few words, and the strangest ones were when she said (for the first time) that she understood why women were starting to protest, what the grievances were that feminists felt. And that was about all she said, a nod to the nascent feminist movement, the one that would begin and then replace both the civil rights movement and the anti–Vietnam War movement, after the war in Indochina concluded in 1975. (And I certainly took some criticism from women friends for my reference to "the Avis girl," in the second line of my book's first chapter. Even I was behind the times.) For the Catholic Left, the Berrigan circle part of it, their movement, because of the trial would disperse in disarray. What seemed to announce that discombobulation most poignantly was Elizabeth's arrest for shoplifting, as *Time* reported it on September 10, 1973:

> Elizabeth McAlister, an ex-nun and the wife of Antiwar Activist Philip Berrigan, and Sister Judith Le Femina were shopping at the Sears, Roebuck store near Glen Burnie, Md. When they left, the store's detective said, they took with them, without paying, a $20.99 handheld electric power saw, a $6.90 package of sandpaper and a $1.90 package of picture hangers. Charged with shoplifting, the pair gave their address as Jonah House, Baltimore, a commune established by Elizabeth and Philip Berrigan for members of the peace movement.

The country as well was falling apart in any number of ways at the time. The Watergate caper had happened in the summer of 1972 after the trial was over—and I have always regretted not mentioning it toward the end of my book, when I discussed Robert Mardian's resignation—but it was outside my time frame: the Watergate burglary appeared to be a typical Mitchell/Mardian bag job. Nixon had been reelected in a landslide against the antiwar candidate, George McGovern, in November 1972, but, in short order, Nixon's hold on power began to unravel, as the White House's involvement was revealed with the break-ins at the Watergate complex and the doctor's office of Daniel Ellsberg, the provider of the Pentagon Papers. Fulfilling that awkward cliché, the White House was being hoisted on its own petard. All the conspiracy prosecutions they had originated against the ranks of the antiwar protestors (scores of grand juries and nearly a dozen trials) had prepared the larger public for a conspiracy trial against themselves. It had been an education for the public, all those prosecutions.

By the time congressional impeachment proceedings against Nixon started in 1974, the Ellsberg trial had collapsed in scandal, after most of the mischief the White House engaged in had begun to come out. The boil had been lanced. The

Camden Twenty-Eight draft board raid trial of 1973 had ended in acquittal, a post-Harrisburg win for draft board raiders. The Camden Twenty-Eight had a sympathetic judge, as well as their own informer, an agent provocateur, named Robert W. Hardy, a fellow defendant, though at the time so much was going on it wasn't covered extensively. (But in 2007 a documentary film on the trial was released.)

At the same time as these events, FBI offices in Media, Pennsylvania, were raided and FBI internal documents were released—a minor WikiLeaks event in a Xerox age, compared with the release of the Pentagon Papers in 1971. Congress finally shut off funding for the Vietnam War and it came to an end in 1975, ignominiously, as our military fled the region, pushing helicopters off ships into the deep blue sea. (The draft, too, had ended by then, after switching in 1973 to an all-volunteer system.) But it wasn't the only thing that ended—the war, that is. The antiwar movement came to a screeching halt, too.

The end of the Vietnam War is what allowed the seventies' protest movements to shift almost entirely to the personal, the leftover business of various civil rights causes: the women's movement, the gay rights movement, issues that are still alive and not entirely resolved today. And those on the Left who were already committed to violence and stayed violent as the war wound down became ludicrous. The Weatherman faction had gone underground, occasionally blowing up a bathroom in a public building. A California group, the Symbionese Liberation Army (SLA), grabbed the heiress Patty Hearst in 1974, ostensibly to highlight the mistreatment of the poor by the rich (not an obscure thing, even then), and demanded the Hearst family feed the hungry. The SLA became a blueprint, unfortunately, for a number of fringe groups, offering an unstable amalgam of white college dropouts and black men with criminal records. The SLA looked like a cartoon version of the Weatherman, but eventually the remnants of the Weatherman group ended up looking like a cartoon version of the SLA. When the last holdouts of the Weatherman emerged to public view it was during a murderous rampage in Nyack, New York, in 1981, the robbery of a Brink's truck and the subsequent killing of policemen at a roadblock, which resulted in one of Leonard Boudin's last trial appearances, when he helped defend his daughter, Kathy, against charges of capital felony murder.

For as much as the left was the dominant force in the world of protest movements from the end of World War II to the mid-1970s (roughly, from the Rosenberg case of 1951 to the end of the Vietnam War), the right has dominated the protest terrain since then. Civil rights and antiwar protestors were the story for three decades until 1975. (The "left," pre–World War II, was largely the Communist Party–dominated left, with more doctrinaire fights between Soviet-dominated party members and native socialists; after the Greatest Generation, it more or less became thoroughly Americanized.) The last three decades have witnessed a turnabout.

After the Harrisburg trial, the New Catholic Left became the New Catholic Right. Again, a lot of subtle things account for that change, but some are not so hard to see. The rise of Ronald Reagan heralded the switch, and Jimmy Carter's one-term presidency is instructive. Carter was a victim of the peace in Vietnam, insofar as the economy no longer ran smoothly on guns and butter. By 1975 the boom years were over. The economic restructuring left Carter with high inflation and limited oil supplies. Gas lines and the bottom line undid him. (There is a parallel here with the situation of our current president, Barack Obama. See below.) Jimmy Carter suffered a backlash for being the president presiding over a country that had lost a war; a substantial portion of the country felt further victimized by the bad economy, stagnating wages, gas lines, and Carter's talk of wearing cardigan sweaters and lowering thermostat settings, and so forth. His handling of the Panama Canal, the Iran hostage debacle, and his amnesty for draft resisters, were all things that didn't endear him to the more martially inclined of the citizenry or to the corporate behemoths of the military-industrial complex that politicians are beholden to. The rise of Reagan and Bush (thanks to both inflation and interest rates under Carter hitting 18 percent) altered the landscape and paved the way for the American Right to gain power. A new sort of conservative would rise from the ruins of the Vietnam War's end.

But the Carter administration did signal the global realignment of the post-Vietnam world. The Iran hostage crisis of 1979 was the harbinger of the geopolitical shift. Indochina would recede and the Middle East would step forward. Oil (which began to stand in for the industrial part of the military-industrial complex) and the economy became prominent in the public's consciousness and in the world's. Reagan's elderly cabinet of Cold War and CIA has-beens began a variety of illegal escapades that would outdo Richard Nixon's earlier schemes. The Central America and the South American drug trade became entwined with the Middle East conflicts during the Iran-Contra period of the mid-1980s. And then the former head of the CIA, George H. W. Bush, became president for one term, following the old Soviet model, in which the head of state security became president, and our country got used to the spectacle of governmental lawlessness, followed by congressional hearings, spectacles that replaced trials for public entertainment. With so many heavy hitters and government officials testifying under oath, the minor law breaking of antiwar Catholics demonstrating against nuclear weapons was hardly considered news.

Meanwhile, in reaction to the appearance of women's and gay liberation, all happening on the periphery of the public's attention, counter groups were established. Large right-wing foundations and like-minded CEOs began to fund all manner of right-wing think tanks and protest organizations. The anti-tax forces assembled themselves, as did foundations dedicated to ending Social Security and Medicare, such as the Cato Institute, begun in 1977 by one of the now notorious Koch brothers. And the legalization of abortion in 1973 (*Roe v. Wade*) gave fuel to the creation of the largest Catholic protest movement, the anti-abortion, or prolife, movement, even though, at the beginning, it was largely an evangelical, white, male, Protestant movement.

The Republican years of the presidency, the Reagan-Bush, then Bush-Quayle, of the 1980s and early '90s let all these movements take root. What derailed this Republican supremacy in the executive branch was the eccentric presidential run of H. Ross Perot, which allowed Bill Clinton to assume the presidency. There were two trials that occupied the public's consciousness during the Clinton years: O. J. Simpson's and Clinton's own impeachment.

Trial reporting changed forever with the Simpson case. Traditional trial reporting more or less stopped and was turned over to television, and the "reporters"—more commentators—on trials henceforth were lawyers, which always produced a conflict of interest, a special kind of moral hazard informed their coverage. And for our recent wars, television networks have hired retired generals to report and comment, another blow to journalism as a whole. The cult of the expert, which had flourished in journalistic circles since the 1980s, had its downside. The Harrisburg trial was one of the last print-only trials.

Cable television was in its infancy in 1972, and few (or none) of the events I wrote about in Harrisburg were recorded for television. Once, I did see a man I took to be an FBI agent (or some branch of intelligence) filming a demonstration outside the federal courthouse, with a small camera, an expensive object back then. He was tall, fit, wearing a suit, but also sported cowboy boots. Camcorders didn't come along till the 1980s and, in the early 1970s, though parents might be filming children at home with 8mm cameras, there wasn't much private use of them to cover public events. *Court TV* first aired on cable in 1991. CNN had televised a sensational New Bedford, Massachusetts, rape trial in 1984; since then television has coopted trials as entertainment and there have been fewer trial books like mine published. That absence is sometimes filled by the occasional decent documentary film.

The start of the Clinton administration was both inauspicious and prophetic. In February 1993 the World Trade Center was rocked by an explosion and soot-blackened faces emerged on television screens from one of the Twin Towers. Two days later four federal agents were killed while raiding a religious compound, that of the Branch Davidians, outside of Waco, Texas, and by April 19 fire consumed the compound, killing men, women, and children. Some twenty years earlier there was a precedent: several members of the Symbionese Liberation Army were also consumed by fire, during a shoot-out with police at their "safe" house in 1974. Burning draft files had long ago receded as effective protest.

During 1993 two more predictive events happened. In Somalia, American soldiers were dragged through the dusty streets, and one captured soldier, Michael Durant, was videotaped by his captors and the video shown worldwide. In September 1994 a small plane was flown into the White House by Frank Corder. A suicide mission, it did little damage, but it did show how easy it was to fly a plane into the White House. Then, two years after the Branch Davidians' immolation, Timothy McVeigh's rental truck bomb destroyed the Murrah Federal Office Building in Oklahoma City. At first, Muslim terrorists were suspected, but then the disaffected Army veteran was apprehended.

So fierce was the determination of the right wing during the Clinton years that they discounted Clinton's abdication of the economy to the Wall Street barons, allowing the financiers to do almost everything they wanted, including wholesale deregulation of the industry. The radical right still treated Clinton as an illegitimate president, managing to turn a cheap real estate deal into a sex scandal, and, finally, actually impeaching him, though they did not succeed in having him drummed out of office.

But the impeachment did affect the voters' judgment of Clinton's vice president, and Al Gore managed to lose the presidential election in 2000, even though he won the popular vote. But Gore, it was clear, never had his heart in the post-election fight, as the forces of George W. Bush obviously did. After two terms of Bush II, Clinton's true legacy, we were able to elect the "antiwar" candidate in 2008, one who then continued his predecessor's two wars. And who would bother to ask, by that point, whither the Catholic Left?

As Carter dealt with an America wallowing in post-losing-war blues, President Obama has had to deal with the collapse of Wall Street and two unpopular wars, as well as the prevailing atmosphere of vulnerability established by 9/11, and the legacy of fear fostered by the George W. Bush administration. Obama was, lest we forget, the antiwar candidate. During the last few months of the 2008 campaign, Obama unleashed a powerful nostalgia for the bygone sixties generation and its children. But the eventual right-wing backlash of 2010 was fueled largely by the same constituency that had hounded Carter: racists and anti-immigration forces, and the whole panoply of right-wing Astroturf protest groups spawned by the economic upheaval.

The religious anti-abortion forces had more or less taken over the strategies of the Catholic Left shortly after *Roe v. Wade* was decided, bringing along the same mixture of symbolic protest that put them on the road to violence. Those on the Catholic Left watched, with great dismay, if not horror, over the years, as the anti-abortion movement adopted the protest tactics of the Catholic Left. Instead of draft boards, it was women's health clinics that were targeted, and eventually attacked. Pickets acting as roadblocks, harassment of women who sought the services of the clinics, "nonviolent" interventions with foul-smelling chemicals to render the clinics inoperable—all the variations that were developed during the draft board raiding period of the Catholic Left.

Men ran these protests, and the women of the Catholic Right didn't seem to chafe at this. Then abortion providers were attacked, and eventually killed, by other men, zealots who often claimed religious motivations.

The Catholic League for Religious and Civil Rights was founded in 1973, but was more or less moribund till the newer wave of right-wing groups and their funders emerged in the early 1990s. But even the earlier incarnation of the Catholic League was a supporter of school vouchers, and by the time William Donohue took over in 1993 (finding a high-paying job for himself), it began to champion conservative causes across the board. Seeing anti-Catholicism everywhere, its board of directors consisted of a gallery of the poster children for right-wing causes. The Supreme Court now boasts six Catholics, five of whom make up its conservative-bloc majority. Radical Protestant evangelicals would have trouble winning congressional approval for the court, but conservative Catholics became their acceptable stand-ins.

The Catholic Left, after a period of regrouping, returned to its first impulses, working primarily on social justice causes, forming Catholic Worker houses, doing "good works," mostly out of the public eye. Philip Berrigan and Elizabeth McAlister created Jonah House in Baltimore and by the start of the 1980s had reconstituted, not as the East Coast Conspiracy to Save Lives, but as the Plowshares movement—beating swords into plowshares, and promoting pacifism. Championing pacifism has not been a popular political stance the last three decades, so much so that the *New York Times* published an article about the phenomenon on August 28, 2011, with this tongue-in-cheek headline: "Give Pacifism a Chance."

From protesting the humble starting point of organized warfare—draft boards, the recruitment of soldiers as good ol' cannon fodder—the Berrigans jumped to the end of the process, protesting the technological height of the military-industrial complex, its most sacred and scary weapons, its nuclear stockpile. In some ways this could be seen as penance for their earlier work. If Gandhi could end the British Empire's colonial domination of a country, why couldn't the Berrigans end our reliance on nuclear weapons? But some of the same draft board–raiding tactics were used in the various actions that the Plowshares group engaged in, beginning with the 1980 King of Prussia, Pennsylvania, GE Missile Re-entry Division episode (GE makes arms as well as medical machines). Daniel and Philip and the usual "six others" came with hammers to pound and blood to be poured. They couldn't abandon the ritual and symbols. But there was limited reaction.

The "Catholic Left," more importantly, had been globalized in the 1980s, along with much else, and Central America had become a cynosure of Left political action. The New Catholic Left had moved south of our border. Four American nuns and a laywoman were killed in El Salvador in December 1980, where Archbishop Oscar Romero had been murdered earlier that same year. "Liberation theology" had become the conservative world's bugaboo. The American Catholic Left did not come equipped with a coherent political-economy analysis at the time it burned draft records, though in England during the same period, what was called there the Catholic "New Left," inspired by Vatican II, attempted to work out a humanistic socialist theory. What I called the New Catholic Left in 1972 placed the emphasis on the "new" Catholics, not the "new" New Catholic Left. A new American Left barely existed in 1972, except as an abstraction, a smattering of undercooked historic impulses. In 1983 Pope John Paul II, while touring Central America, told nuns and priests in El Salvador to cease their political work.

So, back in the USA, the antinuclear actions of the Plowshares group, given their big target, seemed too easy to hit; the Plowshares group may have been David versus Goliath, but this Goliath did not fall when hit by a stone or hammer. Even the American government wanted to limit, eventually, the number of nuclear weapons worldwide.

The fall of the Soviet Union in 1991 got the United States itself into the dismantle-nukes business. But the Plowshares group persisted, and after some fifty lesser actions went off with their hammers and blood in 1997 to the Bath, Maine, ironworks, where a nuclear weapon-equipped destroyer, *The Sullivans*, was moored before being commissioned. The Plowshares people (absent Daniel Berrigan) hammered missile hatches, and eventually blood got poured on guidance instruments of the destroyer. (In 2000 *The Sullivans* was the target of attack in Yemen by al-Qaeda, but the attacking boat itself was too full of explosives and sank before detonating.)

After the *The Sullivans* arrest in 1997, the case did make the news, though more for an exchange between the prosecution and the judge at the bail hearing.

Denying the need for high bail or confinement for Philip Berrigan, Judge Joseph Field said, "Anyone of my generation [the judge was fifty] knows Philip Berrigan. He is a moral giant, the conscience of a generation."

But the trial judge, Gene Carter, thought differently, and after their convictions sentenced Berrigan and the others to two years in prison. But Berrigan's act remained inspirational. John Peck wrote a poem, "On the Sentencing of Philip Berrigan, Portland, Maine, 1997," which contains these lines:

> A *trained efficient* killer
> Berrigan's phrase for himself in the war,
> artillery then infantry. Then the collar
> on a Josephite teacher of black kids in D.C.,
> New Orleans, Baltimore—
> sentenced once more in old age
> for boarding a destroyer at the Bath Iron Works
> in Lenten daybreak.

Persistence pays off in this country and Philip Berrigan persisted till the end. When he died at age seventy-nine in 2002, I wrote the following about him in a column for the *Chicago Sun-Times* (December 17, 2002), which I reproduce in its entirety, so the context will be clear:

> *The bad old days have been much in the news recently: Trent Lott mourning the loss of segregation forever at Strom Thurmond's one hundredth birthday celebration, plus John Snow, President Bush's choice to replace Paul O'Neill as treasury secretary, reviving once again memories of the Ford administration, plus Snow's belated resignation from that other Southern institution of life as it used to be, the Augusta National Golf Club, with its female-free comforts. And, most sorrowfully, the death of Philip Berrigan, the antiwar former Catholic priest, who spent his life attempting to turn swords into ploughshares.*
>
> *There is always a variety of pasts to choose from: Lott's and Snow's versions may still command the attention of the powerful, but Philip Berrigan's concerns were always aimed at benefitting the powerless.*
>
> *Lott, the Senate majority leader to be, unless his paean to the plantation era becomes his undoing, was doubtless infected by the occasion, Senator Thurmond's centennial retirement party, which rendered the minds of many who should know better completely daffy. Thurmond has evolved*

over the years from an out-and-out segregationist threat to a dotty old freak show, though one dutifully reelected term after term by his state's all-too-accommodating electorate.

Treasury secretary designate John Snow's chief virtue, allegedly, is that he will be a more effective PR spokesperson for the president's already-in-place economic policy (Cut taxes! Cut taxes!). Though, even the conservative Forbes *magazine had already labeled Snow an inferior CEO of the heavily government-subsidized CSX railroad, giving Snow a grade of D for performance, noting he paid himself about $30 million, while overseeing a five-year annualized negative 1 percent return in his company. Doubtless,* Forbes *will find something nice to say about him now.*

Philip Berrigan certainly could have been a CEO at a large company, if he had hankered for great wealth. He was tall, good looking, strong, and uncompromisingly certain in his views. He became a CEO, of sorts, of the anti–Vietnam War protest movement. After the somewhat disastrous 1972 federal conspiracy trial of the Harrisburg Seven, which the government lost, insofar as there was a hung jury on the major counts charging Father Berrigan and six others of conspiring to kidnap Henry Kissinger and blow up heating tunnels in Washington, DC, but was won because the trial itself deflated the moral capital of Berrigan's group of Catholic Left antiwar protestors, leaving their movement somewhat splintered and dispirited.

Philip Berrigan was drummed out of the priesthood, married the former nun Elizabeth McAlister, staffed Jonah House, and carried on with a smaller group of like-minded individuals. Their focus of protest became nuclear weapons, since the Vietnam War, which they had fought effectively through many antiwar draft protests—enough so to have brought the wrath of J. Edgar Hoover down upon them—finally ended.

Today, an antiwar movement continues to exist, but, unfortunately, with no greater public profile than Senator Lott's pro-segregationist movement—"if the rest of the country had followed our lead we wouldn't have had all these problems over all these years"—and the anti–women-in-golf-clubs movement advocated by corporate chieftains of various kinds, who enjoy the good life at Augusta.

Strom Thurmond's remarkable longevity is further proof that the good die young. But, fortunately, some of the good still die at seventy-nine, like Philip Berrigan. Given the Catholic Church's current bad press, it is remarkable to think back to the late 1960s and early '70s, when Berrigan and his Jesuit brother Dan, were seen by American bishops as "bad" priests, their dastardly antiwar deeds filling the pages of newspapers. Then they were the public face of the Catholic Church, not today's predatory pedophiles and weak-kneed bishops.

All those involved in the trial of the Harrisburg Seven have scattered, most drifting away from the issues and lives that brought them together. Philip Berrigan, though, stood the course, fought the good fight. Unlike the departure of Thurmond and Lott (if he forfeits his post), Berrigan's inspiring presence will be missed.

Lott did forfeit his post and, thankfully, Thurmond died.

Unlike the liberation theologians of Central and South America, as well as those in Britain, the Catholic Left here at home might have had a hard time attaching itself to a coherent economic ideology, but the Catholic Right has had no trouble whatsoever. The Right goes with winners: the oligarchies, the plutocrats, and so forth. The Catholic Left, at its start, was pacifist and vaguely socialist—though more of the each according to his/her needs, each according to his or her abilities sort. They favored communes, not communism. But one reason such issues weren't much discussed (beyond the fact that our post-industrial society made a mockery of third world economic enthusiasms) was that priests and nuns were already living in a communal socialistic environment, used to if not a "vow of poverty" at least the idea of share and share alike, though the hierarchy of the Church's share was a bit more grandiose than mere clergy enjoyed. Overall, it was a French sort of socialism.

But reverence for the rich returned with a vengeance during the Reagan years, stoked by the religious right's fervor for all things conservative. The Catholic Left's heartfelt pursuit of peace had always been centered on stopping the mechanics of war. But at its heart it was never an economic movement, and during the height of the antiwar protests in 1970, following the killings at Kent State, it was most disheartening to see union workers attacking peace demonstrators in downtown Manhattan. And the history of Catholics' participation in the struggles of organized labor in the twentieth century shows their battles for workers' rights were simultaneously fused to a fierce anti-Communism, which created unresolvable tensions and contradictions.

The rise of Reagan Democrats was also a phenomenon of class interests being betrayed, but was part and parcel of a group (the Reagan Dems) wanting to align itself with winners, rather than losers. In America there always has been a parallel outcropping of protests by populists; populism, too, has its own vacillating history, but in the main it has been more right-wing and racist and, not to put too fine a point on it, fascist.

Again, populist movements usually have a mistaken idea of where their economic interests are located. But if the variety of leftist groups during the antiwar period of the Vietnam War required an enemy, other than the government, to berate, they would choose "liberals" (new Democrat liberals of the Michael Harrington sort), a word uttered only with some derision. Even today the word is spurned, and *progressive* has been resurrected, though it still smacks of its radical roots. But reducing all these matters to two sides required only one standard: the distinction between those who acted and those who remained on the sidelines. Liberals, of whatever stripe, by and large remained spectators, and retreated to the sidelines and to, more or less, terminal superfluity.

Bernhard Schlink, the author of the international best seller *The Reader*, as well as a book of essays, *Guilt about the Past*, was asked recently at a lecture held at the University of Notre Dame if he had any analysis about the American protestors of the Vietnam War period, since he had a such a full analysis of the German student movement of the same time. Schlink said he did not, which I thought strange, since he had talked about how the German student movement was influenced so much by the history of World War II, with the students not wanting to do what their parents had done, and how their reaction to the country's Nazi past had radicalized a generation. They wanted to do something, not sit back and do nothing. And some of that, of course, was full of violence, such as the Baader-Meinhof Group, which operated throughout the 1970s and into the '90s. But it is often overlooked how that German World War II history affected the same generation of protestors in America. It was the Nazi atrocities, the films of concentration camps and victims, the Nuremberg trials, the convictions of war criminals that influenced my cohort, as well as myself. Never again.

But the difference was that World War II itself accounted for the ambivalence shared by so many individuals in the antiwar movement. America had fought the "good war"; but in Vietnam it was fighting a bad war. Nonetheless, many protestors were lost in internal conflict, wanting their country to do right again, instead of wrong.

Leonard Boudin, the civil liberties attorney who represented Phillip Berrigan in the Harrisburg case, died in 1989. The Boudins provided me a link to the pre–World War II left, the internationalist left, the Cold War left, as well as trials that took place before I came along (such as the Boston Five, much less the Rosenbergs' trial). Through the Boudins, with whom I remained friends until the ends of their lives, I was exposed to a living history of America's radical past. They served as a family tree, connecting many generations of left-wing movements. Jean Boudin's sister was married to I. F. Stone (1907–89), so he was often at their house, and I met, in no particular order, Judith Coplon, Alger Hiss, and other notorious figures of that period, as well as dozens of other less famous activists, both of the civil rights era and of the antiwar period.

After the Harrisburg trial Leonard continued to represent Cuba, and then Iran, when the United States seized its assets during the Carter administration. "Fame is nice, but money is better," Leonard told me, during the time he was representing Iran. We shared a cynical humor with each other any chance we could, since we both knew we were less cynical than we seemed. Leonard had, nonetheless, grown quite fond of flying to and from Europe on the Concorde.

He represented Jimmy Hoffa in 1974 over Nixon's imposed ban on Hoffa's holding union office till 1980 (Nixon released Hoffa early from jail in exchange for the support of the Teamsters in Nixon's 1972 reelection bid), and Hoffa fired Leonard when the suit's verdict went against him.

Hoffa didn't understand—and Leonard couldn't get it through his thick skull—that Leonard expected to lose the first round but eventually to win the case on appeal. Yet Hoffa was distraught at not winning. And of course Hoffa doubtless knew it was a more important life-or-death issue than Leonard had considered, one that needed to be resolved quickly; for Hoffa disappeared forever in 1975, shortly after losing in federal district court in Washington, DC.

Ramsey Clark, who had served as attorney general in the Johnson administration, underwent a remarkable metamorphosis (unlike Boudin, who had no such conversion), from orchestrating the Boston Five conspiracy case, full of East Coast luminaries, such as Benjamin Spock (Leonard's client) and William Sloane Coffin Jr., and notable others, to serving as counsel for the Harrisburg Seven. Clark has argued (about his fashioning the Boston Five case of 1968) that he wanted to charge famous people who could afford the prosecution in order to air the issues around the draft.

Be that as it may, Clark has since gone on to defend or be associated with less admirable defendants, including, but not limited to, Radovan Karadzic, the Bosnian Serb war criminal; Slobodan Milosevic; Sheikh Omar Abdel Rahman; and Muammar Qaddafi. Back in the states, Clark also helped the Branch Davidians file for damages against the government, for, as Clark has called it, "the greatest failure of law enforcement in the domestic history of the U.S."

Like Leonard, Clark turned into an internationalist practitioner, even offering assistance to Saddam Hussein when he was on trial in Iraq. Having seen the rule of law abused during the Johnson administration, Clark didn't hesitate to shine a light on any place it is being abused again.

Bill Moyers, also of the Johnson administration, has had a similar change of allegiance since his service as press secretary for LBJ. But Ramsey Clark's transformation has been more extreme, though it wasn't anything like the guilt-racked transformation undergone by the former secretary of defense during the Vietnam War, Robert McNamara (1916–2009).

The only defendant I stayed in contact with after the trial was Eqbal Ahmad, and that had more to do, I suppose, with the academic circles we both traveled in: Eqbal taught at Hampshire College in the late 1970s and early '80s when I was teaching at Mount Holyoke College, a few miles away. Shortly after the trial, Eqbal had an idea for the next book I might do. He suggested I investigate the phenomenon of migrant Muslim labor going on throughout Europe and what the consequences of that might be for all the countries involved. He suggested this in 1973.

Obviously, Eqbal was prescient. In one of the last essays he wrote before he died in 1999, titled "A Jihad against Time," he wrote, "Complexity and pluralism threaten most—hopefully not all—contemporary Islamists, because they seek an Islamic order reduced to a penal code, stripped of its humanism, aesthetics, intellectual quests, and spiritual devotion. Neither Muslims nor Jews nor Hindus are unique in this respect. All variants of contemporary 'fundamentalism' reduce complex religious systems and civilizations to one or another version of modern fascism. They are concerned with power, not with the soul, with the mobilization of people for political purposes rather than with sharing or alleviating their sufferings and aspirations."

He had remained prescient. After he died I spent time correcting a variety of obituaries and tributes, where the writers invariably claimed the Harrisburg defendants had been "acquitted." No acquittals had occurred in Harrisburg.

Of the handful of "others" of the Harrisburg Seven, Tony Scoblick and Mary Cain Scoblick have stayed out of the public eye the most; they, seemingly, had been largely disaffected by the trial, not thinking well of Philip's various pronouncements and what they saw as his high-handedness and hypocrisy on the subject of priests marrying nuns. The Scoblicks eventually divorced. The Reverend Joe Wenderoth, though, has remained active. In 2008 he took part in a panel at St. Joseph Parish in Cockeysville, Maryland, speaking on the sacrament of reconciliation. Perhaps the Scoblicks should have attended. Neil McLaughlin was last reported, by Charles Meconis, to be running an antique store in Maryland, but it was a bookstore, a successful one. McLaughlin is now retired.

Elizabeth McAlister and Jonah House still carry on lives of protest in Baltimore. Protests that now include her and Philip Berrigan's daughter. Information about their actions can be found at the Jonah House website: www.jonahhouse.org. Seeing photos of Elizabeth and Philip Berrigan's daughter, Frida (named after Philip's mother), one is struck by how much she looks like her father.

The other major book on the trial, *The F.B.I. and the Berrigans*, was co-written by Jack Nelson (1929–2009) and Ronald J. Ostrow. Jack was the former head of the Washington bureau of the *Los Angeles Times*. He covered the trial (I don't think I ever laid eyes on Ostrow) and was the consummate traditional-style reporter, the more or less mythical tradition of the *Dragnet* sort: just the facts, ma'am. Jack was born in Alabama and had a distinguished career covering the FBI and the civil rights movement. Our two books were often reviewed together.

My book was never a favorite of the New Catholic Left itself or of the Berrigan group. Nor did I expect it to be. Philip Berrigan, I was told, had circulated a long, seven-page letter about my book (written while he was still in prison—he was released right before Christmas 1972), though I was never able to come upon a copy. And as the years went on, when the Harrisburg trial was mentioned in histories, such as *Disarmed and Dangerous: The Radical Lives and Times of Daniel and Philip Berrigan* (1997) and *Harder Than War: Catholic Peacemaking in Twentieth-Century America* (1992), when my book is referred to it is usually dismissed as less "factual," whereas Jack's book is "the most thorough account of the Harrisburg trial."

Nelson and Ostrow's book may be the most thorough account of the events previous to the trial (they wrote about what they knew, the FBI), but it certainly isn't the most thorough account of the trial itself. The original edition of my book had no index, which, doubtless, altered the facts equation. I had not wanted it weighed down with what I thought then to be scholarly apparatus. But I discovered that historians don't usually consult modern books without indexes, since that would require them to read the whole thing.

The animus toward my book of authors sympathetic to the Berrigans always strikes me as strange, since their analyses (all coming years later) of the trial consistently echo my own. In *Disarmed and Dangerous*, Jim Forest, a Catholic Left activist, is described as abandoning a publisher's contract for a book on the trial, because of his being "estranged" from the Berrigans. After my book came out, however, Forest told me that he abandoned his own book, because mine had made the one he intended to write superfluous. But my position vis-à-vis activists was always clear to me. Shortly after the book appeared I was with some contemporaries who were connected to the case at McSorley's, the off-Bowery saloon. One young man, my age, asked me plaintively, How could I have exposed the defendants as I had, since they had befriended me? We had even gone sledding together on a snowy hill in Harrisburg. Long before Janet Malcolm—who had become famous because of her remarks about backstabbing journalists in her 1990 book *The Journalist and the Murderer* (I had written my version of them in my third novel, *Criminal Tendencies*, in 1987)—I understood how journalists were guilty of "selling somebody out," as Joan Didion famously wrote in 1968.

So, in response to my acquaintance's complaint (he was in law school at the time), I just reminded him of my line in the book about dancing on their graves. And, though I liked them, I never thought the defendants were my friends.

I wasn't invited, but I attended the celebration of the Berrigan/McAlister earlier wedding (which supposedly happened in 1969, the self-marriage, officiated by Philip himself) held in Montclair, New Jersey, in June 1973. Diane Schulder had been invited and asked me to come along. Paul O'Dwyer, in attendance, was also unhappy with me, since I had alluded to some facts about his brother, William O'Dwyer (1890–1964), the former mayor of New York City, in my book. Paul was the youngest of eleven children; he died in 1998, at age ninety.

Irish Americans often take offense at the truth, if it happens to be uncomplimentary. So I lost my chance to be part of the Irish American mafia in NYC back then, while I was still doing manual labor in the South Bronx. The most memorable thing about the party, except for the good weather, was that a couple of male members of the McAlister/Berrigan extended family got in a fistfight in the backyard.

Daniel Berrigan, S.J., has been threatening to die the last twenty years, but amazingly he still is alive at this writing. He published books in 2007, 2008, and 2009 and had been working with hospice patients for a decade or more. His 2008 book is called *The Kings and Their Gods: The Pathology of Power.*

Of the small group of writers I was in the "pool" with, all have continued their trade in admirable fashion, with, of course, the unfortunate exception of Paul Cowan, who died of leukemia at the age of forty-eight in 1988. Garry Wills has written at least a couple dozen books (including a novel!) since 1972; Francine du Plessix Gray has turned her pen toward fiction (*Lovers & Tyrants*), memoir (*Them*), and biographies of famous women. Ed Zuckerman went into writing and producing for television. His script was used in the first episode of *Law & Order* ever aired, and he wrote for that show on and off for its entire existence. One of the best episodes of *Law & Order* was about an underground radical being caught late in life (ripped from the headlines!), notable for the cops' lines joking about J. Edgar Hoover wearing a feathered boa. When it first aired, Hoover was of course long dead, but what he always feared had finally come true. Hoover had controlled and manipulated the image of the FBI and himself in television and radio, and a couple of decades later, there he was, being treated as a figure of fun.

Unfortunately, that other cause of the trial of the Harrisburg Seven, Henry Kissinger, is not being treated as a figure of fun. His mischief continues to be legion.

From his shop, Kissinger and Associates, came L. Paul Bremer, its former managing director, who had been an assistant to Kissinger from 1972 to 1976, the years the Vietnam War was "winding down." From K and A, he moved to the Coalition Provisional Authority in Iraq, where he became the U.S. administrator and managed to bungle everything there was to bungle, besides setting in motion most of the privatized corruption and ethnic cleansing that cropped up during the first few years after George W. Bush's invasion.

Most of Hoover's mistakes were buried back in 1972 when he died, but Kissinger's are ongoing. Publicizing his most recent book, *On China*, Kissinger told *Time* (June 6, 2011), "It may turn out that Iraq will be the only country in the region with a representative government. But would I have recommended fighting for 10 years in order to achieve this? I would have said no." Yet another of Kissinger's self-aggrandizing pronouncements, while simultaneously claiming blamelessness.

The FBI continues to be busy, conducting its business with the same level of competence it displayed during the Harrisburg case; and, since 9/11 and the creation of Homeland Security, the country and its citizens are hardly without daily internal scrutiny. The Office of the Inspector General, in September 2010, published a lengthy document, *A Review of the FBI's Investigations of Certain Domestic Advocacy Groups* (I love that new coinage, "Domestic Advocacy Groups"; the review itself is redacted in parts), defending the bureau's aggressive tactics. The groups in question were: "The Thomas Merton Center of Pittsburgh, PA; People for the Ethical Treatment of Animals (PETA); Greenpeace USA; *The Catholic Worker*; Glen Mill (an individual); and, The Religious Society of Friends (the 'Quakers')." Sound familiar?

So, don't worry, the FBI, if no one else, is keeping track of the remnants of the religious and do-good Left. A footnote in the 191-page report tells us that "PETA was the only one of the groups we reviewed that the FBI had investigated during our review period as a terrorism enterprise."

The FBI still behaves in its traditional way, especially with potential protest groups, exploiting informers and agent provocateurs. One such case involved antiwar protestors at the 2008 Republican National Convention in Minneapolis–St. Paul, two of whom (Bradley Crowder and David McKay) eventually pleaded guilty to lesser offences and served time. Their case received little national attention and what notice they did get was hostile to the two young men. There was no defense committee, crowds supporting their actions, and so forth. One oddity, though, was that they had documentary filmmakers contemporaneously on the scene filming and interviewing them as their case wound down to a conclusion. The "documentary" aired on PBS's *POV* series on September 6, 2011 titled, "Better This World."

Precious little journalism infiltrates this particular genre of filmmaking; for the viewer, it's a kind of make-up-your-own-mind experience.

The FBI had an unstable volunteer informer (Brandon Darby) who continually provoked the two young men to consider acts of violence, which then never actually occurred. But they did make old-fashioned Molotov cocktails (the limit of their weapons sophistication), the offense that resulted in their convictions. But their informer was reminiscent of, and even more egregious than, Boyd Douglas in creating the case, but, from the amounts of money mentioned, he appeared to be paid less than Boyd was paid back in 1972. *Plus ça change, plus c'est la même chose.*

And Boyd Douglas, the other preeminent cause of the trial? Taken up in the federal witness protection program, he is lost to history, but not to some records somewhere. I used to wonder if Boyd would ever pop up again in my life, but like most Americans he may never have read my book and felt no need. In any case, Boyd Douglas has now, too, reached geezer status, and he is no doubt collecting Medicare and Social Security benefits.

And the Catholic Church? John Paul II let his native anticommunism run roughshod over liberation theology and progressive clergy, and the current pope, Benedict XVI, has in his biography the unfortunate facts of having been once a member of the Hitler Youth, a conscript in the German army, and an inmate of a POW camp; he has been a later-in-life supporter of the most right-wing aspects of the Catholic Church, which has resulted in the gentle handling of such archconservative organizations such as the Legion of Christ and Opus Dei, as well as the defective oversight of the molestation crisis of the John Paul II era.

The solace one usually attempts to draw from the deeds of good men and women that largely go unrewarded at the time is that, without their "brave and foolish" acts (to quote myself), the world would be a worse place today if they hadn't done what they did. It's difficult, though, to think the world has turned out better today because of the New Catholic Left, though they did certainly affect the fortunes of the past.

We are engaged in a number of wars, fought by 1 percent of our countrymen, the result of the "volunteer" army; if one is cynical enough, that can be seen as the triumph of all that youthful protesting. America's young can choose not to participate in the killing, if they wish. And what has changed from the Vietnam era, because of the volunteer military, is the average age of the dead; we are no longer killing teenagers but young men and women in their early twenties who have lived a bit of life, had jobs and marriages, and so forth. And beyond that fact, we now wage preemptive wars, though the Vietnam War was largely that too, though never advertised as such.

And where is the Catholic Left? Nowhere, it seems, except for the remnants of the original groups that are now slowly dying off. Protest went global in the decades following the trial: civil rights turned into human rights and went back to health, survival, the most basic freedoms.

NGOs have replaced the SDS or the SLA, in the protest alphabet wars. There are now protest groups of the Green, eco sort, marked by sporadic anarchistic blowups around G-20 meetings. Yet the religious right is everywhere, throughout the world. We now have a Department of Homeland Security (the Bush family and administration rekindling its alliances with its German past and its love of homeland; see Kevin Phillips's *American Dynasty*), and the public has gone along with the disregard of a number of our civil rights, as well as condoning torture. America's prisons are so full that courts are ordering the release of more prisoners than protest groups ever managed to set free. Secularism wanes and religion waxes everywhere. Religious conflicts and political conflicts are now so intertwined throughout the globe it is fruitless to try to disentangle them. Abroad the major religions fight each other for survival, and back home, sectarian splinter groups, evangelicals, charismatics, both Protestant and Catholic, vie for control over how people live, what laws they will follow.

Meanwhile, as our ninth president, William H. Harrison, said when a candidate in 1840, "I believe and I say it is a true Democratic feeling, that all the measures of the government are directed to the purpose of making the rich richer and poor poorer." One depressing fact: forty years ago, when the Harrisburg trial concluded, marked the peak of the rise of male earnings. Then the slide began, and a widening gap opened up between the rich and poor, resulting in the present concentration of so much wealth at the very top. President Harrison's characterization of government has never been more true.

When I concluded the Harrisburg book by crying out, "O America," I never thought the country would be worse forty years hence. But it is hard to conclude otherwise. The trial was thrust upon its defendants in 1972. It was nothing they wanted. Perhaps it is just their fate that they were among the last, best, hopeful protestors, wanting only for the country to do right. They were living through an actual golden age of protest. Let me repeat: it was a golden age of protest. Whereas, those who protested after were clothed mainly in self-interest and megalomania springing from a variety of twisted motives: for notoriety, for economic advancement, for exhibiting private pathologies. And at the most extreme, from Timothy McVeigh ripping the face off the Murrah Federal Building, to the men who brought down the Twin Towers, they no longer came in relative peace to protest wrongs; they came with fire and brimstone to punish.

Profile: R. D. Skillings, Resolute Character

My friend Roger Skillings is one of a kind. He is rooted to a single place and that is true both literally and figuratively. He is also attached to a place in my head and heart, but his physical presence remains anchored in P-town, insofar as that is where we first met and where he still is today. I've never seen him anywhere else, even though I know (or think I know) he's gone elsewhere, into New York City and, doubtless, other sites, especially the town where he grew up in Maine, and here or there along the East Coast, and in New England.

We met in 1970. Stanley Kunitz had shanghaied me and Louise Glück, two fresh graduates from the recently founded (at the time) graduate creative writing program at Columbia University, to come to Provincetown, Massachusetts, and become part of the new organization Stanley and Robert Motherwell (so I recall being told) had started, called the Fine Arts Work Center. A center that was nowhere and a circumference which was everywhere, since I can't recall what physical location the Work Center occupied that first year. It may have been (and probably was) the large, blunt, foursquare building covered with gray shingles at the corner of Standish and Bradford, depicted on the back of one of the early issues of *Shankpainter*. But I recall meeting Roger on the street, headed for a bar, with a small group of us newly minted fellows, most likely the Fo'c'sle.

Provincetown in 1970 was not a bustling place in late October. By January it was a village near total abandonment, where you knew most everyone who was seen on the street, either Commercial or Bradford. Stuart Land, who was the husband of one of the painters at the Work Center, Sharli Land, delivered heating oil in a reassuringly stout tanker truck, a source of heat that was sorely needed. The stipend the Work Center passed out back then was a mere token, a hundred dollars a month, which may, or may not, have been enough for most fellows to cover rent. I first worked that winter at a place called the Atlantic Coast Fisheries, which was half an ice house, the other half a processing operation. We packed lobster tails, among other creatures of the sea, for delivery to grocery stores, chains (like the A&P). I, coincidentally, lived in an actual store, one converted to an apartment during the winter, part of a complex that ended on the beach of the harbor bay, across from the Chrysler Art Museum, now, at long last, the refurbished library.

Then, the town's little library was directly across from the Fo'c'sle, sheltered by its comforting linden tree. It afforded a bucolic respite while staring out the large front windows of that bar.

On one of those days Roger and I sat in the window table of the Fo'c'sle, when the weather was finally breaking from winter's hold, and there were a couple of young women with us at the table, strangers to us, who had managed to find the place. It must have been the weekend. They were of a literary bent, I recall, since they were looking for famous writers, namely Norman Mailer, an author they had heard of. Roger suggested to them they should look for writers who weren't famous yet, but who would be one day. "Oh, yeah," the friskiest of the two young women said, "and where would they be?"

"Well, there's one," Roger said, pointing to me. I was staring morosely at my stein of beer, but managed to look up at that point. "And there's another," I said, roused, pointing at Roger. Both young women looked skeptical, but the one who was addressed did manage a smile.

It's not Roger's gift of prophecy I want to highlight by recounting this tale (which, in any case, was slightly defective), but his large gift of generosity.

Because, since the beginning, as thin as he was (and is), Roger was an unending source of excess generosity. It marked him. And his generosity was, in consequence, fruitful. When Roger decreed, I believed. It's almost impossible to think of the Fine Arts Work Center, nearing its half century of existence, becoming what it is, without the generosity and involvement of Roger Skillings. And this generosity is not of the usual American sort, money, but the sort that nurtured young writers more than the paltry stipends fellows received. At the start, those funds were so inadequate that the Work Center continued on only through the will and stamina of the fellows who made it up, but they only managed to do that because of people like Roger, and when I say people, I think of only two or three additional individuals; and, in any case, Roger outpaced the others by far in the long run. And it has been a long run, with the year fifty coming before the end of this decade.

In elementary physics they speak of a "strong force," one that holds the neutrons together, along with the protons, and neutrons to protons, which, in turn, keeps the nucleus where it is, at the center of the atom. Well, Roger is the center, the strong force's major triumph, and he remains exercising the strong force that the Work Center emits, helping to hold it all together, the writing side, while remaining for me, and scores of others, the center of the Center.

And, as the decades passed, we both became late fathers; Roger has his wonderful daughter Marissa and I my own son, Joe. Some years ago we were all at a beach in Truro and Marissa was upset, at age six or so, that my Joe, then around nine, was paying more attention to the brand new Harry Potter installment than to her. She came up to us and said, with a quiet indignity, glaring over at Joe, who sat apart reading, "How does it feel to have an adult as a child?"

Since Marissa has two writers for parents, it was easy to see where her native wit came from. But it's difficult to accurately weigh so many similar small pleasures over the years provided by my friendship with Roger. When you meet someone when you're young it is hard to predict how much their lives will mean to you as time goes by. And, from this distant vantage, I can only be thankful. A man of substance doesn't lose what he has, no matter how much he gives away. And Roger has been a profligate giver.

Looking back over four decades from that day at the Fo'c'sle, when Roger and I had only barely begun to publish, but were both full of hope, is exhausting. But it's reassuring to count all the books that followed. Fiction is often more an honest historical record than nonfiction accounts and Provincetown has its twentieth century (and twenty-first) chronicler in Roger's work, from the early stories in *P-town Stories*, and two additional collections, to the monumental novel *How Many Die*, to his latest collection of stories to be, *The Washashores*. Roger is no more a regional writer than Provincetown is a provincial place, but he does speak for the town, unique as it is.

How Many Die, his masterful chronicle of the AIDS epidemic marching through P-town, begins with an epigraph from Aeschylus—"And grief's hardly more pitiable than joy"—and concludes with an Author's Note, the last paragraph of which is: "In terrible times, when the absolute seems to rule, resolute character is all. At the mercy of unfledged imagination an artist may have small freedom, less power. But as George Kennan says, 'If humanity is to have a hopeful future, there is no escape from the pre-eminent involvement and responsibility of the single human soul, in all its loneliness and frailty.'"

I remember thinking the first time I read that how much it was like Roger, leaving the last word to someone else. (And George Kennan, no less!) How generous. So unlike so many writers. Resolute character, indeed. Thank the world for R. D. Skillings.

Profile: Judith Shahn, Greenwich Village, circa 1973

All the good art I own has been given to me, most often by the artists themselves. How Judith Shahn came to give me her 1954 painting, which I have titled *Man and Shop Window* (titling it in the manner of the rest of her titled paintings), happened like this: It was the early 1970s and I was living at 4 Milligan Place down in the Village. Milligan Place was/is a small, gated courtyard on Sixth Avenue (the Avenue of the Americas, it was/is also called) between 10th and 11th streets, nearer 10th. The more famous Patchin Place, on 10th Street, abutted the back of Milligan Place. I lived in a one-room apartment in the front looking out onto the courtyard and a corner of the playground of an elementary school on 11th Street. I moved there because my friend in the building, Craig Nova, told me an apartment had just come open when I returned to the NYC after finishing *The Harrisburg 7 and the New Catholic Left* in 1972. The building, before it was cut up into small apartments, had, supposedly, once been the home of Theodore Dreiser.

I was living, as I described it back then, an economically immature existence. In other words, I was poor, cash poor, but I realized it was a special kind of poverty, the bohemian existence I always pined for as a kid growing up in the Midwest. I had no money, but my book was on the *New York Times Book Review*'s New and Recommended list. Craig had just published his first novel, *Turkey Hash*, and we pooled our funds and purchased a foot-long lettuce sandwich to share at the Blimpie's (now long gone) at the corner of 11th and Sixth, all we could afford, and after that thin meal Craig vowed *this would never happen again.*

Well, I got a job, more or less, at Feller's Scenery Studio in the South Bronx building Broadway scenery, making use of the theatrical skills I had picked up in my youth. And I recall Craig trying his hand at ghostwriting. We both forged ahead.

It was around this time I was contacted by Judith Shahn. Judy, after some sort of legal battle, was being evicted from her studio, which happened to be around the corner from where I lived. I had known her and her husband, the poet Alan Dugan, since 1970, while a fellow at the new Fine Arts Work Center (FAWC) in Provincetown, Massachusetts. I had some youthful experience with Cape Cod, but not much with Provincetown, but, having few other prospects in 1970, I went merrily along. My first year was mainly spent working in the fish factory there (gone now) and then guarding the Chrysler Glass Museum (also long gone), but the following summer in P-town managed to change my life, when I met a young lawyer who led me to Harrisburg, Pennsylvannia, and the Catholic Left.

Judy and Alan were big supporters of the FAWC, from its beginnings to the end of both their lives, Alan helping to anchor the poetry side of the operation and Judy the art side. I never had known or knew at the time that Judy had a studio down in the Village, as well as a separate small apartment that she and Dugan had kept for years. But she asked if I could help move her out of the studio. Dugan had been hitting the Heaven Hill a little hard and had gotten into fisticuffs, or some altercation, with the landlord and was banned from the building.

Sure, I said. I had actually done a similar job before, when I was a graduate student at Columbia. I had moved an artist from one studio to another, employment that turned up for me after I observed a notice on a student bulletin board. Fay Lansner, primarily a print maker, had a studio on the East Side, above a tony restaurant (Sign of the Dove), which was expanding and she too was being forced out. That was 1969. Fay was moving to a new studio on lower Broadway. It turned out that Fay's husband was Kermit Lansner, then the editor of *Newsweek*, which resulted, after my Harrisburg book came out, in me being invited to a number of fancy parties.

But Judy wasn't moving to another City studio, but taking most everything back to Truro, where a studio was to be built, enlarging the house they owned there, a house which I presume had been in her family, once owned by her father, Ben Shahn.

So some things went to the apartment, but most went into storage, or was prepared to be shipped to the Cape. I did the work during the night in the main, having a day job at the time, and it took a couple of weeks. The loft space was to be taken over by a baker, a baker whose specialty was "erotic" bread. This, obviously, was a sign of things to come, and at the time I presumed erotic bread was sculptural, though I thought there might be only so much that could be sculpted in dough. The wealthy, oddly, were somewhat subdued in the 1970s. But the nascent one percent was preparing to invade and occupy Manhattan. Doubtless all this was a forerunner of the artisan food movement. Isn't "toast" hot now?

In any case, Judy and I labored away and when we got to nearly the end, after taking down two-by-four partitions, etc., packing canvases, etc., we reached the back of one wall not seen for a number of years and she spotted something, reached down, and extracted a small framed canvas. She said to me, "Well, this will take us through old age."

What it was was a painting of her brother done by her father. It was a portrait, dark with the accumulated dirt of decades. I saw it a year or so later hanging on their dining room wall in Truro, all bright and clean. She had sent it to Yale and its experts had restored it.

And it was when we got down to the last two or three things left to pack in the studio, she said, "You can have one of these. Pick." I may have protested, since I was doing this for a friend, not for any kind of pay. But, nonetheless, I chose the largest one, the canvas that is on the cover of the *Notre Dame Review*, volume 39. It was framed, which was maybe why I picked it, whereas the two smaller ones were not.

Nearby, in another corner of the loft, were three sculptures by Marisol, who once shared the studio with Judy. And I pointed to the group, squarish wood constructions, pillars of a sort, with faces painted at the top, about three or four feet tall. "Can I have one of those, too?" I meant it as some kind of joke, but Judy said, nonplused, "No, she's going to come by to get those."

I didn't have to pack Judy's painting, since I only needed to carry it around the corner.

So I have had it for over forty years, somehow managing to take it, unharmed, with me in numerous relocations, and I'm not sure if it has ever been reproduced, or cataloged, anywhere. I certainly would have lent it for any sort of show, but Judy—no one—ever asked me. Judy died when she was eighty in 2009, predeceased, as they say, by Alan, some six years earlier. An obituary can be found here: https://www.provincetownartistregistry.com/S/shahn_judith.html.

Until the last years of her life she mainly did illustrations for the *New Yorker*, small sketches that filled white space breaking up and at the end of articles. And she continued to produce a number of prints, in a far different style than her early oils, which may well be her ongoing artistic legacy. The *New Yorker* has changed, New York has changed, everything has changed, and I am flummoxed to look back at those years, my poverty years, that were so rich.

Irish Times Times Two: On Michael Collins

I. March 16, 2017

I was a university professor for over forty years and Michael Collins was the only genius student I ever encountered. I certainly had any number of smart ones, bright ones, utterly successful ones. Too much ability can be a burden of sorts and what Michael possessed in excess he lacked in what some might call common sense—at least the American variety of common sense. He was then and now the classic outsider.

He came to Notre Dame by way of the university athletic program, insofar as he was recruited as a long-distance runner. He turned up in my beginning creative writing class after a falling-out with the track coach, or so I heard. His scholarship had been yanked and a priest had to intervene to recover some of that—mere secular professors had no influence there.

Michael, at that time, was also a computer prodigy and what could be termed a "premature hacker," since the term wasn't in use back then. I heard he got into the university's system and changed some grades. I had never met a student who had such diverse high-level abilities: in prose literature, in world-class athletics, and in computer know-how. He defied C. P. Snow's "two cultures" split; in fact, he was dancing in three cultures.

Writers, especially novelists, tend to be outsiders. Insiders often turn into journalists, if they have any literary talent. The outsider point of view is almost de rigueur for the critical mind, though the paradox of knowing what you're talking about while observing it nonetheless pertains.

In my creative writing class when Michael was a junior he would turn in short stories with sentences like these:

> Father Sheamus gorged down a greasy fry and washed it back with three cups of watery tea. His heavy coarse beard was splattered with the yellow of egg and specked with crumbs from burnt toast. The waiter stood idly by in amazement. The priest gulped down the last drop of tea and then slamming the cup against the table with great satisfaction, he belched and wiped his sleeve across his mouth. The jostling train

now set on track four, crawled like a great armored centipede into the station.

It's highly unusual to have a student with such a gift: description that is dynamic rather than static. "Gift" is usually what displays of early talent is called, since no one can believe that the youngster is able to do something like that without outside intervention. Irish writers have a long, glorious history in the short form, the short story, so Michael's competence didn't seem out of place. Here a sort of racism and stereotyping provided him a background that didn't make him seem an outlier, but a writer emerging from a tradition.

Humans tend to mask their ignorance by inventing similarities. A year later I tried to get Michael into the premier graduate creative writing program at the University of Iowa, by contacting T. C. Boyle, who had influence there. Boyle was a writer I had met, but he balked at my entreaties by saying, "But, he's so Irish!" Michael, on his own, applied to the University of Alaska, a choice few native Americans would have made. They, no surprise, accepted him. He left a few months after he began, selling his only suit in order to arrange transportation back to the lower forty-eight.

He showed up at my office door later and his at-sea-ness led me to do something I had intended to do all along, to start a graduate creative writing program at my university.

Michael and a young man who was in the PhD program became Notre Dame's first two graduates of the new program, which has since flourished. Upon graduating (Michael only needed a year, since I had given him graduate credit for all the advanced creative writing courses he had taken with me as an undergraduate) he went back to Ireland and England and I learned that a small press there was bringing out a book of short stories, some of which he wrote as an undergraduate, titled *The Meat Eaters*. It was called *The Man Who Dreamt of Lobsters* when it was published a couple of years later in the states by Random House.

It turned out that Michael had created the small press that brought out the original volume, attempting to get notice, which only succeeded in getting my notice and the help of my agent who managed to sell the book both in England and America after *Esquire* magazine ran a story from it, accompanied by a large picture of the young, handsome author.

Presumably, Michael had arrived. But the literary world is a fickle place and nothing went smoothly thereafter. Though a critical success, a hardback of short stories, all set in Ireland, only attracts a discerning, but limited audience. It received as much praise as any collection of short stories had that year, though, unfortunately, as a debut book especially, there is, in America, a ceiling on how much such a collection will sell. Cause and effect are tossed about and Michael found himself dismayed that his fresh fame didn't make his life similar to members of the band U2.

Michael and his young wife went to Chicago and he enrolled as a PhD student at the University of Illinois at Chicago Circle. She went to medical school. Michael didn't publish another book in America until eight years later (*The Man Who Dreamt of Lobsters* had appeared in 1992). When *The Keepers of Truth* was short-listed for the Booker Prize the attention it generated prompted a US edition, a paperback, of the novel to appear in 2000.

By then Michael had acquired a PhD from Illinois and still was running about, winning long races and found himself working for Bill Gates in Washington state, where his wife practiced medicine. He wrote *The Keepers of Truth* out West while employed at Microsoft, and the corporation wasn't aware they had let an actual writer into its midst (an asp in its bosom!) until the notoriety of the Booker Prize accolade reached someone's ears out there.

Michael and Microsoft parted ways, a fact that became apparent when his swipe card no longer opened up any doors. Microsoft may want to run the world, but the literary culture wasn't high on any of its lists of specific interests. They do like to kill mosquitoes, though.

Michael had signed nondisclosure contracts with the company and hasn't to my knowledge written about the place, since they would likely send two hundred lawyers to ruin his life if he dared. Talking about outsiders! One of Norman Mailer's best books (and least read) is *Of a Fire on the Moon*, about NASA's moon landing. Employees of NASA seem to be denatured of any novelistic ambitions as they rise in the ranks, and it was necessary for them to bring in someone from the outside to chronicle their daring do.

Mailer possessed sufficient reputation, so he was called in and given remarkable access to the goings-on. Hidden cultures make for interesting novels and books, but we have come a long way from the days of Upton Sinclair, or, for that matter, muckrakers in general. Modern corporations, obviously, take steps not to open themselves up to critical scrutiny.

There are many reasons for the relative scarcity of work literature. In 1977 I put together an anthology titled *On the Job: Fiction about Work by Contemporary American Writers*. I was surprised by the paucity of possibilities. One reason that trend has continued is that so many writers of my generation have found work in American universities. Life in academia has been well covered.

Michael ended up living in lower Michigan, teaching at what was more or less a community college in Dowagiac, while his wife doctored in South Bend, a half hour away. Michael's outsider status, like many an author, had multiple sides, at least a pentagon's worth, all equally distant. His publishing history reflects that. After the Booker short listing, American publishers again took interest in him. Scribner's published *The Resurrectionists* in 2002. One Irish critic commented on the British edition, saying, "Collins is a chronicler of small Americana and the downbeat drifters that have been passing through ever since *The Grapes of Wrath*."

Of course, it was Michael who has been passing through. Dowagiac is a hard-scrabble town, not quite the upper-scale Microsoft suburban world of Bellingham, Washington. The American economy in this part of the country has become a cliché, saddled with its own tired vocabulary, cinched by its "Rust Belt" label. First there was automation, then nationalization, then globalization. Michael has been writing about the region's Donald Trump voters for a long time.

The Keepers of the Truth is set, evidently, in South Bend, Indiana, seen, of course, from the serene woods of Washington state, where it was written. The writer as outsider often needs to be literally outside the geography where a novel is located. His next two novels, *The Resurrectionists* and *Lost Souls*, form a trilogy of sorts, all dealing as they do with our country's down and almost out. Alas, given low sales, American publishers abandoned Michael's neo-proletarian novels once again after *Lost Souls*.

By the early 2000s American publishing had changed utterly. Large publishing had coalesced into the minor businesses of three or four giant conglomerates. And computers, technology, the internet, had done their insidious work. America no longer has a literate culture, but an oral-visual one, a media, platform culture and the so-called serious writers remain out of luck, unless they are billeted at some stable university. Reading rich prose became as much of a specialty in the common culture as being able to play a musical instrument, not a universal ability.

There was, still is, a Noah's Ark sort of hopefulness for authors, where at least two examples of each literary species will be saved, given the flood of all the "content" overtaking the average American who can read. One barcode villain can be identified: Bookscan, which can accurately chart every sale any book in the country makes. Publishers use this data point as a decision maker or breaker. Oddly, as discerning readers began to vanish, the number of publishers began to rise, since writers, primarily those attached to universities, began to create coterie presses, a great number of them. Virginia Woolf, I keep claiming, is to blame, given that she too invented a press and published her friends. That model the last twenty years has been employed by American writers without shame.

But authors make mistakes, too. Very few noncommercial writers know how to successfully advance their careers. Michael was no exception. He changed agents, publishers, gave up writing short stories—a critical mistake in this country, if you want to continue to be noticed as a literary writer—and attempted to jump into the crime genre to entice the vagrant reader. If best sellers were easy to write there would be more of them. Michael, unfortunately, had, has, too much talent to succeed as a crime writer. He doesn't possess the fatal lack of talent required. He asks too much of a reader. America really doesn't possess enough of a literary culture anymore to maintain a writer like Michael.

England, Ireland, France (the French love Michael's books), are small enough countries (geographically small) to still contain literary cultures that are contiguous, somewhat centralized. In the United States we have no such organic whole. What literary culture that is here is not united, but, shattered, dying off, only functioning in the redoubts of two or three big cities, controlled by fashion-setting gatekeepers, one or two national critical organs that still exist to examine authors (the *New York Times Book Review* and the *New York Review of Books*). The country might be too big to fail, but it fails its writers. They are largely superfluous. The academic world houses them in universities across the country, but universities are largely insular and have little effect outside their boundaries.

And it is also true that here in the states you will only be read by the many, not the few, if you are telling the culture something it wants to hear. Michael isn't doing that. Here is almost a random sentence from his current novel, *The Death of All Things Seen*:

> He stood amidst his daughters' clothes from years earlier, the rows of imported cashmere cardigans, the Izods in the pastel colors and pop-up collars that were no longer in fashion, along with the obscene number of dresses, shoes, boots, sneakers and sandals, many in their original boxes, never worn, or worn once. In their totality, they suggested a great fraud had been committed, in the way Imelda Marcos and her three thousand pairs of shoes had sparked true moral outrage in a world grown too accustomed to mass graves.

Not something most readers hunger to be told.

The Death of All Things Seen, with its mix of high and low characters, hasn't penetrated the American publishing world, even though it is in the tradition of the great Chicago writers, midwestern writers, such as Saul Bellow, Theodore Dreiser, James T. Farrell, other chroniclers of the American underbelly, its teeming sites of production and consumption, its portraits of the used and used-up many who both populate the place and produce its products.

One difficulty is that Michael, unlike the three writers mentioned above, is not a Dead White Male (a category anathema in U.S. literature departments for the last thirty years), but a Live White Male, not a demographic entity that is much in fashion these days. Though globalized in actuality, Michael is not globalized by background or genetics.

The Outsider writer is both a fact and a curse. If you're outside, in the cold, there you may well remain. His last novel published here was *The Death of a Writer* (2006). I bought it in London when it was published and titled *The Secret Life of E. Robert Pendleton.* Though an "academic" novel (which likely got it published here) Michael makes use of a crime to drive the plot and I was happy to see he took a line of mine, giving it to the soon-to-be-disposed-of dyspeptic author to remark that he stopped writing novels since he didn't want to give people "more not to read."

Again, Michael, by this time, given the spate of novels published in the United States, had finally gotten interviews at decent universities to teach writing, but he made the mistake of reading the early chapter of *The Death of a Writer* that is an excoriating attack on English departments and their incompetent professors. Not surprisingly, he didn't get any job offers.

Michael's career has been singular, since he is singular, though there is an American writer, Craig Nova, who Michael, in some ways, resembles. Craig is also a writer of indelible prose, lyrical and trenchant. And, in his search for an audience, Nova has dipped into the crime genre and certainly writes in those novels, mainly, of the dispossessed and marginal. But, being American, Craig is not an outsider; he knows how the system works and is currently an endowed chair at a North Carolina university.

Craig, too, does not have a large audience reading him and is known only by the well-informed, but not hugely populated, literary circles. Large publishers, though, have thus far stuck with him, a rarity in itself, and his novels have piled up, like Michael's. Needless to say, Craig is also a Live White Male.

I, too, have outsider status, at least in one novel, *Notts*, which appeared in the states in 1996. It is set during the last great strike, the NUM strike of 1984–85, in and around London and Nottingham, where I spent time during the strike. The novel has never been published in England, or anywhere else but America, though when it appeared here in 1996, I discovered that though there was a long tradition of coal mining novels, there was no current interest.

Terry Eagleton, at the time, was visiting Notre Dame for a few months at great expense to the university, and I gave him a copy, eventually copies, of the novel to no effect whatsoever. Eagleton dipped into Notre Dame's treasury for a number of years and not so long ago in the early 2000s I refreshed his memory of the book, saying it was the only novel that used the NUM strike as a subject. He said, No, I just reviewed a book about the strike recently, so I adjusted my remark to say, well, it was the first novel about the strike, published a decade earlier. I looked up his review of what I considered (of course) an inferior treatment of the strike (*GB84*, by David Peace). Nothing like being an outsider, especially to one's own sometime colleague.

The French may well like Michael's writing because they translate it into their own language, a cultural absorption of sorts. Between England and Ireland and America there is no need for translation and that makes being an outsider a more abstract thing. Both American and UK and Irish writers who go back and forth easily are the celebrity writers. There is no denying that Ireland and England still have vibrant literary cultures, especially compared to what an invalid that passes for literary culture in the states, but like so many of Michael's characters, what makes him and them outsiders is largely an economic question and not a literary one.

II. March 22, 2017

I am pleased that my "aside" prompted so many, in the main, thoughtful responses—and surprised that there are so many self-described "crime writers" at the ready. When I use the term I am, was, thinking of those formulaic, genre writers, who turn them out yearly, if not monthly. I worked in New York City publishing when I was in graduate school way back when and proofread and copyedited quite a few.

My remark—"He doesn't possess the fatal lack of talent required"—is the sentence, actually the phrase, everyone seems to object to. Though, given the literate audience involved, I would have thought that such a description—"fatal lack of talent"—would alert the reader (since it is a mixture of direct statement and hyperbole) to the realization that I might be aware of its provoking ambiguities. This particular notion—fatal lack—is a perennial hobbyhorse of mine, though I have never written about it. As an old friend, the noncrime writer Irini Spanidou, said to me long ago, "Genius is a gift and talent is a curse."

Michael Collins, if one reads the phrase in context, is the one bereft of the fatal lack of talent, saddled with the curse, in other words, hampered by too much talent. Not the mob of crime writers out there. Everyone is a crime writer, in the largest sense. Shakespeare is a crime writer. I published a novel titled *Criminal Tendencies*; there is a crime in it. The novel I have just completed has a crime in it—adultery, though most people no longer consider adultery a crime.

Let us be reasonable here. I am too old and have published too much to be thought ignorant enough not to be aware of the objections put forward by the miffed thirteen. But, I contend, writers who publish are always writing at the top of their form. No one writes down. It's difficult, almost impossible. Writers cursed with too much "talent" are unable to stoop to conquer.

The crime writers I was thinking of are the sort whose principal object is not to get the reader to stop in his or her tracks and ponder some remarkable aperçu, or paradox of the moment, be stunned to stop and think, but to keep turning the pages.

At my university I am part of a College of Arts and Letters. Though in our current age it is mainly Arts and Entertainment. I am not on the side that thinks awarding the Nobel Prize in Literature to Bob Dylan (né Zimmerman) is an appropriate thing, even though it is certainly of the moment and is the epitome of the mix of high and low culture that reigns, evidently, everywhere. But, as a Yank, in a jingoist mode, I certainly think his winning preferable to giving it to some author I've never heard of residing in one of the Baltic states.

The examples of writers of announced stature who write, allegedly, superior crime novels under pseudonyms, is a matter of judgment. In any case, there are a number of counter-examples. Here are three, all by happenstance female: Doris Lessing, Joyce Carol Oates, and J.K. Rowling. All published in different genres under pen names and those books went nowhere, until the actual celebrity author was revealed. And, in Oates's case, it was revealed pre-publication.

I am not bothered by the success of others. In fact, it's one of my few good traits. But I am well aware of the limitations of writers and if one is addicted to metaphor, prose residing in the neighborhood of belles lettres, it is difficult, if not impossible, to go cold turkey and write otherwise. As one of the respondents (Barbara Nadel) pointed out, I, too, categorize writing as either fiction or nonfiction and, secondarily, whether it is good or bad.

The real cause of literary success, if one wants to go there, is contained in my remarks about telling the culture what it wants to hear. That's a subject that needs to be discussed more deeply, rather than the offense taken at the phrase "fatal lack of talent." And, I must admit, I am a bit surprised so many have such a low threshold for feeling belittled by my passing remark.

It proves the central point of my article on Michael, that there is an active and vibrant and cohesive literary community across the pond, but not in the USA. Such a display of insults and ire would never happen in America, because I am not a celebrity. The chief reaction to perceived literary rebuke by an unfamous author in the states is not to be bothered. Neglect has always been the preferred weapon of choice here.

Part I was originally published as "Michael Collins: A Genius Student but Classic Outsider," Irish Times, *March 16, 2017; part II was published as "William O'Rourke: 'I'm Not Bothered by the Success of Others,'"* Irish Times, *March 22, 2017. For the thirteen Irish crime writers' responses, see Martin Doyle, "'Untalented' Crime Writers Respond to Their No 1 Critic: 13 Thriller Writers Take William O'Rourke to Task for Dismissing Them and Their Readers,"* Irish Times, *March 20, 2017, https://www.irishtimes.com/culture/books/untalented-crime-writers-respond-to-their-no-1-critic-1.3017198.*

Making Poverty More Bearable

■ First presented as a talk at Lone Star College, Houston, Texas, April 2, 2016

The humanities have always played one important role in income inequality: they can make being poor more bearable. Unfortunately, I have lived long enough to see, or have gone through, a number of changes in how poverty is viewed, and what roles poverty plays in our culture.

I am not quite a baby boomer, since that category officially starts on January 1, 1946. I was born in December 1945.

Let me enumerate a quick list of generational name tags I've seen applied as I have aged. The first, as a late teenager—in fact, the word *teenager* is a label that was also an invention, coming into use in the early twentieth century; its emergence had to do with the growth of high school education, the prevalence of automobiles, changes in social mores, etc.—in any case, the generation ahead of me were so-called beatniks; that subculture morphed into hippies; then, by the time of the 1980s, the term *yuppies* was coined. More recently there has been Generation X and, popular today, the less interestingly named millennials. Hipsters are a subset, though they mainly live in Brooklyn.

OK. What's in a name? Here's my point concerning these labels: the first three, *beatniks* and *hippies*, even *yuppies*, denote a class, or, at least, a sociological orientation. For the first two groups, though, poverty was not shameful, not entirely crushing, or feared.

Indeed, both categories at heart had traditions supporting them and at their centers sat the humanities. If *beatniks* and *hippies* have any meanings, associations, for college-age students today, it may well be, for the first, Allen Ginsberg, perhaps poetry readings, for the second, communes, Woodstock.

Beatniks were continuing the older nineteenth-century heritage of bohemians. According to the *Oxford English Dictionary*, the first use of the word *bohemian* turned up in 1848 and described the manner of living of so-called impoverished writers, journalists, artists, musicians, and actors living in major European cities.

The American beatnik period was also the era of folk songs, from decidedly downscale guitar plunkers up to even stars like Joan Baez, Pete Seeger, and a few others who appeared just above the commercial horizon. But very few of their recordings went, as we would say today, viral—just vinyl. Poetry and guitar playing, then, were certainly technology-light.

The bohemian tradition shared one thing with hippies, insofar as bohemians set out to make poverty fun. Both beatniks and bohemians were urban phenomena, since you needed some excess capital around to make being poor fun; it required a few rich friends, acquaintances, and/or patrons to sometime feed you and buy drinks. That the arts are being cut from grammar and high school curriculums is further proof of the situation at hand.

I've spent my entire adult life writing about the intersection of politics and literature and I want to point out that a number of things happened in this country because of the bohemian tradition. The sixties happened. Protest happened. The civil rights movement happened. The anti–Vietnam War protests happened. Universities were temporarily shut down, people were in the streets. Change happened.

And a good bit of this was the result of the bohemian tradition and what it wrought. The young college students in the sixties didn't find poverty crippling. There was enough surplus capital around in the sixties and early seventies that allowed students in the North to travel down to the South, and students from the West to start free speech movements and, in the Midwest, to organize the Students for Democratic Society (SDS).

Jack Kerouac had published *On the Road* in the late 1950s and students took to the road in the 1960s. During the sixties, the number of people experiencing higher education tripled. I have been pointing out that statistic for years. It had never doubled in the decades previous. That demographic change, it can be argued, is responsible for what we call the sixties. A meaningful percentage of these students began to protest an unpopular and useless war, partly out of self-interest, since so many of them, the men that is, were vulnerable to the war because of the draft, but also because their educations—teach-ins that took place on campuses—made them question what the government was doing.

College campuses in the 1960s and '70s had become bohemian redoubts; they were their own examples of a new sort of urbanity, where educated people could coalesce and, in most cases, get by on very little income. For four years a lot of the population became bohemians. Not all, of course. There was always the fraternity/sorority side. But, thanks to Sputnik in 1957, the federal government started dumping money into land-grant universities across the country. The whole sixties generation profited from that. Again, recall the tripling of that population. For a few years ingrained American anti-intellectualism was put aside. And during the years that followed, though short lived, antimaterialism prospered.

Eventually, all that more or less ended. Hippies suffered self-immolation; communes were saddled with the bad image of the Charlie Manson murders, publicized most vividly in 1971. The modern women's movement percolated out of the chauvinist protest world and all the contradictions that experimentation with communal living and protesting had highlighted.

But what really altered this trajectory was the alarm experienced by the powers that be. They saw what happened when you began to educate the nonelite in state universities with low cost to the students. An important document that was privately circulated back then was the Powell Memo, written by the future Supreme Court justice, Lewis F. Powell, Jr., in 1971. A call to action for corporate America, spurred by what Powell saw as an attack on the free-enterprise system, the memo spelled out the countermovement to the counterculture that was then arising.

A college education wasn't free in the 1960s, but costs were low, mostly from so-called fees. An important date to reckon with is 1973, when Nixon signed Sallie Mae legislation, guaranteeing all sorts of student loans with federal money. That, more or less, was the birth of the modern history of for-profit colleges. Changes had begun earlier in the 1960s under Lyndon Johnson, when he signed the Higher Education Act of 1965.

That law's purpose was "to strengthen the educational resources of our colleges and universities and to provide financial assistance for students in postsecondary and higher education."

Amended over the years, the law strengthened banks far more than student interests.

But it was during the Reagan years when prevailing cultural attitudes about poverty were completely upended. Beatniks, hippies, college students be damned. The bohemian tradition went into permanent eclipse. Being poor was no longer fun.

Ronald Reagan is often held up as being a great leader and one bit of film is offered as evidence and, during this 2016 election year, it is being reshown now and then: Reagan objecting to having a microphone shut off. "I paid for this microphone," he says sternly in grumpy-old-man objection. It's a curious bit of proof to hold up as an example of Reagan's leadership qualities: I bought it, I own it, money talks, everyone else walks. Reverence for the rich came in with Reagan in spades. It's no coincidence that the word *yuppies* originated in the early 1980s, so much so it became a cliché in that decade. Again, this chain of events was not a coincidence. The point was, is, to burden the educated young with debt: to take away their free time and mobility.

Debt is an odd concept: to go into debt requires, usually, resources. To be in debt signifies a certain sort of economic status. The poor are robbed even of debt. There is a difference between loans and debt. Not that the near poor aren't eventually saddled with permanent poverty, via rising rents, so-called payday loans, which imply their customers have a job. Those storefront enterprises are backed up by the largest banks, which provide the necessary credit. Like so much else, how things work in this country remains behind closed doors, or at least obscured, quite deliberately. There are no Chase logos, or any other big banks' signs, on those gaudy storefronts.

We've gone from Michael Harrington's 1962 *The Other America*, to the current hot poverty book, *Evicted*, by Matthew Desmond. Though Michael Moore's hit 1989 documentary, *Roger & Me*, featured a number of evictions during the 1980s in Flint, Michigan.

Even Michael Moore's career can be seen as indicative of the larger cultural problem. His presentation of the poor in that film, formerly working-class individuals, both white and black, of Flint, highlights, at the end of the Reagan era when it was released, the grotesque aspects. It's the working-class post work, meaning the individuals involved really never had secure working-class jobs. The film doesn't show poverty out of the bohemian tradition. *Roger & Me* is poverty in all senses, of education, income, spirit. Moore himself, early on and currently, was costumed as a bohemian; he might have been out of the educated arts tradition, but not his subjects.

Reverence for the rich by 1989 was everywhere. The baseball-cap beheaded, overweight, disheveled Moore may have been the bull in the wealthy's china shop, yet he had become one of the first modern branders. His look was a uniform, a persona, as much, in the same period, as the dandy Tom Wolfe's white suit. And Wolfe was, is, foremost a chronicler of the rich and status conscious.

Another popular figure, one first out of the folk tradition, was Bob Dylan, but in 1965 he came on stage with an electric guitar. What was perceived, but not necessarily articulated, was his abandonment of the folk tradition, its humble ambitions, and his embrace of popular music, desiring mainstream acceptance and sales. Recall the Beatles hit our shores big time in 1963.

Popular arts strive to be popular. However scruffy the bands back then, most all wanted to be rich. Music is the humanities and its history tells its own tale. Rap and hip-hop started their rise in the 1980s, during the Reagan years. It may seem counterintuitive, but what held the Beatles and Bob Dylan and rap artists together was their love of contracts, rights, ownership, capitalism. The Beatles were big suers. Grunge, at its start, was a label in music meant to point out a contrast to the prevailing money-grubbers.

Tom Wolfe is credited with popularizing the label "the me generation," which meant to brand the post–Vietnam War remnants of the baby boomers as individualistic cultural narcissists. A variety of cultural figures were reorienting an entire generation away from its bohemian roots and attempting to put them back on the materialist fast track. The larger culture moved away from the bohemian model with relief.

Republicans and libertarians during this period set out to privatize whatever they could. They've largely succeeded. They're all for private wealth, not public wealth, and public wealth allowed for bohemian culture. It's a large subject, privatization, but it tracks with all the economic trends of the last three decades. The military is now largely privatized; NASA, the space program, is getting there. Privatization, in the main, makes a few people very rich, and leaves most everyone else anxious and dependent. Wonder how Russian oligarchs were made? The former state-owned industries were captured by the Russian well connected. Universities, both private and public, now have independent contractors doing much of the grunt work. So these lower-paid workers can't blame bastions of higher learning for their lack of benefits and low salaries.

The first personal computers appeared in the late 1970s, early '80s, too. The counterculture began to turn into the cyberculture. It's not too large a claim to point out that the heroes of Silicon Valley were, are, new versions of late nineteenth- and early twentieth-century robber barons, all capitalists par excellence.

Who are the heroes of educated millennials? Steve Jobs, Mark Zuckerberg, Bill Gates. Recall the early years of Microsoft. Stories back then about the firm concerned the legions of lawyers employed to secure Gates's rights and patents. These days business school enrollments are up, English majors down. Lately, everyone wants to run a hedge fund, or be at a private equity firm. The get-rich-quick dream of American hustlers everywhere had real-life counterparts by the 1980s; the new technologies created a handful of the stupendously wealthy—J. D. Rockefeller and Henry Ford would have been impressed.

Even philanthropy is privatized, a paradox of sorts. *60 Minutes* used to be a news show, but recently the program had a group of billionaires on air to congratulate themselves on giving away, supposedly, half of their fortunes. The *60 Minutes* interlocutor, hardly a journalist, never bothered to ask them if they would be willing to pay more taxes.

Here, for your contemplation, are the tax rates at the end of Bill Clinton's two terms: 31 percent applied to all income over $51,900. The Omnibus Reconciliation Act of 1993 created a new bracket of 36 percent for income above $115,000, and 39.6 percent for income above $250,000. Those were the rates Obama wouldn't revert to by letting Bush's tax cuts expire. Clinton's rates weren't onerous. Remember, Bush pushed through his tax cuts and didn't pay for the Medicare part D drug bill that had passed nor for the wars he started. He cut elsewhere. Those rates were sunset-ed, made to retire, because even bought-and-paid-for Republican economists couldn't hide their deleterious effects on the deficit.

The anti-tax crowd, a mixed bag, but mainly Republicans, succeeded beyond their dreams, but their dreams (flat tax! Banish corporate taxes! Abolish the IRS!) never die. Obama's biggest mistake, I hold, is that he didn't let all the Bush tax cuts expire. It was the most powerful card he held at the beginning of his presidency and he didn't play it.

A March 7, 2016 Bloomberg *QuickTake* article points out that Wall Street "bonuses began their climb in the 1980s, when deregulation allowed commercial banks to expand into more stock and bond trading and boost profits by buying and selling with the bank's own money. Eat-what-you-kill traditions meant professionals reaped bonuses in line with the profit they generated. Top bankers argued that their skills made them as valuable as professional athletes."

A graph published in the *New York Times* in 2011 shows that the average "securities industry" NYC salary in 1981 was less than $50,000 a year; though that was about double of all other private-sector jobs there, on average. By 2008 the figure was nearly $400,000; everyone else's average yearly pay in NYC that year was slightly above $55,000.

What I contend, and Bloomberg doesn't point out, is that this rapid rise, this rate of growth, going from double to six times the size in less than thirty years, just didn't affect the securities industry. Other company CEOs, top executives across industries, including academia, saw the bonuses and salaries of those young Wall Streeters rise in the 1980s and '90s, and felt, deep in their souls, they were all being underpaid. In the 1970s the ratio of CEO pay to the company's workers was around 20 to 1. In 2012 the *Los Angeles Times* reported that the average CEO-to-worker pay ratio was about 350 to 1. Some companies were higher. The three-hundred-plus figure is the average.

It was during the Reagan years that income inequality everywhere began to take off. No wonder Occupy Wall Street happened in 2011; the question is, Why did it take so long? Occupy was largely a feckless movement that had one lasting effect: it brought publicity to income inequality. Occupy more or less made the mantra "the one percent, ninety-nine percent" ubiquitous.

Again, what I'm trying to point out is that this cultural shift didn't happen by accident. Various commentators claim the Powell Memo of 1971 "influenced or inspired the creation of the Heritage Foundation, the Manhattan Institute, the

Cato Institute, Citizens for a Sound Economy, Accuracy in Academe, and other powerful organizations. Their long-term focus began paying off handsomely in the 1980s, in coordination with the Reagan Administration's 'hands-off business' philosophy." The Powell Memo is a remarkable document, prescient and alarming, though it was not in general circulation till the 1990s.

The 1980s and '90s saw a concerted reaction against the 1960s and '70s. No more of that: time to reduce the number of idealistic young who didn't seem to care that much about money. The cultural landscape was now filled with one percenters, all heroes of the new generation: musicians, athletes, money managers, Silicon Valley barons.

The growth of for-profit colleges is just one of the hallmarks of the last twenty some years; they were helped along by the parallel decrease in state support for college and universities. Again, public education was being privatized. The debt that students began to accrue they were not able to shed, since laws made it exempt from bankruptcy protection.

Add to that our country's condition of permanent war, predicted long ago by one of the greatest humanists, George Orwell, that we have been enduring since the end of last century, the twentieth, that is. Orwell's essay, "Politics and the English Language," is still seminal, but, evidently, completely ignored. Rhetoric and antigovernment propaganda from the right has been almost completely successful; nonetheless, the most startling growth of for-profit colleges has been in the last ten years or so. They tapped into the GI Bill population of veterans minted by our Middle East wars, primarily the Afghanistan war onward.

Speaking again of language and labels, words or phrases that drop out of common speech are also significant. *Beatniks, hippies*, even *yuppies*, since that word always had some derision in it, are long gone, more or less. Way back in the early twentieth century, there was a certain group written about, and that label has dropped out of the vernacular, too. It was *capitalists*; you can look up, say, the *New York Times* pre–World War I, and see headlines such as "Capitalists Meet." After the First World War the use of the word, designating a localized subgroup, a class apart, decreased and then disappeared. Capitalists wanted their title and presence to be mainstreamed and it was. Another common phrase that disappeared just before the Vietnam War was *war profiteer.*

Kevin Phillips's two books on the Bush family (*American Dynasty* and *American Theocracy*) show quite clearly that both branches of the Bush family have been war profiteers for generations. Bring in a Bush, bring on a war.

What was the Iraq War about? It made the upper class millions and the lower classes dead and maimed. This isn't Marxism, it's just facts. History is the humanities. An old remark by Randolph Bourne, made around the turn of the century, the nineteenth to the twentieth, "War is the health of the state," is still on target. What American industries continue to manufacture are the machines necessary for war: planes and bombs, armaments generally. These businesses employ a lot of people. And the government isn't eager to outsource arms sales to China.

I've had what passes for a secure job since 1978 when I began teaching at universities and private colleges. Before then I had manual labor jobs. But I began teaching full time in 1975 at a public university, Rutgers–Newark. Public universities aren't quite as safe as private ones. I take the *South Shore* into Chicago now and then, and the train travels by Chicago State University where all the teachers have been fired recently because of Illinois Republican governor Bruce Rauner; Rauner cut state funding and continues to quarrel over Illinois's education budget. Rauner was, what else? the chairman of R8 Capital Partners and chairman of the private equity firm GTCR. And now, as governor of Illinois, Rauner retains his mad focus on privatization, doing his best to ruin higher public education in the state. He, more or less, bought his governorship (he reportedly spent $26 million of his own money on his campaign), though the Democrats did help by putting three of their former modern governors in prison.

One might ask, How do these people get elected to high offices and why do so many midwestern states have Republican-controlled state legislatures (though not yet Illinois's), along with school boards, city councils, all the smaller bodies that control so much of people's lives? One reason is that, in many ways, Republicans change a vice into a virtue. Conservatives tend to be parochial, thinking not very much beyond their noses, but just that sort of parochial self-interest lets them get more deeply involved in local politics. Whereas liberals, bless them, have longer horizons, see the world as interconnected, are more macro than micro, and, alas, do not get involved as intensely in the nitty gritty of small-time politics and civic positions. If you want to save the whales, you're thinking of oceans; if you want to combat climate change, you're thinking of the planet. You can see the problem. If you want to prevent evolution from being taught in the school down the street, you attempt to get on the state board of education; you become Mary Lou Bruner, the Texas woman who believes President Obama was a gay prostitute to pay for his drug habit back in his college days.

One, I suppose, could write a book called, "How the One Percent Became the One Percent," tracing the history of laws and deregulations that took place, often enacted below most people's radar. Remember, everyone wanted to be a lawyer back in the 1980s; now, not so much. But what sort of legislation is currently in the news? It's all voter-suppression laws. If the general population might finally begin to catch on—"Feel the Bern"—make it harder for them to vote is the answer. The disruptions (i.e., Trump) that are going on in both parties show something at long last has gotten through to the disgruntled.

Our culture values persistence and Bernie Sanders has been persistent, as I have pointed out elsewhere in print. Bernie has two or three things to say and he's been saying them since he began to run for office in Vermont during the 1970s. What is amazing to me is that it has taken nearly five decades for his message to be heard. Bernie is the revenge of the sixties, a pied piper who has captured the young, with the distilled elixir of his (and my) youth. He has stepped out intact from a sixties' time capsule. Though he doesn't look like a hippie, a beatnik—no serape or beads, no candles in Chianti bottles.

Bernie Sanders wears suits, but the excesses of the right and the one percent over the same time span have become so egregious, brazen, and successful, that no one, even the least sophisticated (i.e., Trump supporters), can miss or deny it, especially college students who are footing a lot of the bill—alas, just to be educated. They may not be under the gun of the draft, but the draft for this generation has been replaced by debt.

After winning the Indiana Democratic primary, Sanders said, "I'll tell you what is extremely exciting for me, and that is that in primary after primary, caucus after caucus, we end up winning the vote of people 45 years of age and younger. And that is important because it tells me that ideas that we are fighting for are the ideas for the future of America and the future of the Democratic Party." He didn't point out that they were also the ideas of the past.

Even the Supreme Court chimed in in 2013 on voter suppression, gutting the civil rights–era voting rights legislation. Do you think the current Republican-controlled Congress will fix that? But one trouble with voter suppression is that the voters themselves are so good at it, given that only about 50 percent of the eligible even vote. Democrats seem to forget about elections unless a presidency is at stake. Midterms have been fertile harvests for Republicans, especially in flyover country.

At Rutgers–Newark way back when, my first full-time teaching job, it was like teaching night school during the day, insofar as a majority of the first-generation students enrolled seemed to have full-time jobs that they worked their daytime classes around. But now even the faculties at public colleges and universities can be poor, if they are adjuncts, a growing trend over the last twenty years.

How can the humanities affect poverty? the theme of this event. As I started with, it can make poverty more bearable. But the important thing is fundamental and twofold. Knowing how to read, of course, is the first requirement. My students at Rutgers had some problems with that, yet even a handful at the private schools where I've taught did, too. We have been an aural-visual culture for some time now, especially so, since the flourishing of the internet and so-called smartphones. A picture is worth a thousand words, certainly, but now a lot of people lack those thousand words.

I have tried to point out one thing to my students: words are free if you can get a hold of a dictionary somewhere. It used to be in America that a couple of material things were free: ballpoint pens and T-shirts. You could usually find one or the other being given away somewhere. Now, unfortunately, there is a third free thing: books. It's easy these days to find a free book, if you're not too picky. But words have always been free. What you would frequently find in the bohemian world was the so-called autodidact. Someone self-educated, meaning the person read a lot, often across a wide, and fairly crazy, spectrum.

IQ tests of yore were largely built on the size of a person's vocabulary. I guess the old SATs still pushed that. I would tell my students that one answer supplied to that old game of "What two books would you want if stranded on a desert island?" was given by Emily Dickinson. Her two books were the Bible and a dictionary.

Culture largely comes from one great book; all literate cultures have one. The Bible, the Talmud, the Koran. I had a few religious fundamentalist students at Rutgers who, though lacking a lot of ideas, had interesting prose styles, since all they ever read was the King James Bible. But this theory can also produce unfortunate examples, since a lot of destruction has come about by people who swear by one book, doing God knows what in its name. Beyond the religious texts noted above, there is, for example, Mao's *Little Red Book*, Hitler's *Mein Kampf*.

Certainly, you could get an argument that culture comes out of technology. Creating fire doubtless was a matter of primitive technology. Making a tool. The silicon chip, and the devices that have resulted, has created its own culture, one that is still in formation. Indeed, regarding language, we are going backward. Emoticons are proliferating. We're back to drawing pictures on the walls of our flat-screen individual caves. Literacy allegedly triumphed over the oral by the middle of the twentieth century, but since then orality has come storming back.

There is nothing sadder than the statistical studies of how many words children of poverty hear, are exposed to, and how infrequently adults, if they happen to be around, read to such children.

Even the young I encountered in classrooms are, on average, no longer as well read as those I dealt with twenty, thirty years ago. Of course, there are exceptions. There are always exceptions.

The culture, because of technology, has replaced knowing with Googling, often on small machines made by the largely poor in China. I use a computer, write on one, so I can't complain that people would rather read off a piece of glass than hold a book in their hands, since I, too, type words on a screen.

It is easier to think if you have a lot of words in your head and have many words from which to choose. Even though they are free for the taking, they deserve your respect and attention. Nonetheless, I've told my students for years if words were expensive, more people might want them. If words were sold, that is, they would be valued.

Edward Dahlberg: Letters to a Young Would-Be Writer

The letters found below are those I still have from the writer Edward Dahlberg (1900–1977), who was my teacher for two courses one semester at the University of Missouri at Kansas City (UMKC). I had what is usually called a checkered history as an undergraduate. I went for one year to Rockhurst College (now university) in Kansas City, Missouri, did badly, and, after spending the summer working for the Santa Fe Opera, barely managed to transfer to the state university branch in my hometown, then a so-called streetcar university, insofar as it educated local students, not being the residential campus it is now. After a listless academic year there, with the exception of the classes I took with Dahlberg in the spring semester of 1965, I went to Cape Cod to work as part of the annual migration college kids take to become cheap seasonal labor. Though, unlike most of the hundreds who did so, I stayed on the Cape, in Hyannis, after the summer, rented a room "fit only for suicide," as a friend put it back then, eventually secured a job at a craft shop that remained open for the fall, and changed apartments to a cozier one above the store. The owners had decamped to Boston for work during Christmastime, making enamels on copper in a downtown department store window.

I was attempting to write my version of the great American novel, a long piece of juvenilia titled The Armless Warrior. *The Vietnam War, needless to say, was raging at the time. In order to delay being drafted I returned to Kansas City in January 1966 and reenrolled at UMKC.*

Dahlberg had already written a great American novel/memoir, called Because I Was Flesh, *which appeared in 1964 and is one of the most prominent of neglected and unread masterpieces by an American writer. There are a number of reasons for that, some revealed in his letters to me, others the product of the literary culture and marketplace. Dahlberg had returned to UMKC for the fall semester that I had forgone. When I returned in January, I learned that Dahlberg had left before the semester's end. It evidently took me a few months to summon the strength to write him. Dahlberg was sixty-five and I was twenty when the correspondence began.*

I do not have copies of my letters to Dahlberg. They are among his papers kept at the Harry Ransom Humanities Research Center at the University of Texas, Austin, so what I wrote to him remains speculative to me. I'm sure they were inflamed and appropriately jejune. The letters that I have from Dahlberg are all similar in their physicality, mailed in small-sized Air Mail prestamped envelopes (eight cents!), chevroned around the edges with red and blue slashes, the letters themselves often typed on cheap yellow paper half the size of standard ms. paper. In between Dahlberg's letters that follow in chronological order I comment, I hope where helpful, supplying context and explanation, if not excuses. It was on the phone, not in these letters, where Dahlberg once thundered into my ear, "O'Rourke, all excuses are perjuries!"

May 9, '66

Mr. William O'Rourke,
5431 Wyandotte
Kansas City, Missouri.

Dear O'Rourke:

I have your very good letter and thank you for what you say about me. Our situation at the university was almost similar. You had no human being there except myself and I no gifted student but you. I became so discouraged that I told Dr. Ryan, my only friend on the faculty, that I could not stomach the mediocrity of the teachers and the people who never came to learn anything and were quite successful.

These are doleful days, and I should feel quite crestfallen were you to be drafted. I read in the papers (if you can believe anything that is in them) that students now can either go into the peace corps or join the poverty program. Maybe this would be a solution, not the most felicitous one, for you. Unfortunately, it does not matter what college you attend the studies are a humbug; you might in the east meet more intelligent young women and men, but the professors, with the rarest exceptions, are dunciads everywhere.

Should you want me to write to Dr. Ryan in your behalf for any sort of kindness, be sure that I will do so at once. My influence in New York colleges is unmentionable.

I have three books coming out this fall, *Edward Dahlberg Reader*, a volume of my letters, and if I can repair some very bad sentences I wrote a few years ago, and put that logic into the words that is never in life, there should be another volume of mine appearing in Autumn, *The Leafless American.*

Believe me, in one way or another, those have feeling and do their utmost not to be stupid (for no man is wise except by accident) we are all torn piecemeal every day, and often each hour.

I am very glad that you wrote to me, for I had hoped you would return, and that maybe I could be useful to you.

Everybody wants to write, but very few wish to read, and so you know I never minded the fact that you chose to study good books instead of the usual, hackneyed scrawl one gets from students and most of our so-called celebrated writers.

Write me when you feel like doing so. Be sure that I always appreciated your character. Had I five O'Rourkes in Kansas City I would have remained there, but then I am demanding miracles of a surd universe. I repeat, thank you very much for your letter; that is far better than the fusty and tepid best regards that one gets in an epistle nowadays. I lived on the Cape for 6 years, and just about lost my senses during the long, obituary winters when the small snowy hamlets were peopleless.

Edward Dahlberg

64 Rivington Street
New York, 2, N.Y.

UMKC, back in the midsixties, was a much more parochial institution than it is now. Of course, all of America was more parochial in 1965. Dahlberg didn't gather too many friends, or acquire them easily. Academics are famously sensitive about their accomplishments, however puny, and often are prickly in the presence of large, imposing figures who come from either coast to the hinterlands. I hyperbolically ended a reminiscence of Dahlberg a year after he died with the remark, "At the end of his long life he had fewer than six people he would have called 'friend.'" When Jonathan Lethem in 2003 wrote about Dahlberg in Harper's *he titled the piece, and the eventual book (2005) it appeared in, "The Disappointment Artist." Lethem quoted from my earliest pieces on Dahlberg in his article, but it was clear Lethem had no notion of anything else I had written.*

I had returned in the summer of 1966 to the Santa Fe Opera, where I toiled as a scenic technician. Because of my friendship there with Susan Scott, who worked at the opera as a "volunteer," I came to know her parents, the heiress Eleanor Metcalf Scott and the poet Winfield Townley Scott, who out of the blue Charles Baxter called earlier this year (February 19, 2015) toward the end of a book review of H. P. Lovecraft in the New York Review of Books, *a "grievously neglected American poet." Good for him. Scott (who had written early in his career on Lovecraft) was the second prominent writer I had come to know after Dahlberg, and I don't find it entirely out of place at this point that my earliest encounters with authors involved the seriously neglected. What my letter from the opera (the technicians lived at the ranch annexed to the theater) complained of specifically, I do not know, though I had a lot of complaints.*

July 30, '66

Mr. William O'Rourke
P.O. Box 2408,
Santa Fe, New Mexico

My dear O'Rourke:

I have your doleful letter, but what remedy is there for life at your age or mine? You know what feelings I have about our execrable education. But then there is bread, and how to get it, and into I have known many writers who fell into depravity of one sort or another, to fetch lucre.

There is a Hollywood scribbler whom I see on rare occasions who imagines he can debauch his own spirit and that of the populace and at the same time compose an honest book glutted with the truths of a soothsayer. While I was starving, he earned much money, but now that his hopes are wan, and he is hungry, but for fame!

The other day I wrote to a man at the University of Texas who is editing a small volume of miscellaneous essays and a tale, to excise some of my remarks about pathics. Then along came galleys of letters of mine to appear in the *Edward Dahlberg Reader* (which the editor had selected) and there are droll and harsh words about homosexuals, and so I now think I made a mistake, and must write him again to let it be, and take the consequences, for this brood of unnatural half-men, governs reviews and one's book is likely to be interred should one be as offensive as I have been. There will also be a volume of my epistles to be published in November by Braziller, and I have not the scantiest idea which ones are to be printed.

What else can you do but read the wise authors, and somehow you will come out of your tedious perplexities. There were long seasons of drought when no matter what I did I had no luck with women. I earnestly hope you will find one, but not a venomous bitch, and don't get married too early, for it takes a long time to understand anything at all about one's self, and by the time you have the least comprehension of your nature, you are likely to discover that you have wed a woman who is absolutely alien to you. But all advice is worthless, but I give it, anyway, for I have no other choice; for should I be mute I would blame myself if you blunder, and of course offering you counsel may be wrong too.

This is a barbarous, sullen town (no pun), and I feel that soon as I commence to write I go into exile. But I think every man of feeling is banished. Don't imagine that it is easy for me to compose a book, or that I am any less of a worm than you. It is always hard, and you do not know whether you are putting down elegant platitudes, wandering, or if you should not cast the whole idea away. Even so, what is a man to do with his life? I cannot be a drone, and have no thought of being a drudge either. The two dilemmas are: the woman who inflames the heart and the flesh, and the talent to do something with those heavy, endless hours. Auden is another pseudo-male, and so you are quite right in rejecting him.

Write me whenever you wish to do that. I would suggest other books for you to read, but I imagine you have by no means consumed the list I gave you; however, if there are ancient sages you desire to be familiar with please let me know. Wish my rejoinder were more useful to you; the truth is I have been in the dumps, since for months I have been taking elaborate notes and scrabbling what lines I know not for a literary autobiography.

Be sure of my friendliest regards, and that I always like to hear from you. I shall be here until about the middle of September.

Edward Dahlberg

820 Arguello Road,
Santa Barbara, California 93105

Well, I can only surmise I mentioned that I was drawing the attention of a number of men at the opera, but none of the women. Some elegant paradox I was attempting, no doubt. In any case, Dahlberg's attitudes regarding gays in the 1960s mirrored the mainstream's (only in his prejudices was Dahlberg ordinary), though complicated, I'm sure, by those gay men who most admired him and were his patrons. And, however Dahlberg spoke, wrote, about women in his letters, and in person, what was clear to me was that he thought about them quite a bit. I've always considered the most common sort of misogyny displayed by men was their thinking about women not at all. And lest anyone thinks I rejected an overture from W. H. Auden, the reference, I'm sure, was to Auden's libretto, or some part of it, to Stravinsky's The Rake's Progress, *which Santa Fe was mounting that summer. When I encountered Auden a few years later at Columbia University (he was visiting a poetry workshop there), I refrained from telling him I had worked on* The Rake's Progress, *and had studied his libretto closely. I did, though, sit silently fascinated by the length of ash he maintained on the cigarette he was smoking, while a student, I think it was Hugh Seidman, recited a poem.*

November 29, '66

Mr. William O'Rourke,
5431 Wyandotte,
Kansas City, Missouri.

My dear O'Rourke:

I am always pleased to get your letters, and cannot help but notice some of the sharp and deeply-felt phrases. Would that I could in some way heal your despondency, but that is impossible. Each one carries his sack of suffering, and even could another help him, he would not know how to do it. A pity too that your friend has been drafted. I prize my few friends, and who claims he has more than that is a liar and a braggart.

The Reader and a volume of my Letters will be published the latter part of January; and three of my books will be issued as paperbacks. There is another volume of mine, The Leafless, which a San Francisco publisher will bring out in the close future.

Meantime, I am at work on a literary autobiography, and at this writing am dealing with those young enthusiasts of the Muses, Ernest Walsh, Kay Boyle, Robert McAlmon and Emanuel Carnevali, forgotten this day, but then that is the way it is. A parcel of this is supposed to appear in the *New York Times* in their Sunday Book Supplement.

Have been invited to go out as a Distinguished Professor (their wording) to a California university, but am fearful of accepting this. One has either to contend with academic bottleheads or untalented students. And the experience at Kansas City was a remorseless ordeal, and quite unreplenishing. I am not really a schoolmaster, for writing is my life, and my life otherwise is zero, except when friends come. I am very delighted to hear that you admire Dr. William M. Ryan; he is the only scholar out there and my dear friend.

I know this is a surd reply to your epistle; and what makes it so is that I would like to be useful to you, but at least now don't know what to do. Words should be curative, but it is hard to tell what they may be. Maybe, if you can manage it, you ought to get out of Kansas City unless that means relinquishing affectionate companions. I may be doing some teaching at an eastern college, nearby, but don't know yet. Then there is that devil, lucre, which always haunts us. But tell me what you would like to do, and let me see whether I can help. Be sure I want to do that if possible.

I don't hesitate to tell you about a brother, but there is little to divulge, would that it were not so, but then our real kin are those who share our conceptions and feelings. Anybody who thinks is an orphan in the earth.

A renowned Italian author came here with two other people and we did a tape-recording together and this will be heard on the principal Rome radio. The Italian translation of *Because I Was Flesh* has had a real reception among serious readers and the intelligentsia in Italy. This I did not know until I was informed.

Write when you feel inclined to do so. Be sure of my warmest thoughts for you. I always had a strong feeling that you had a different sort of nature, not at all average; I consider the mediocre man insane.

Edward Dahlberg

64 Rivington Street,
New York 2, N.Y.

Dahlberg had returned to New York City from Santa Barbara, and I had returned from Santa Fe to UMKC. It was, officially, my junior year of college. Looking back it is clear I seesawed from remarkable summers to below ordinary college semesters. Dr. Ryan taught Chaucer and other medieval subjects. I had retained from Santa Fe a 1946 Studebaker pickup truck, with a metal load bed, painted turquoise in the New Mexican manner, equipped with Atomic Energy Commission tires (they were so stenciled on the sidewalls). I had a cowboy hat and cowboy boots, but soon realized that this getup was no draw on anyone wandering the campus, since all my fellow midwesterners at UMKC were fleeing such rural and roughshod backgrounds, hoping to be educated and economically advanced. Had I been a student at an East Coast university it may have been different. I would have been the other, not the all-too familiar. This is doubtless why Dahlberg keeps referring to my missives as "doleful," as I went on about my somewhat self-imposed cloistered existence. Given the time lapses between letters their doleful qualities might not seem quite so redundant as they do now read collectively. All these "doleful" years I recounted in my 1981 novel, Idle Hands, *which I demi-dedicated to Dahlberg. During the later 1960s Dahlberg was having something of a renaissance, at least in the publishing world, since* Because I Was Flesh *had been widely praised, if not read.*

February 10, '67

Mr. William O'Rourke,
5431 Wyandotte,
Kansas City, Missouri 64112

My dear O'Rourke:

I believe you know how sympathetic I am with your perplexities. Nor can I tell you how pleased I am that Dr. Ryan is your friend. This pedantic noddle, I am referring to French, of course, who calls me pompous, would not associate with students as Dr. Ryan or I do, and even that sounds, as I write it, like a bombastic remark. This hack was motivated by ferine jealousy and malice. I would not trouble about it except that he was assailing not my book but my character. Not that I go about babbling about my paltry virtues. Be sure, I have been assailed all my life, for one cause or another; that I ever desired to be respectable, a pecuniary adjective, is a foul lie. Since my youth I fled from the petit-bourgeoisie in the academies or in the business world.

I know nothing about the draft board. But I am to be a professor at Columbia University in the Fall and am supposed to teach writing, if one can do that, or be a benison to one human being in the earth.

I believe I told you I had the most rueful experiences with women at your age, and am not suggesting that all the darlings now are falling at my feet. There are scholarships at Columbia, and I could endeavor to secure one for you. But as you say, there is conscription, and then I don't know what you would be relinquishing should you leave Kansas City. I don't think much, except, of course, your family, and that is extremely important. And should you have friends there, and even one female who fetches your imagination, that, too, is a vital consideration.

As Dr. Ryan is a learned medievalist, and language so important to the living waters in the soul, I should not like to see you lose the advantage of hearing his lectures and learning from him, everything is a dilemma, and a Burden of Tyre.

You might, if you have a mind to do so, write to Thorpe Menn, the book-editor of the K.C. Star, provided you do not afterwards become the victim of his boundless spite. Never fear the strong, but be on guard against the weanling and the feeble mind.

You have, as ever, my very warm thoughts, and if you at any time think I can be useful to you, well, that is what man is born to do.

Edward Dahlberg

64 Rivington Street,
New York 2, N.Y.

I was living at my family home while attending UMKC and that condition obviously affected my mood and demeanor. I read a lot, but wasn't attentive to my studies and was, more or less, affronted by having to sit in, say, a Shakespeare class. I wandered in one day and discovered that there was to be a midterm exam on three plays I had yet to read. I did summon enough chutzpah to ask the professor if I could take the exam the next class. I wasn't sure I would ever finish the degree. Dahlberg, meanwhile, published one of the volumes he had mentioned and it was lambasted in the Kansas City Star, *and I dispatched my own attack of the review to the* Star, *which, no surprise, ignored it. The "French" Dahlberg mentioned in the letter would be Warren French, who may have done the referenced* Star *review. He taught eighteenth-century literature at UMKC, which I took, having, at least, exhausted all the literature courses the English Department offered. Attacking one of my own professors wouldn't have been out of character for me back then.*

April 2, '67

William O'Rourke,
5431 Wyandotte
Kansas City, Missouri.

Dear O'Rourke:

Please forgive me for being so dilatory in replying to your letter. It was kind of you to send a letter to the Star, but by now I think enough people know how squalid and malicious was his review.

I rejoice in hearing that you have found female companionship, and hope she is the darling you require. Women nowadays are not very good. It was Homer who called the serving-maids of Penelope bitches, and everything is about the same, but just worse since the days of Attica.

Students are supposed to be coming from England and Europe as well as the United States to attend these alleged courses in writing. I understand the director is endeavoring to secure scholarships for those who cannot afford the tuition. It might be good for you, and maybe I could get this for you. I don't know. There is another and real quandary. Should this girl be what you deeply need, I would be most hesitant to suggest that you come to New York, for here you might be lonely, and though I could introduce you to people, who can take the place of a woman? Let us see what will occur?

How much shall I relish the task? I came to New York when I was twenty-three, and I was a solitary, a halved male for a year, and it was a bleak experience. So I don't want to give you counsel that might be hellebore for you. This is a garbaged, septic city, where you can meet people with whom you can talk, but the women I see are savages in skirts half a meter in length, and though they look like amorous morsels you are likely to starve to death on such a sparse meal. I wish I could be clear about this. But I am endeavoring to do the best I can. I still don't know how desperate is your desire to be a writer, a good one. We have a plethora of scribblers and require no more. Then I would not like you to pay the cruel price I had to become an author, and then to be reviled by a pismire like French. Should he have a particle of the masculine in him I would be startled. Quite oddly, what raised his bile was my divulgation of Melville's homosexuality. Had he been willing to accept my challenge, then I should have cut him to pieces. For he has neither with nor learning. Nobody in American letters ever heard of French, and almost every pedant scrabbles a few drossy books which are forgotten within a few weeks after they have come off the university presses.

I expect to go to Long Island to the shore the fag-end of May, and to continue writing, and, of course, reading. I'm not always so tardy in answering your epistles, and please don't think I was indifferent. I myself was in the dumps despite the national encomia I have received for my books. The Leafless American went back to the printer who was drunk when he was setting up type, and so at the end of the book there are one or two lines missing.

You have, as always my warm thoughts; write whenever you have a mind to do so, and I promise to respond straightway.

Professor Edward Dahlberg

64 Rivington Street,
New York 2, N.Y.

Who was the "darling I require" mentioned in his letter? I have no recollection of any relationship in Kansas City at the time. I was getting out a bit more, in my fashion, and had a few friends and I was aware I could make women laugh, my best trait. The reference must have been to Susan Scott, whom I may have mentioned to him. She was writing me and we had been a suspect item for a short period toward the end of the previous summer in Santa Fe. But, in December, I received a Dear John letter and recklessly took off over Christmas break in the Studebaker pickup for Santa Fe in order to attempt to reclaim her.

The pickup threw a rod near Wichita, Kansas, and, after selling a truck I did not own, I continued on to Santa Fe by train. Susan refused to see me, but her mother made me a cup of hot tea, after Susan left me standing, abandoned, on East Alameda as she drove away with her new beau. I was standing forlornly on the dirt road by the meager river with a dunce cap of snow on my head.

In the summer of 1967, instead of returning to Santa Fe (the opera had asked me back), I traveled to the Cape to work for my friends, the shop owners, the Karekas, who were doing well. The Santa Fe Opera burned to the ground that summer. But the season went on and they rebuilt. At the end of the summer I left the Cape and visited Dahlberg at his apartment on Rivington Street. New York City in the sixties hadn't gone through any real estate revolution yet and much of it, including the Village, appeared unchanged, remaining as it had been for a number of decades.

Rivington Street, though not in the Village, certainly retained the atmosphere of the shtetl in the late 1960s, and Dahlberg's narrow apartment could have housed fresh immigrants. I recall black accordion metal gates guarding the two long front windows that abutted a fire escape. I suppose one of them must have been open, since this would have been the window where Fanny Howe claimed in Poetry *magazine a few years ago (July 2008) to have jumped through, escaping Dahlberg's pants-down advances back then. For my visit, Dahlberg sat rooted at his desk, which was prominent in the apartment's front room, and I in a chair across from of him. If we had a meal I don't remember it, but there might have been cheese, crackers, fruit. This was the first time I had seen him apart from a classroom in Missouri. Dahlberg spoke as he wrote, whereas I, at the time, strove for mere coherence, lacking eloquence. Though it was my early inchoate talent for aphorism that I showed which doubtless interested him in the first place.*

January 26, '68

Mr. William O'Rourke,
5431 Wyandotte
Kansas City, Missouri 64112

Dear O'Rourke:

I have filled out the forms and am mailing them this day. I shall not be at Columbia, but am going with my wife to Ireland, and we expect to remain in Europe for a year.

You can get a student's loan; that I have learned from those in my group. What you will learn in the department of writing is zero. The teachers are dunderheads, with no passion or erudition. Actually, though Kansas City is a corpse town, you will not find a Dr. Ryan in this profane institution. I wanted you to study medieval English with Dr. Ryan, and learn a good deal about the origins of language just about at its end today. But I know you must have feminine companionship, and I don't understand why it is so difficult to find a savory and delectable female in the mid-west. I certainly am not telling you that they are there, and that the onus is upon your head. I should be most unkind and not truthful were I to speak so to you.

Please forgive me for not replying to your last letter; I had some accursed sickness, and was so phlegmatic thereafter that I did no work, could not read, and was entirely worthless.

I knew your direful plight when you were here, and even then I could not help you, and that made me quite ill. We are not born for ourselves alone, says Cicero.

It is a fierce tomb to be alone, and I have known it and been in that sepulcher too often in my life not to appreciate deeply your own sorrow. The tragedy is that we can do little or usually nothing for others. I believe you know that if I knew someone here who would be a companion for you I would convey her to you. It is futile to console you, and even dishonest. And I won't do it.

I send you my affections for what they are worth, not much, and wish I could at this time be advantageous to you. I have had numerous mishaps myself, but won't bore you with them.

My book, *The Carnal Myth* will be out in May, and in the meantime I am laboring over the literary autobiography, sidereal drudgery, and I can't be sure that I know what I am doing.

Professor Edward Dahlberg

64 Rivington Street,
New York, N.Y.2.

I had returned to UMKC for my last year and applied to the fledgling graduate creative writing program just begun at Columbia. Dahlberg wrote me a letter of recommendation, and I applied to one other school's program, the University of Iowa, its storied Writers' Workshop. In both cases I had applied as a poet, of all things. I was admitted to both, but wanting to flee the Midwest I turned down Iowa and accepted Columbia. I was elated by the acceptances. At the same time I had entered a volume of poetry in the Yale Series of Younger Poets contest and it was eventually rejected, but even the rejection seemed like something. Dudley Fitts was the judge that year, his last (really his last—Fitts died the same year). Dahlberg, however, had only lasted a year at Columbia and, after I arrived there, I heard stories about the cause of his departure, though the one I believed is that he had failed Piers Paul Read, Herbert Read's son, and that got him fired. Years later I heard other stories. Read published in 1974 Alive, *a book about disaster-inspired cannibalism. Cannibalism everywhere.*

March 21, '68

Mr. William O'Rourke,
5431 Wyandotte,
Kansas City, Missouri 64112.

Dear O'Rourke:

Please forgive me for not replying to your last epistle. Since I had the virus, of some kind or other, I have been lumpish, and have found it very hard to work, though I have. But after that I am undone, and this as a paltry apology, but please accept it.

I was glad to speak for you; but then what will you derive at Columbia University? There are four she-professors who know nothing and cannot talk about it eloquently. So you would not find their humid lectures of any value. Would you find feminine companionship here? You know I would have introduced you to one did I know her. It is woeful that I can give you no counsel that is beneficial, and this is hurtful to me. It always has been this way, as far as I can recollect. I knew these long spasms of stupor and solitude, and that is the way of the one and not the many, though I believe the disease of the multitude is solitude.

We leave on May 28th and it is very kind of you to suggest that you see me before leaving. Two young women are in my group, one married, and the other is looking for lucre and a man of social position, so that is very fine to tell you. Meantime, I have been taking elaborate notes making ready to attack American education and our tepid females, and love in North America, pretty sodden and moldy.

Now I have to correct page-proofs, and they came so late that the publisher will not allow me to mend a sentence here and there or even take care of the errors of printers. The other volume, *Edward Dahlberg American Ishmael of Letters* should be issued shortly, within a few weeks.

This contains sundry essays written about my work.

To repeat, it is good that you have Dr. Ryan as a friend. He doubtless has told you what Kansas City is as if you required more empirical evidence than you already have.

I wish I could be your teacher, for I notice that you strain for your language, a metaphor or a trope, and though that is inevitable at the start, and many authors who should know better still do it, you might go on doing it. Try if you can to be a natural prose stylist, and that is hard, very. Study Swift's *Journal to Stella.* Write sentences that fetch you, and also jot down idiomatic phrases.

I guess one should ask another to pardon him when he is unable to be useful to him.

You have my affections which would be had you a young nymph in your arms.

Professor Edward Dahlberg

64 Rivington Street,
New York, N.Y. 2.

I doubtless had written thanking him for opening Columbia's doors to me. I am sure his recommendation made the difference. During my time at Columbia I learned 1) that I was the student who had the lowest undergraduate grade point average ever admitted to any of Columbia University's graduate schools, and 2) that Dahlberg's recommendation consisted of one sentence, saying that I was the only intelligent person he had met in the Midwest. It did feel odd that he left the City just as I arrived, but his absence, doubtless, let me settle into Columbia unencumbered.

October 30, '70

My dear O'Rourke:

Thank you very much for your epistle gorged with a rare probity in a putid, raging, and nihilistic age. How rueful it is to hear that you are alone. It is even related that one of the great sorrows of Our Blessed Mary was solitude. Well, you will have to make your own mistakes although I had fervently hoped you would commit mine! But do, though nobody takes advice, try to compose your novel in a noble English. One can be a Bottom Dogs in fiction, or in life and language it well.

Do you have the *TriQuarterly*; it will also be published as a book. Any number of persons have spoken of your tribute to me, and in a most complimentary vein. But my dear O'Rourke, when did I ever ask a student of mine to peruse my books. Never! That is a trifling matter, and though every author is vain, I did not indulge in that sort of egolatry.

Do you wish me to send you a copy of *The Confessions*, now ready, that is, the trade edition, but to be published February 1st. You are right you can't be a reviewer whilst hoping also to be a man of letters. Of course, you can say what you must about books in the *Nation*, though also your load of Babylon since most of your books offered to you by the editor, are draff.

Am glad you wrote to me; it was no pleasure to rebuke you, but it is said in the Book of Proverbs that if you reproach fat Jeshurun he will kick you, but if you reprehend a wise man he will thank you. Forgive me anyhow for being so severe with you. I always wanted you to have only a trull or a tart if that is what was available, but I felt that your other simple was work. Love.

Edward Dahlberg

[In handwriting in the letter's margins:] If you're ever hungry, or out of pocket, you know that though my querdon *[?]* from books have been small, I'll never turn away from you. If you're ever in trouble call me collect—724–1108. I'll do my best to find a publisher for you if you wish me to do that.

57 West 75th Street
Apartment 5 H
New York, New York 10023

Dahlberg had returned to New York City in late 1969. I became an aide-de-camp *of sorts, helping out however I could. Some of this was amusing, some not. I've written about these times before, so I won't recount them here (see my* Signs of the Literary

Times [1993]). *While at Columbia I began to publish prose; one of the first things to appear was the reminiscence of Dahlberg that appeared in the fall 1970 issue of* TriQuarterly. *(I wrote the piece in 1967, having been told by Dahlberg around the time of my visit to his Rivington Street apartment that some sort of volume was being put together and I might submit a recollection.) I also began to do short reviews for* The Nation *in 1970, having met the poetry editor, Allen Planz, at a party, and we furthered our drinking at a bar on lower Broadway (the St. Adrian Company in the Broadway Central Hotel, which collapsed, the entire building that is, in 1973). Planz then introduced me to the literary editor, Beverly Gross. She liked what I did, always a necessity, having an editor who likes what you do. I saw Dahlberg intermittently through the spring, finished at Columbia, and, after working during the summer for the New York Shakespeare Festival, took myself off to Provincetown at Stanley Kunitz's suggestion. Kunitz taught at Columbia, and even though I had switched immediately from poetry to prose, he had me to his townhouse for a memorable night with Robert Lowell and Elizabeth Bishop. Kunitz was involved in the creation of the Fine Arts Work Center, and in 1970 he persuaded two brand new Columbia MFAs, myself and Louise Glück, to quit the City and spend the long, vacant off-season in Provincetown. For whatever reason, I have no letters from Dahlberg to me at my initial New York City addresses—I lived on West 76th Street and on East 8th Street, between B and C, when I was a student.*

November 5, '70

William O'Rourke,
355 Commercial Street,
Provincetown, Mass.

My dear O'Rourke:

I replied to your very good letter the other day, and this feature article just arrived, and I hope that it will give you some pleasure. So if I am laconic, I've been toiling over notes for the book on The New World for hours and my back is sore and fatigued.

You have my love, and although I've been your taskmaster, I never reproached you with vipry thoughts, Never; be sure of that, although in the main nobody has one certitude.

Anyway, I want to get this off to you; cleave to, my fine boy (this is not patronizing but affectionate), and you'll one of these days, if you'll now heed my exhortation, read, read, read, and then write, and write and write. Chase any lissome trull that you fancy, that you fancy, drink a bottle of small beer, if it eases your entrails, but as I have oftentimes told you, By Zeus earn the right to be a lecher.

With love,
Edward Dahlberg

[On back of envelope:]
Edward Dahlberg
57 West 75th Street
Apartment 5H
New York, New York 10023

Unfortunately, the Fine Arts Work Center only provided the smallest of stipends in its infancy ($100 a month), and, having no other source of income, I worked for a fish-packing enterprise (Atlantic Coast Fisheries) in Provincetown for three months and then, more comfortably, as a night guard for the Chrysler Glass Museum. At the museum I wrote a short story, my first to be respectably published, set in the fish factory, called "The Maggot Principle"; first and last, insofar as I abandoned the short story as a form (or it abandoned me), and I turned henceforth only to book-length fiction.

November 18, '70

William O'Rourke Esq.,
355 Commercial Street,
Provincetown, Mass.

My dear O'Rourke:

This won't be a reply to your own enchanting epistle, for which I thank you very much. But I must get this to you with the same haste. As the Angels demanded of Lot, that he flee Sodom at once.

I want to see about 40 to fifty pages of your novel about Kansas City, and if it's good (no patronizing remark; for one is always a prentice; beware of the writer who calls himself a Master), I think I can get it published for you.

So please forgive this laconic note, and along with this, I am mailing to you a copy of The Confessions of E.D.

So forgive this drossy note; what is important at the moment is haste, or as the Angels said to Lot: Haste thee out of Sodom.

Love,
Edward Dalhberg

[And in handwriting below signature:] I earnestly hope you will be able to laurel Sorrentino's book; simpleton that I am I told him O'Rourke is reviewing it! Alas, I shouldn't have said it; for if you impugn it I'll be to blame! But one must not tell lies! Should I so counsel you what a sharper your teacher must be! I wrote a moiety of that scurrile book of mine, *From Flushing to Calvary*, on Commercial St., Provincetown in 1931.

I was still doing the short reviews for The Nation *and was sent Gilbert Sorrentino's novel* Steelwork *(1970) to review, along with a few others. It never ran, or the one I wrote never ran. It must have been critical in some way, and Sorrentino (who died in 2006) was a favorite of the then literary editor, and, I presume, he (it was no longer Beverly Gross) just killed the review and ordered up another. The fact that Dahlberg had written some of his early proletarian second novel on the same street in Provincetown I was writing from must have startled me, though since P-town was a place many writers had passed through over the decades (as well as the entire East Coast, all of New England), it shouldn't have been surprising, even to a youngster like myself.*

December 13, '70

William O'Rourke
355 Commercial Street,
Provincetown, Massachusetts.

My dear O'Rourke:

I did not reply straightway for two causes: one I have had a plethora of work, really, no nonsense or bombast about this, and the most sovereign reason is that I do not wish to hurt you.

What I importuned you to do you did not do: eschew figures of speech; only in one or two instances were you lucky. Then I begged you to write about your own experiences, a poor Irish Catholic in Kansas City; if later on you portrayed your life, and that of your father, mother and sisters, I cannot in all fairness to you, tell you, since I did not get beyond fifty pages. What is the point of humdrum conversations you offer the reader which he can hear in the streets every day, and that which he wishes above all to shun. I had emphasized this to you, namely, that colloquies should be ideal rather than real, and that not one line should be written that does not nourish the soul, enhance the wisdom of the auditor. This too you failed to do. Now, I am still of the mind, and without equivocation, that you have talent, a friend of mine, not much older than you, said the best piece of writing in the *TriQuarterly* is your portrait of me as a professor at Kansas City. And he's no simpleton. Should I be your flatterer, or dissembler, and really harm you. That I cannot do. But I can say soon as you do what I ask of you, and that is to divulge the secrets of your own identity, and experience in Kansas City, I shall peddle your heart. But not yet; when will you be ready? when you are. Now, I have no dicta to proffer you but do, please, as I ask, do not make my squalid mistakes. And you will then display the regal talent I believe you have. Is this guess-work. doubtless. But what else is there?

Now, you lauded the work of Sorrentino, and in some large measure, the fault and onus are mine. You wanted to please me, but I told you not to tell lies, and alas maybe you didn't. One cannot ascribe your weak judgment to me; it is always your defect. It is a very bad and salacious book, not erotically, or genuinely masculine. No, I am not asserting that Sorrentino is not a ripe male, but that he is somehow or other though a man in the depths of his forties, or so I suppose, had adopted the cult of youth, and one nowadays is young if he employs four letter words, or composes a latrine novel.

What am I to say to Sorrentino, the truth? What will it bring me, maybe a foe who is at present a friend of my work. Have I any other choice? So I become the hard, the truculent man, and not the flaccid, pragmatical one. Once more I exhort you, do what I suggest; this is not egolatry, but a great desire on my part to see you write a book, and not acquire a quick reputation, and be a churl among upstarts, or mushrooms in our merchant agora.

Do not for one moment imagine I like writing to you in this vein. Do you not think it would be a cornucopia of pleasure for me to relate that you have genius, and that nobody except a fool would or could gainsay it. I know how difficult it is to be obscure, impoverished, and to get a letter of admonition instead of a laurel of parsnip from me. But be patient; it is very stony counsel. Meantime, if I can get some money for you, I shall do it, but I am not certain of this. I must ask someone.

You have my love, and please believe me, it pains my pulses to write you so, and to tell you to sit down and write what you know, the Kansas City blood in your veins, and not scrawl all sorts of talk that is useless to you, me, and anybody else.

Should I, far older than you, and yet with the same quandaries, be your pickthank friend, you would abhor me, later.

Edward Dalhberg

57 West 75th Street,
Apartment 5 H
New York, New York 10023

Will return your MS.

Evidently I sent Dahlberg the pages he requested. And I must have sent what I wrote on Sorrentino, though Dahlberg thought it was praise enough, unlike The Nation. *The novel I was working on was my first, published eventually, truncated, in 1974, entitled* The Meekness of Isaac. *I had written a long unpublished novel my first year at Columbia called "The Armless Warrior." I am not clear on what I sent Dahlberg, since I was looting the earlier novel here and there, though* The Meekness of Isaac *was, in its final version, written mostly fresh. I did send the same pages doubtless to an editor in New York who had contacted me, and he repeated more or less the same thing Dahlberg said, though of course, more simply. Even then I had no desire to emulate Dahlberg's prose; I only wanted to write as well as I could, which I thought then was well enough.*

December 22, '70

William O'Rourke
355 Commercial Street,
Provincetown, Massachusetts,

My dear O'Rourke,

I have just filled out the form you sent to me, and be sure I have offered the warmest words about you. Make no mistake about it. It is the least that I can do.

It was a deep pain to return your MS., for I had hoped, and quite fervently, that you would write about your early boyhood as a poor Irish Catholic in Kansas City. Build your experiences as a mason might; don't wander here and there, or set down lines that reader can relinquish. A book must be essential to a person's identity; any other sort is deceit. I am glad you did not laud that scurrile book; I feared your own perceptions might be marred by my own desire that he receive laurels, but not false withered ones.

I know a man who says there is some foundation that gives money to talented young men who have not yet published a book, and soon as he is out of hospital I shall speak for you. Please know that I'll do all within my paltry powers to help you. Alas, I have small influence in this fell and caitiff world, but I have a few friends, and I'll do all I can. Know that you have my love, and my profound concern.

Poor Dr. Ryan has just lost his Mother, a very dear Woman, and he is in the dumps; it is a wound that can never be healed. Be sure to write of your Mother and Father as they are, and also of your sisters and brothers, and the harsh penury that both of us have known. Please know, above all, that I am not the Moses of the Muses bringing down the ten commandments the canons of prose style; break my tablets if you must, but abide by our great English.

As you see this letter was written on the 22nd of this month; many ills, and also the depravity of melancholia prevented me from finishing this epistle. If I've hurt you I beg your pardon; we must ask forgiveness of those whom we have not harmed, lest they suppose we do not love them.

Edward Dahlberg

57 West 75th Street,
Apartment 5H
New York, New York 10023

Again, I'm not sure what forms I sent him. For a Guggenheim? Hardly, since at the time I had published almost nothing. Most likely it was a general recommendation for a file I was opening at Columbia, a service the school provided to its graduates, future job seekers, of letters of reference. Dahlberg didn't unlock any monies from his patron, or, at least the one he seemed to have in mind (Coburn Britton?), though he did extract some funds for me a few years later from the Authors Guild (the Authors League Fund) around 1974. I think it was $2,500. He then did it again, but I refused the additional money, and both he and the Fund took some offense at that. Over the years I have donated money to the same Authors League Fund that had funded me back then.

May 13, '71

William O'Rourke,
355 Commercial Street
Provincetown, Massachusetts 02657

My dear O'Rourke:

At last I have word from you; you must needs know that it was a load of pain for me to annul your manuscript. But you must, and nothing else, write about your experiences as a young, impecunious Irish Catholic in Kansas City. But in a traditional English, no jargon, and no counterfeit spermal lines. I had to write just as plainly to Sorrentino, and after he had inscribed his book to me with genuflexional words. What else could I do? If I lie to you I'm your foe, should I be truthful you're silent as the sphinx. What should be my conduct? I cannot be other than I am, and take the blows of one who is morose. Again and again I implored you to do what I am now asking of you. What the Grub Street hacks tell you at Columbia is dross, and they have duped you. You were a glory there, and some day you may be, but not at this writing. You must be a novice, now and always, as I am. Each book is a battle, and nobody knows whether it will be won or lost, no matter how many books of worth he has published. Nothing helps; you blunder, stumble, or as Gloucester says, "I stumbled when I saw."

Now, don't be perverse; take my counsel though you pay no Mammon for it; despite the fact it is good advice, for people commonly heed a varlet, a criticaster, and though you are an oracle at the moment, and know that what he's doing is wrong, he will return you a peevishness, a long night of stillness.

I am now writing a novella for Harcourt Brace Jovanovich, and with a plethora of luck should complete it within six months, but I have been mumbling this for a lustrum, beginning it at Soller de Majorca, then in Dublin, again in Santa Barbara, in Kansas City, New York, and Barcelona.

You see then I do not write easily, but fumble just as you do. Age does not make you wiser nor does youth. If the Muses are kind, then you'll compose a book to be laureled.

Please don't expect falsehoods from me. I try not to decoy myself, and why you?

When the book is right it will pleasure my soul to tell you so and on the heels of Mercury.

Of course, your plight troubles me, but I must perforce gamble my heart, here and there, peddling it for francs as Stendhal said, and I have never reached that reposeful El Dorado. But I must write one book, then another, or else Rumor advises me, I shall soon be forgot, although never remembered.

Why did you not review *The Confessions*? I never saw what was said about me in the *Nation*, and only have read about six or seven articles about me, some were panegyrics, others worm-eaten and scullion attacks, with no comprehension of the book. To be quite candid, the *Confessions* has been widely noticed from coast to coast but never divulged. Here you could have done me a signal service. Why no, do not ask me. How do I know anything about another person, even my student whom I have friended best I can. And still wish to do so. So this is no pile of spleens, just wonder.

You have, as ever, my warm affections, and when You do what you are, for what deeds, good or bad, are the consequence of your character, I think you'll get off an autobiographical novel that will be worth the time and expense of the soul, and then I shall do all that I can to find a publisher for you.

Edward Dahlberg

General Delivery
Post Office,
Sarasota, Florida.

I'm not sure why I didn't review his Confessions. *My book review connections were not many and* The Nation, *I think, did have someone else in mind for the book. I did review a book for the* New York Times Book Review *in 1971, arranged by Richard Elman, one of my former teachers at Columbia. It was the only review I ever did for the* Times, *being, as it was, as my friend Craig Nova would have put it, a "vicious attack." I had stopped working at the Glass Museum and got a job for the summer as a dune buggy driver, taking tourists for rides over the high parabolic dunes outside, or astride, Provincetown. And, during that summer, I met the woman who led me to Harrisburg, Diane Schulder, one of the lawyers for the defense.*

YALE CLUB
FIFTY VANDERBILT AVENUE
NEW YORK, N.Y. 10017

[early October 1972, via postmark]

William O'Rourke,
4 Milligan Place,
New York City 10011.

My dear O'Rourke:

I am exceedingly sorry that I failed to reply to your last two epistles. Fearful of this criminal city, I went to Florida, which I could not stomach. I had withal two bouts of Hong Kong influenza, and a hemorrhage.

Now, I am very delighted that you have published your book. Frankly, I know nothing about the two unfrocked priests and the nuns save what I have read in the press, which is to say, I know nothing.

Your book just arrived, and I haven't had a chance to look at a line to see whether you have eschewed our boorish jargon, or if you, my fond hope, have consulted the masters of the English language. I realize this is not a work of literature, but let me inform you that there is more politics in belles lettres than there is literature in political writings. Balzac was alluded to as a statesman.

Of course, you can use a sentence, or more, from *The Confessions* as an epigraph to your novel, and I am heartened to learn that you are relying upon your own experience (Whose else can you borrow?). When we fail to comprehend a work of a seer the cause is that our feelings and life do not equal his. I have said somewhere is that all I have to do is to open my mouth to sow dragon's teeth. So if you have not sufficient character to acquire foes you're sure to be a nobody as an author.

You can call me almost any day at about one o'clock of the afternoon. Why not do me a signal kindness and review *The Sorrows of Priapus* which has just been reissued a brace *[of]* days ago. The publisher is Harcourt Brace Jovanovich. Ask for Mrs. Lindley. Tel: 572–5000.

Spite of my silence you've always had my friendship and love.

Edward Dahlberg

128 East 91st Street
Apartment 2B
New York, N.Y. 10028
Tel: 289–4339

The book was The Harrisburg 7 and the New Catholic Left. *The trial was over at the beginning of April 1972, and the book was published in October 1972. The haste, oddly, was not a hindrance, at least from my point of view. It was written entirely on the Cape, in Provincetown and in Barnstable, at my friends', the Kareka's, new home on a bluff overlooking the salt marshes of Sandwich. I wrote it with intense, single-minded concentration, and it showed.*

YALE CLUB
FIFTY VANDERBILT AVENUE
NEW YORK, N.Y. 10017

December 21, '72

William O'Rourke,
Thomas Y. Crowell Company
666 Fifth Avenue,
New York, New York 10019

Dear O'Rourke:

I replied soon as I received your epistle. I only licked a page here and there. Of course, I believe it's cruel and ludicrous to imprison men for burning draft cards. But what dismays me is that you have now become a paper-bullet writer. There's more politics in literature than letters in the economics and politics of the State.

It is kind of you to cite me at the conclusion of the volume, but do you realize in your opening line you are closely paraphrasing me. And though I had no part in the making of this book, I believe, without bombast, that I have had a good deal to do with the making of William O'Rourke's mind. Atheist that I am, I add, For God's sake return to belles lettres, and bear in mind that a journalistic prose has nothing to do with a man who wishes to be a litterateur.

My affections,
as always Edward Dahlberg

128 East 91st Street
Apartment 2 B
New York, N.Y, 10028

The opening line Dahlberg refers to is: "In the logic of our time, it is better to have a bad experience that turns out well, than to have just a plain good one." I'm not sure why he sent the letter to my publisher. I may have been traveling. A biography of Dahlberg was being prepared at the time and he set its author, Charles DeFanti, to scour my book, looking for examples of my plagiarizing of his words. As I have written elsewhere, on reflection years later, that line, my own, owes a bit more to Camus than Dahlberg, but it's probably a toss up. DeFanti's forced reading of my book did lead to our friendship that continues to this day.

April 11, '74

William O'Rourke, Esq.
306 Front Street,
Key West, Florida 33040

My dear O'Rourke,

I never looked for such a benison as an epistle from you. St. Augustine said he would never have become a Christian had he not believed in miracles. A brave man and also a gullible one.

I tremble when I ponder your return. The age is void of truth. The quandary is: how can I be useful to you. I've spoken to Nick of another contract for you which you can gulp down in a brace of hours.

You always can utter your woes to me. I'm not that sort of poltroon. I hope you've been the kindest weather for your companion. Everybody, except liars are alone nowadays, so you're quiet. Ruskin asserted that inaction was the ruin of a nation. But what's that to do with Hecuba or you.

The meanwhile, you have my deepest affections.

Edward Dahlberg

[On back of envelope:]
128 East 91st Street,
New York, New York 10028

This was the last letter I received, or have, from Dahlberg, and it is entirely handwritten. Though sent to the Kareka's shop in Key West, it was forwarded to me when I returned to my apartment at Milligan Place. By then my first novel must have been in production and I had gone to Key West for a visit, and not alone. I took Joan Silber, my girlfriend at the time. (You'll have to ask Joan if I was "the kindest weather" for her.) I always thought it strange that I had arranged for a publisher for Dahlberg, rather than he arranging one for me. I introduced him to my Harrisburg 7 *editor at T.Y. Crowell, Nick Ellison, whom I had met when he was an editor at William Morrow, while I was a student at Columbia. I, along with Craig Nova and Irini Spanidou, worked there as part-time (at least Craig and I, Irini being full-time) copyeditors, more or less rewriting* Temple Fielding's Guide to Europe *during that period. He is the "Nick" that Dahlberg refers to in the letter. Nick published Dahlberg's* The Olive of Minerva *(1976), which I reviewed in the* SoHo Weekly News, *and I got Nick to bring out, at the same time, an omnibus volume of Dahlberg's three early novels. I was often at Dahlberg's 91st Street apartment during the early seventies (1972–74). He returned abruptly to Ireland around the end of 1974, then rushed back to NYC and stayed at the Hotel Chelsea for a while (circa 1975), and I helped him find a small apartment on the Upper East Side, which he abandoned suddenly and then went, finally, to Santa Barbara, California. I'm not sure why there aren't—or I don't have—any California letters from him, or any written reaction to the publication of my first novel. I did document my last conversation—on the telephone—with him in a eulogy I wrote that appeared in the* San Francisco Review of Books *a year after he died, his last words to me before he emphatically slammed down the phone ("No university has ever paid me $12,000!"). I had just told him I had been hired by Rutgers University in Newark for my first real academic job. So we must have spoken on the phone in 1975/76. His many chastisements in the letters were always a delight to me, whereas in person, or on the phone, the same sort of lambastements were more painful, revealing to me the stark difference between the literate and oral forms. Perhaps we were estranged. And it was on a PATH train to Newark in 1977 that I learned he died, during my second year teaching at Rutgers. I was reading the* New York Times *on my commute and happened upon his obituary. The train car was filled with dusty bright sunlight. I looked up and away from the paper that I had let fall onto my lap. The great man who had buoyed my youth and stoked my nascent ambitions and who had paid me all that unwarranted loving attention like no other, gone.*

Acknowledgments

Grateful acknowledgment is given to the following publications in which earlier versions of these essays first appeared:

REVIEWS

National Catholic Reporter: "Days of Rage" (as "Days of Rage: Ignores Larger Forces" ©2015 THE NATIONAL CATHOLIC REPORTER); "The Miracle of Dan Berrigan" (as "Lions' Den Details Dan Berrigan's Life"); "O'Connor/Giroux" (as "O'Connor, Giroux's 'Partnership' Succeeds" ©2018 THE NATIONAL CATHOLIC REPORTER); "Patty Prevails" (as "Setting the Patty Hearst Record Straight"); and "Reporting on Anti-war Catholics and the FBI."

Notre Dame Review: "Instructs and Entertains"; "The Media Burglary and the Media"; "The Miracle of Dan Berrigan"; "Patty Prevails"; "Richard and Roger"; and "Up Against the Workshop."

RANTS

Huffington Post: "Accidental Presidencies"; "Barney Rosset U."; "The Birther Business"; "Bye Bye Bernie"; "Clinton Exhaustion"; "Contraception Wars and Woes"; "Cuba and Carnage"; "Halftime in Pink America"; "The Haunting of Hillary"; "It's the Voter Suppression, Stupid!"; "Ken Burns, Boy Capitalist, and *The Vietnam War*" (parts I and II); "My Hillary Problem—and Yours"; "Not Saving Social Security, Again (an Update)"; "Oh, Rush, Poor Rush"; "Our Postsatirical Primaries"; "Pensive Pence"; "A Primary History Primer"; "Revenge of the Sixties"; "Richie Rich, Baby Boomers, and, Look Out, 2018 Looming"; "Similarities"; "The Superfluity of Iowa"; "Ted's Excellent Mansplaining"; "Transforming The Donald"; "Trump Monkeys"; "Trump Rising"; "Trump, Trumped, Trumpery"; and "'What a Dump!' the Presidency, That Is."

The Nation, Greg Mitchell (blog): "The Oak Ridge Three."

NUVO: "The Great Refudiator"; "Mourning Becomes Them"; and "Reality-Based Shooter."

South Bend Tribune: "It's the Voter Suppression, Stupid!"; "My Hillary Problem—and Yours"; "Saving Social Security, Not" (as "Pandora's Box Opened on Social Security"); "Torture? What Torture?"; and "To Kill a 'Second' Novel." ©2012, 2015, 2016 The South Bend Tribune Corp.

The View from the Couch: "Brett Kavanaugh, a Suit, and the Bro Culture"; "Class Warfare"; "Dr. Gingrich and Mr. Chucky"; "The First Lady's Lack of Firsts";

"Hillary's Voice"; "Keyes to the Caindom"; "Mommie Baddest"; "The Oak Ridge Three"; "Saving Social Security, Not"; and "The Superfluity of Iowa."

COMMENTARY

Irish Times: "*Irish Times* Times Two: On Michael Collins" (part I as "Michael Collins: A Genius Student but Classic Outsider," part II as "William O'Rourke: 'I'm Not Bothered by the Success of Others'").

Notre Dame Review: "Edward Dahlberg: Letters to a Young Would-Be Writer"; "Making Poverty More Bearable"; "Profile: Judith Shahn, Greenwich Village, circa 1973"; and "Whither the New Catholic Left?"

Provincetown Arts: "Profile: R. D. Skillings, Resolute Character." ©2011 Provincetown Arts, Inc.

A version of "Whither the New Catholic Left?" appeared as the afterword to the fortieth anniversary edition of William O'Rourke, *The Harrisburg 7 and the New Catholic Left* (University of Notre Dame Press, 2012).

I also thank the editors, Christopher Busa at *Provincetown Arts*; Martin Doyle at the *Irish Times*; David Hoppe at *NUVO*; Jamie L. Mason at the *National Catholic Reporter*; Greg Mitchell at *The Nation*; editors over the years at the *South Bend Tribune*, especially Alesia Redding; and all my colleagues then and now at the *Notre Dame Review*, first and foremost, Kathleen Canavan.

And I thank the usual suspects, some connected to Notre Dame, some not: Linda DeCicco, Corinne Demas, Valerie Sayers, David Black, Ed Zuckerman, Charles DeFanti, John Matthias, Jaimy Gordon, Craig Nova, Irini Spanidou, Joan Harris, David Matlin, Betty Signer, Robert Kareka, R. D. Skillings, Susan Blum, Laura Haigwood, Chris Vanden Bossche, Katie Lehman, Cynthia Landeen, John Weber, and others who should be named, but aren't.

Index

The use of **bold** page locators in the subentry field indicates an essay by the author.

Abbey, Edward, 20
abortifacient, 101
abortion, 67, 100–101, 152, 177, 179
Abrams, Robert, 140
"Accidental Presidencies" (O'Rourke), **117–118**
Accuracy in Academe, 213
Adams, Alice (née Vonnegut), 17
Adams, James Carmalt, 17
Aeschylus, 194
"The Afterlife Is Only Strange" (Elman), 59–60
Age of Obama, 108
The Age of Surveillance (Donner), 34
Ahmad, Eqbal, 65, 186
Aldridge, John, 28
Alive (Read), 230
Allred, Gloria, 83
All the President's Men (film), 33, 165
Alternative Lives (Skillings), 60
Amazon, 44, 57
American Dynasty (Phillips), 213
American Healthcare Act, 146
American Heiress: The Wild Saga of the Kidnapping, Crimes and Trial of Patty Hearst (Toobin), 50–53
American Machine Foundary (AMF), 39
American Theocracy (Phillips), 213
Ann-Margaret, 130
anti-abortion lobby, 152, 179
antimaterialism, 209
antinuclear protests
  "The Oak Ridge Three," **107–110**
  Plowshares movement, 109, 179–180
Arizona shootings, 75–76
The Armies of the Night (Mailer), 34
The Armless Warrior (O'Rourke), 237
Arthur, Chester, 133
Asekoff, Louis, 61
atomic bomb, 43
Auden, W. H., 222
audiences, acquiring, 26–27
Augustine, St., 243
author, test of an, 24
Authors League Fund, 238
avant-garde, 27

Baader-Meinhof Group, 184
baby boomers, 150–152
Bachmann, Michele, 88–89
Baez, Joan, 208
Bagdikian, Ben, 32
Bailey, Blake, 21
Baltimore Four, 170
Balz, Dan, 77
Balzac, 103, 241
Bank of America, 157, 159
Bannon, Steve, 144, 149
Barnes v. Glen Theatre, 106
"Barney Rossett U." (O'Rourke), **103–104**
Barrett, Amy Coney, 165
Barthelme, Donald, 61
Bartiromo, Maria, 148
Battle Hymn of the Tiger Mother (Chua), 79–80
Batuman, Elif, 28, 30
Baxter, Charles, 220
Bayh, Evan, 124, 135
Beatles, 82, 210
beatniks, 207–208, 209, 213
Because I Was Flesh (Dahlberg), 218, 224
Bellow, Saul, 15, 202
Benedict XVI, 190
Berlin Wall, 172
Bernstein, Carl, 33, 165
Berrigan, Daniel, 107–108, 170–174, 179–180, 182
  The Kings and Their Gods: The Pathology of Power, 188
  At Play in the Lions' Den: A Biography and Memoir of Daniel Berrigan (Forest), 65–68
Berrigan, Frida, 186
Berrigan, Philip, 37, 45, 66–68, 107–108, 170–174, 179–184, 186–187
Beschloss, Michael, 77–78
The Best American Poetry (McHugh, ed.), 30
"Better This World" (documentary), 189
Biden, Joe, 137
The Big Dance (Castellucci), 46

The Big Rich (Burrough), 48
"Bird Feeder in the Rain" (Skillings), 62
"Birth Control, Bishops and Religious Authority" (Gutting), 101
"The Birther Business" (O'Rourke), **132–134**
Bishop, Elizabeth, 233
Black Liberation Army, 46
Black Panthers, 42, 49, 171
Black Power movement, 172
bohemians, 195, 207–211
book advances, 15
books
  censored, 75
  culture and, 216
  newspaper's literary book review section, 55
  numbers published, 57
  paperback revolution, 103
bookstores, 57
Borges, Jorge Luis, 104
Boston Five, 159–160, 170, 185
Bottom Dogs (Dahlberg), 58
Boudin, Jean, 162, 184
Boudin, Kathy, 175
Boudin, Leonard, 34, 68, 162, 175, 184–185
Bourne, Randolph, 172, 214
Bowdler, Thomas, 75
Bowles, Paul, 104
Boyle, T. C., 199
Brady, Tom, 98
brainwashing, 52–53
Branch Davidians, 51, 76, 178
Bread Loaf, 30
Bremer, L. Paul, 188
"Brett Kavanaugh, a Suit, and the Bro Culture" (O'Rourke), **165–168**
Britton, Burt, 19–20
Britton, Coburn, 238
bro culture, **165–168**
Brooke, Edward, 137
Brooks, David, 154
Brown, H. Rap, 47
Brown, Sherrod, 136
Broyard, Anatole, 21
Bruner, Mary Lou, 214
Bryan, C. D. B., 156
Buchanan, John, 133
Buchanan, Pat, 124
"Builders" (Yates), 24
Burger, Knox, 18
The Burglary: The Discovery of J. Edgar Hoover's Secret FBI (Medsger), 31–45, 50
Burns, Ken, **156–161**
Burrough, Bryan, 46–50
Bush, George H. W., 75, 111, 117, 136, 167, 176
Bush, George W.
  2000 election, 178
  "Accidental Presidencies," **117–118**
  contributions of, 12
  the entitled, 142, 150
  Kavanaugh and, 166
  rise of, 176
  tax reform, 212
  "Torture? What Torture?" **112**
  voters, 148
Bush, George W. administration
  appointments, 181
  financial bailout, 97
  Iraq war, 189
  legacy of fear, 178
  Social Security and the, 85–86
  torture during, 22
Bush, Jeb, 136
Buttigieg, Pete, 151
"Bye Bye Bernie" (O'Rourke), **130–131**
Bye Bye Birdie (film), 130

cable television, 177
Cain, Herman, 83–84
Camden Twenty-Eight, 43, 175
Campaign America '96: The View from the Couch (O'Rourke), 88, 98, 105, 118, 140
Cantor, Eric, 29
capitalism/capitalists, 157–158, 213
  bro culture, 165
  crony, 92
  hero, 82
  heroes, 28, 210
  "Ken Burns, Boy Capitalist, and *The Vietnam War*" (O'Rourke), **155–161**
  Madonna, 98
  MFA programs, 29
  musical, 210
  predatory, 92
  term use, 213
  Trump, Donald, 157–158

capitalism/capitalists, cont.
  Vonnegut, Kurt Jr., 22
  weapon of choice, 33
Carlin, George, 105
The Carnal Myth (Dahlberg), 229
Carter, Gene, 181
Carter, Graydon, 46
Carter, Jimmy, 52, 126–127, 141, 160, 176, 178, 185
Carver, Catherine "Katy," 70
Casey, Bill, 160
Castellucci, John, 46
Castro, Fidel, 126, 163–164
Castro, Raul, 163–164
Catholic antiwar movement, 109
Catholic Church, **100–102**, 106
Catholic League for Religious and Civil Rights, 179
Catholic Left. *See also* New Catholic Left
  anti-abortion strategies, 179
  Berrigan brothers and the, 171
  economic ideology, 183
  globalization of the, 180
  ideology, 183
  liberation theology, 180, 183, 190
  protest movement remnants, 108
  protest movement strategies, Right's adoption of, 179
  violence and the, 49
Catholic Right, 49, 101, 183. *See also* New Catholic Right
Catholics
  Hearst, Patty, 52
  O'Connor, Flannery, 69
  protest movements, 177
  Supreme Court, 179
Cato Institute, 177, 213
Catonsville Nine, 65–66, 107, 170
The Catonsville Nine (Peters), 66
Catt, Patrick, 37
celebrity, 24, 61
censorship, 33, 75
Challenger disaster, 77–78
Chamber Music (Joyce), 58
Chaucer, 64
Chekhov, 60
Cheney, Dick, 111–112
Cho, Seung-Hui, 75–76
Chua, Amy, 79–80, 167
Church Committee hearings, 36
Cicero, 229
Cinque, 51
Citizens Commission to Demilitarize Industry, 39–40
Citizens for a Sound Economy, 213
civil disobedience, 42
civil rights movement, 42, 46, 48, 171, 172, 174–175
Clark, Leonard, 185
Clark, Ramsey, 32, 185–186
"Class Warfare" (O'Rourke), **81–82**
Cleaver, Eldridge, 48
Clinton, Bill
  anger of, 121
  father of, 133, 142
  legacy, 150
  Limbaugh and, 105–106
  marriage, 137–138
  mentioned, 12, 167
  Senate win, 140
  Trump on, 128
  Vietnam War, 96
  voice of, 138
  Whitewater, 128
Clinton, Bill, presidency
  "Accidental Presidencies," **117–118**
  Hearst pardon, 52
  Hillary and the, 90–91
  permanent campaign, 153
  tax rates during, 211
  winning the, 136, 177
Clinton, Hillary
  2008 primary, 96
  Carter compared, 127
  child of the meritocracy, 142
  "Clinton Exhaustion," **128–129**
  Clinton fatigue, 128, 150
  Crooked Hillary, 141
  defeat, 151, 154
  "The Haunting of Hillary," **121–122**
  "Hillary's Voice," **137–138**
  "It's the Voter Suppression, Stupid!" **139**
  marriage, 91, 137–138
  mentioned, 74, 118, 132
  "My Hillary Problem—and Yours," **115–116**
  "Revenge of the Sixties," **119–120**

Clinton, Hillary, cont.
Sanders and, 115, 118, 121–122, 128–129, 130–131, 149, 154
vice-presidential pick, 136
voters, 150
"Clinton Exhaustion" (O'Rourke), **128–129**
Coats, Dan, 124, 135
Coffin, William Sloane Jr., 185
Cold War, 172–173, 176
colleges, for-profit, 209, 213
Collins, Michael, 11, **198–205**
Collins, Michael, works
The Death of All Things Seen, 202
The Death of a Writer, 203
The Keepers of Truth, 200–201
Lost Souls, 201
The Man Who Dreamt of Lobsters, 199–200
The Meat Eaters, 199
The Resurrectionists, 201
The Secret Life of E. Robert Pendleton, 203
Collins, Susan, 167
Columbia University, 230–231, 233
Complete Poems of Richard Elman 1955–1997 (Goode-Elman), **54–64**
computers, 33, 43–44, 211, 216
Confessions of a Guilty Freelancer (O'Rourke), 9
The Confessions of Edward Dahlberg (Dahlberg), 232, 234, 240–241
"Confidential Memorandum: Attack of American Free Enterprise System" (Powell), 120
congressional elections (2018), 150–152
CONINTELPRO, 35–36
Conspiracy to Save Lives, 50
Constitution, U.S., 75
contraception, 100–102, 106
"Contraception's Con Men" (Wills), 101
"Contraception Wars and Woes" (O'Rourke), **100–102**
Coplon, Judith, 185
Corder, Frank, 178
Cosgrove, Joe, 66
counterculture, 211
Court TV, 177
Cowan, Paul, 32, 45, 188
Coyote, Peter, 157
Crane, Alexandra, 17
Crane, Hart, 59
creative writing programs, 57–58
crime writers, 11, 202, 204
Criminal Tendencies (O'Rourke), 162, 187, 204
Crowder, Bradley, 189
Cruz, Ted, 119, **123–125**
Cuba, 162–164, 172
"Cuba and Carnage" (O'Rourke), **162–164**
Cuban Missile Crisis, 172
Cuban refugees, 126–127
cultural heros, literary, 15
culture
aural/visual, 36, 57, 61, 138, 159, 177, 201, 216
bohemian, 207–211
books and, 216
celebrity, 61
me generation, 211
science vs. humanities, 16
technology and, 211, 216
"A Cup of G.I. Joe" (Dowd), 41
cyberculture, 211

Dahlberg, Edward, letters to O'Rourke, **218–244**
apartments, 228, 233
at Columbia, 230
on education, 229–230
friendships, 223
health, 230, 238, 241
on homosexuality, 221–222, 227
on mediocrity, 224
O'Rourke on, 233
on O'Rourke's writing, 235–237, 239, 242–243
on suffering, 223
at UMKC, 219
on women, 221–222, 225–227, 229
on writing, 221–222, 232
Dahlberg, Edward, test of an author, 24
Dahlberg, Edward, works
Because I Was Flesh, 218, 224
Bottom Dogs, 58
The Carnal Myth, 229
The Confessions of Edward Dahlberg, 232, 234, 240–241
Edward Dahlberg American Ishmael of Letters, 231
Edward Dahlberg Reader, 219, 221

From Flushing to Calvary, 58, 235
The Leafless American, 219, 223, 227
Letters to a Young Would-Be Writer, 10–11, 218–244
The Olive of Minerva, 58, 244
Sorrows of Priapus, 241
Those Who Perish, 58
Daley, William, 76
D'Amato, Alfonse, 83, 140
Daniels, Mitch, 135
Darby, Brandon, 190
Davidon, William, 36–39, 40
Davis, Bette, 153
Day, Dorothy, 67
"Dear Heart" (Elman), 59
The Death of All Things Seen (Collins), 202
The Death of a Writer (Collins), 203
debt, 209–210
DeFanti, Charles, 243
Department of Homeland Security, 189–191
Desmond, Matthew, 210
DiCaprio, Leonardo, 94
Dickinson, Emily, 216
Didion, Joan, 188
"The Disappointment Artist" (Lethem), 220
Disarmed and Dangerous: The Radical Lives and Times of Daniel and Philip Berrigan (Forest), 187
Dohrn, Bernardine, 48
Dole, Bob, 117
Donnelly, Joe, 150–152
Donner, Frank, 34
Donohue, William, 179
Dostoevsky, 103
Douglas, Boyd, 190
Dowd, Maureen, 41
draft, end of the, 175
draft deferments, 159
draft protest movement, 65–66, 107, 109, 159–160, 170, 185
Dreiser, Theodore, 202
"Dr. Gingrich and Mr. Chucky" (O'Rourke), **92–93**
drug trade, 176
Dubliners (Joyce), 58
Dugan, Alan, 195–196
Dukakis, Michael, 117
Dump Trump movement, 119
Dylan, Bob (née Zimmerman), 61, 205, 210
Eagleton, Terry, 203
East Coast Conspiracy to Save Lives, 39, 179
The Easter Parade (Yates), 23
Eastwood, Clint, 98
economics
civil rights movement, 48
privatization, 211
of protest, 48, 109, 173, 208
Reaganomics, 48, 109, 183
tax rates, 211–212
economy
Carter administration, 176
Clinton presidency, 178
Obama administration, 178–179
education
cost of, 173, 209
Dahlberg on, 229–230
enrollment, 15, 173, 208
privatization, 213
Reagan administration policy, 119
space race and, 172–173, 208
Edward Dahlberg American Ishmael of Letters (Dahlberg), 231
"Edward Dahlberg: Letters to a Young Would-Be Writer," **218–243**
Edward Dahlberg Reader (Dahlberg), 219, 221
Eisenhower, Dwight David, 153
elections. *See also* presidential election (2016); the primaries (2016)
close, 73–74
congressional (2018), 150–152
The Elephants Teach (Myers), 28
Eleven Kinds of Loneliness (Yates), 20, 24
Ellison, Nick, 244
Ellsberg, Daniel, 34, 37, 43, 44, 174
Elman, Richard, 58, 63, 240
Elman, Richard, works
"The Afterlife Is Only Strange," 59–60
An Education in Blood, 63
Little Lives, 60
"The Man Who Ate New York," 59
Namedropping, 54–55, 59
Tar Beach, 54–55
Engdahl, Horace, 27
Engle, Paul, 69
entertainment, trials as, 177
Every Secret Thing (Hearst), 50
Evicted (Desmond), 210

"Faces of the Old" (Skillings), 63
Fahrenheit 451 (film), 71
The Falcon and the Snowman case, 44
false equivalency, 154
fame, 20–22, 29
Farber, Don, 19
Farrell, James T., 202
fascism, 183
fatal lack of talent, 11, 202, 204–205
Faulkner, William, 33, 61
The F.B.I. and the Berrigans (Nelson & Ostrow), 32, 187
FC2, 27
FCC v. Pacifica Foundation, 105
Federal Bureau of Investigation (FBI)
  The Burglary: The Discovery of J. Edgar Hoover's Secret FBI (Medsger), 31–45, 50
  Catonsville Nine trial and, 66
  Days of Rage: America's Radical Underground, the FBI, and the Forgotten Age of Revolutionary Violence, 46–49
  The F.B.I. and the Berrigans (Nelson & Ostrow), 32, 187
  The Federal Bureau of Investigation (Lowenthal), 43
  Harrisburg Seven trial and, 67, 107
  informers, 190
  minority representation, 47
  protests, tracking, 189
The Federal Bureau of Investigation (Lowenthal), 43
Feingold, Judi, 43
Feldman, Michael, 105
feminazis, 106
feminist movement, 32, 174
Ferraro, Geraldine, 140
Ficciones (Borges), 104
Fiction Collective, 27
"Fiddler's Reach" (Skillings), 62
Field, Joseph, 181
"The 15 Most Overrated Contemporary American Writers" (Shivani), 26
financial crisis 2007, 178–179
Fine Arts Work Center, 61, 192–193, 195–196, 233–234
Fink, Liz, 47
Finnegans Wake (Joyce), 58
Fiorina, Carly, 123
First Amendment, 106
"The First Lady's Lack of Firsts" (O'Rourke), **90–91**
Fitts, Dudley, 230
Fitzgerald, F. Scott, 79
Flannery O'Connor and Robert Giroux: A Publishing Partnership (Samway), 69–71
Fliegelman, Ron, 47
Flowers, Gennifer, 83
Fluke, Sandra, 106
Flynn, General, 149
Ford, Christine Blasey, 166
Ford, Ford Madox, 54
Ford, Henry, 211
Forest, Jim, 65–68, 187
Foster, Marcus, 51
Foster, Vince, 129
Fox News, 81
Francis, Pope, 68
Francis Xavier, 52
Freedom of Information Act, 35
Freedom Riders, 172
French, Warren, 225–226
Fuerzas Armadas de Liberación Nacional Puertoriqueña (FALN), 46–47
Fuhrman, Mark, 51

Gandhi, 171, 180
Gates, Bill, 82, 156–157, 200, 211
gay liberation, 177
gay literature, 56–57
G8 protests, 108
Generation X, 207
genre, 58–59, 60–61
Gingrich, Newt
  "Dr. Gingrich and Mr. Chucky," **92–93**
  Limbaugh and, 105
  "Our Postsaterical Primaries," **94–95**
  "A Primary History Primer," **96–97**
  vice-presidential pick, 135
Giroux, Robert, 69–71
Glick, Ted, 40
globalization, 51
Glück, Louise, 192, 233
God Bless You, Mr. Rosewater (Vonnegut), 16
Going after Cacciato (O'Brien), 156
The Golden Bowl (James), 103
Goode-Elman, Alice, 54–64

Gordon, Jaimy, 11
Gore, Al, 96, 136, 140, 148–149, 150, 178
Gorsuch, Neil, 143, 148, 151–152
Go Set a Watchman (Lee), 113–114
Gould, Jay, 81–82
government, measures of the, 191
Gowen, Sue, 40
Gravity's Rainbow (Pynchon), 114
Gray, Francine du Plessix, 188
Greatest Generation, 15, 66
The Great Gatsby (Fitzgerald), 79
Great Recession, 97
"The Great Refudiator" (O'Rourke), **73–74**
Gregg, John, 124
grief porn, 145
Gross, Beverly, 230, 233
Grove Press University of the Arts, 103–104
grunge, 210
Guilt about the Past (Schlink), 184
guns, 75–76
Gutting, Gary, 101

Haley, Nikki, 122
"Halftime in Pink America" (O'Rourke), **98–99**
Handel, Karen, 99
Harder Than War: Catholic Peacemaking in Twentieth-Century America (McNeal), 187
Hardy, Thomas, 60
Harrington, Michael, 184, 210
"Harrisburg, Pennsylvania: Ballad for Americans" (Cowan), 45
The Harrisburg 7 and the New Catholic Left (fortieth anniversary edition, 2012) (O'Rourke), 9, 34, 50, 107–108, 169
The Harrisburg 7 and the New Catholic Left (O'Rourke), 9, 31–34, 65, 101, 114, 156, 187, 195, 241–242
Harrisburg Defense Committee, 39–40
Harrisburg Seven trial
  anniversary event, 35, 107
  attendees, 34
  attorneys, 34, 68
  convictions, 170
  convictions and acquittals, 45, 186
  Hoover and the, 94
  informers, 67
  jury deliberation, 39
  kidnapping discussion, 171
  Medsger's mistakes about the, 45
  model, 52
  Plowshares movement from, 108
  print-only coverage, 177
  underlying the, 67, 107, 182
  "Whither the New Catholic Left?" **170–191**
Harrison, William H., 190
"The Haunting of Hillary" (O'Rourke), **121–122**
Hawthorne, Nathaniel, 18
Haymarket Riot, 159
H-bomb, 43
HD, 123
Hearst, Catherine, 53
Hearst, Patty, 48, 50–53, 175
Hearst, Randolph, 53
Heller, Joseph, 15
Hemingway, Ernest, 79, 152
Heritage Foundation, 212
heroes
  capitalist, 28, 82, 210
  citizen jurors, 45
  cultural, 15, 22
  millenial, 211
  one-percenters, 211
  of Silicon Valley, 211
  war, 160
Hersh, Sy, 36
higher education
  cost of, 173, 209
  enrollment, 173, 208
Higher Education Act, 209
"High Flight" (Magee), 77
Hill, Anita, 83, 165–166
Hill, Baron, 124
Hillarycare, 87
"Hillary's Voice" (O'Rourke), **137–138**
hippies, 207, 209, 213
hipsters, 207
Hiss, Alger, 185
history
  as entertainment, 50–52
  great man vs. violent theory of, 47
  Orwell on, 50
Hit & Stay: A History of Faith and Resistance (documentary), 45, 66, 108–109
Hoffa, Jimmy, 185
Hohoff, Tay, 113

Holtzman, Liz, 140
Homer, 103
homosexuality, 56, 70, 94, 186, 221–222, 227
Hoover, J. Edgar
The Burglary: The Discovery of J. Edgar Hoover's Secret FBI (Medsger), 31–45, 50
On China, 189
Days of Rage (Burrough), 48
in film, 94
Harrisburg Seven trial and, 67, 107, 182
homosexuality, 94, 186
mentioned, 165, 189
Hoppe, David, 152
Horton, Willie, 117
Howe, Fanny, 228
How Many Die (Skillings), 56, 194
Huckabee, Mike, 88
Hugo, Victor, 103
humor writing, 22–23
Humphrey, Hubert, 120
Hussein, Saddam, 185
hyperliterary, 23

Idle Hands (O'Rourke), 224
If I Die in a Combat Zone (O'Brien), 156
immolation tactic, 66, 178
income inequality. *See also* wealth gap
"Making Poverty More Bearable," **207–217**
"Revenge of the Sixties," **119–120**
indexes, 34, 48, 187
Indiana Toll Road, 135
infinite monkey theorem, 145
"Instructs and Entertains" (O'Rourke), **14–25**
internet, 33, 36
Iowa primaries, 88–89
Iowa Writers' Workshop, 16, 29, 69–70, 199, 230
Iran-Contra, 141, 159, 176
Iran hostage crisis, 127, 176
Iraq war, 121
"*Irish Times*, Times Two: On Michael Collins" (O'Rourke), **198–205**
The Iron Lady (film), 94
"It's the Voter Suppression, Stupid!" (O'Rourke), **139–140**

Jackson, Andrew, 133
James, Henry, 103
James, LeBron, 133
J. Edgar (film), 94–95
"A Jihad against Time" (Ahmad), 186
Jindal, Bobby, 137
Jobs, Steve, 82, 156–157, 211
John Paul II, 180, 190
Johnson, Lyndon Baines, 41, 160, 172, 184–185, 209
Johnson, Samuel, 72
Jonah House, 67, 179, 182, 186
Jones, Jim, 52
journalism
degradation of, 138
establishment vs. anti-establishment, 35
O. J. Simpson trial, 177
present-day, 36
The Journalist and the Murderer (Malcolm), 187
Joyce, James, 58
"Judith Shahn, Greenwich Village" (O'Rourke), **195–197**

Kaine, Tim, 136
Kantor, Jodi, 90
Karadzic, Radovan, 185
Kareka family, 228, 242–243
Karr, Mary, 64
Kasich, John, 122
Kavanaugh, Brett, **165–168**
Keats, John, 54
The Keepers of Truth (Collins), 200–201
"Ken Burns, Boy Capitalist, and *The Vietnam War*" (O'Rourke), **155–161**
Kennan, George, 194
Kennedy, John F., 76, 172–173
Kennedy, Robert, 172
Kennedy, Ted, 142
Kent State, 183
Kerouac, Jack, 208
Kerrigan, Anthony, 104
Kerry, John, 40–41, 96, 166
Keyes, Alan, 84, 101, 117
"Keyes to the Caindom" (O'Rourke), **83–84**
kidnapping
Hearst, 50–53
Kissinger, 37–38, 52, 107, 171, 182
Lindbergh Jr., 52
SLA model, 52

"To Kill a 'Second' Novel" (O'Rourke), **113–114**
King, Martin Luther Jr., 42, 171–173
King, Rodney, 115
King, Stephen, 24
The Kings and Their Gods: The Pathology of Power (Berrigan), 188
Kissinger, Henry, 37–38, 52, 107, 171, 182, 188–189
Koch, David H., 157
Koch brothers, 177
Komen, Susan G., 98–99
Kozinski, Alex, 166
Krementz, Jill, 14, 21
Kristol, Bill, 84, 117
Kunitz, Stanley, 192, 233
Kushner, Jared, 149

Lady Chatterley's Lover (Lawrence), 103
Land, Sharli, 192
Land, Stuart, 192
language, GOP appropriation of progressive, 92
Lansner, Fay, 196
Lansner, Kermit, 196
Lauren, Ralph, 161
Lawrence, D. H., 103
Lawrence, Seymour "Sam," 18, 21
The Leafless American (Dahlberg), 219, 223, 227
Lee, Brenda, 130–131
Lee, Harper, 71, 113–114
Le Femina, Judith, 174
Lehrer, Jim, 77
Lessing, Doris, 205
Lethem, Jonatham, 220
Lewinsky, Monica, 121–122
liberation theology, 180, 183, 190
Limbaugh, Rush, 81, 105–106
Lindbergh, Charles, 124
Lindbergh, Charles Jr., 52
literary life, generational changes, 57
literature, purpose of, 23
Little Lives (Elman), 60
Lost Souls (Collins), 201
Lott, Trent, 181–183
Loughner, Jared Lee, 75–76
Louis-Dreyfus, Julia, 123
Lovers & Tyrants (Plessix Gray), 188
Lowell, Robert, 15–16, 69, 233
Lowenthal, Max, 43
Luntz, Frank, 92

Madonna, 98–99, 129
magazines, literary, 15
"The Maggot Principle" (O'Rourke), 234
Mailer, Norman, 15, 17–18, 34, 55, 193, 200
"Making Poverty More Bearable" (O'Rourke), 120, **207–217**
Malcolm, Janet, 187
Malcolm X, 48, 171
Manafort, Paul, 149
Man and Shop Window (Shahn), 195–197
mandala effect, 33
Manhattan Institute, 212
Manhattan Project, 43
Manning, Bradley (now Chelsea), 44
man of letters, 55–56
Manson, Charlie, 173, 209
"The Man Who Ate New York" (Elman), 59
The Man Who Dreamt of Lobsters (Collins), 199–200
Marcos, Imelda, 202
Mardian, Robert, 174
Mariel boatlift, 126
Marisol, 197
market economy, 30
Matthews, Chris, 88
May Day, 159
McAlister, Elizabeth, 45, 67–68, 107–108, 170, 173–174, 179, 182, 186
McAuliffe, Christa, 77
McCain, John, 96–97, 117, 121, 132
McClanahan, E. Thomas, 87
McConnell, Mitch, 133, 148, 154
McCullough, Fran, 19
McDougal, Jim, 129
McGovern, George, 174
McGurl, Mark, 28
McHugh, Heather, 30
McKay, David, 189
McLaughlin, Neil, 186
McNamara, Robert, 186
McVeigh, Timothy, 76, 178, 190
The Meat Eaters (Collins), 199
Media burglary, the, 31–45
Medicare, 177
Medonis, Charles, 186

Medsger, Betty, 31–45, 50
The Meekness of Isaac (O'Rourke), 114, 156, 237
me generation, 211
Melville, Herman, 225–227
Melville, Sam, 46
Memory for Marisa Rose (Skillings), 56
men
  earnings of, 191
  White Male Privilege, 168
Merton, Thomas, 67
MFA programs, 26–30
military, US. *See also* Vietnam War
  1960s, 172
  spies, 44
  volunteer, 158, 175, 190
military-industrial complex, 176, 179–180
millennials, 207, 211
Miller, Henry, 103
Milosevic, Slobodan, 185
Milwaukee Fourteen, 66
"The Miracle of Dan Berrigan" (O'Rourke), **65–68**
Mitchell, John, 42
"Mommie Baddest" (O'Rourke), **79–80**
Montgomery, Lori, 87
Moore, Michael, 140, 210
mothers, Chinese, 79–80
Motherwell, Robert, 192
Mourdock, Richard, 150
"Mourning Becomes Them" (O'Rourke), **77–78**
Moyers, Bill, 185
Murrah Federal Office Building bombing, 178, 190
music, 210
Myers, D. G., 28
"My Hillary Problem—and Yours" (O'Rourke), **115–116**
My Lai, 36

Nader, Ralph, **120**
Namedropping (Elman), 54–55, 59
natural law, 101–102
Negroponte, John, 160
Neier, Aryeh, 42
Nelson, Jack, 32–33, 186
New Bedford rape trial, 177
New Catholic Left. *See also* Harrisburg Seven trial
  ascendency, 107
  beginnings, 101
  draft protest movement, 65–66, 107, 170
  "Whither the New Catholic Left?" **170–191**
New Catholic Right, 176
New Republican Party, 105
newspapers, literary book review section, 55
New Yorker, 24
Nike, 161
Nixon, Richard, 34, 41, 97, 120, 160, 165, 174, 176, 185, 209
Nobel, Alfred, 109–110
Nobel prize, 109–110, 205
non-voters, 139, 152, 154, 215
Noonan, Peggy, 77
Norris, Chuck, 141
"Not Saving Social Security, Again" (O'Rourke), **87**
Notts (O'Rourke), 203
Nova, Craig, 12, 19, 195, 203, 240, 244
novels, academic, 203
Novick, Lynn, **156–161**
NRA, 76, 139, 152
nuclear energy, 44
nuclear proliferation, 37
Nuns on the Bus, 108

Oak Ridge Three, 40
"The Oak Ridge Three" (O'Rourke), **107–110**
Oates, Joyce Carol, 205
Obama, Barack
  Age of Obama, 108
  "The Birther Business," **132–134**
  challenges, 178
  child of the meritocracy, 142
  Clinton (Bill) compared, 142
  counter-terrorism speech, 110
  election history, 117, 122
  endorsing, 98–99
  "The Great Refudiator," **73–74**
  "high-road" behavior, 139
  mentioned, 137, 141, 144
  "Mourning Becomes Them," **77–78**
  National Defense University speech, 110
  nomination, 96, 121
  Notre Dame commencement speech, 101

presidency, successful, 12, 96, 127
really good at killing people, 118
second term, 84
Senate race, 117
seven-year presidency, 154
too good to be true, 122
Trump tour, 153
Tucson speech, 77–78
undoing the presidency of, 148
voters, 89, 150
why-can't-we-all-get-along presidency, 115
Obama, Barack, administration
American Healthcare Act, 146
appointments, 76
"Contraception Wars and Woes," **100–101**
Cuba, opening, 162
financial bailout, 97
payroll tax extension, 85–88
tax reform, 211–212
Obama, Michelle, 90–91, 123, 139, 153
O'Brien, Tim, 156, 160
obstructionism, GOP, 133
Occupy Wall Street, 44, 66, 68, 108, 120, 173, 212
O'Connor, Flannery, 69–71
"O'Connor/Giroux" (O'Rourke), **69–71**
O'Dwyer, Paul, 188
O'Dwyer, William, 188
"Oh, Rush, Poor Rush" (O'Rourke), **105–106**
Old-Age, Survivors, and Disability Insurance Program, 85, 87
old Catholic Left, 101
old New Catholic Left, 67
The Olive of Minerva (Dahlberg), 58, 244
O'Malley, Martin, 118
Omnibus Reconciliation Act, 211
O'Neill, Paul, 181
one percent, 29, 44, 81–82, 109, **119–120**, 146, 191
The Onion, 74
"Only Bones" (Skillings), 56, 62, 64
On the Job: Fiction about Work by Contemporary American Writers (O'Rourke, ed.), 20
On the Road (Kerouac), 208
"On the Sentencing of Philip Berrigan, Portland, Maine, 1997" (Peck), 181
O'Reilly, Bill, 81, 106
O'Rourke, Joe, 193
O'Rourke, William, letters from Dahlberg. *See* Dahlberg, Edward, letters to O'Rourke
O'Rourke, William, works
The Armless Warrior, 218, 237
Campaign America '96: The View from the Couch, 88, 98, 105, 118, 140
Confessions of a Guilty Freelancer, 9
Criminal Tendencies, 162, 187, 204
The Harrisburg 7 and the New Catholic Left, 9, 31–34, 65, 101, 114, 156, 187, 241–242
The Harrisburg 7 and the New Catholic Left (fortieth anniversary edition, 2012), 9, 34, 50, 107–108, 169
Idle Hands, 224
On the Job: Fiction about Work by Contemporary American Writers (editor), 20, 200
"The Maggot Principle," 234
"Making Poverty More Bearable," 119, 207–214
The Meekness of Isaac, 114, 156, 237
Notts, 203
Politics and the American Language, 9–10
Signs of the Literary Times: Essays, Reviews, Profiles 1970–1992, 9, 232
Orwell, George, 10, 50, 56, 112, 116, 213
Oshinsky, David, 42–43
Ostrow, Ronald, 32, 186
Oswald, Lee Harvey, 51, 75, 172
The Other America (Harrington), 210
"Our Postsatirical Primaries" (O'Rourke), **94–95**
Owens, William "Ryan," 145

Page, Carter, 149
Palin, Sarah, 74, 77–78, 92, 117, 121
Pamuk, Orhan, 27
Pane, Aylesha, 30
Parini, Jay, 30
Paul, Ron, 88, 97
payroll tax, 85–88
Peace, David, 204
Peck, John, 181
Pelosi, Nancy, 84
Pence, Mike, 124–125, **135–136**, 143, 145–146, 148, 151

"Pensive Pence" (O'Rourke), **135–136**
Pentagon Papers, 34, 174–175
Perot, Ross, 117, 177
Perry, Rick, 83, 88, 92
PETA, 189
Peters, Shawn Francis, 66
philanthropy, 211
Phillips, Kevin, 213
photographs vs. prose, 36
pink America, 98–99
Planned Parenthood, 98–99
Planz, Allen, 233
Player Piano (Vonnegut), 20
At Play in the Lions' Den: A Biography and Memoir of Daniel Berrigan (Forest), 65–68
Plowshares movement, 107–109, 179–180
poets, learning from, 59. *See also specific poets*
police forces
  immolation tactic, 51, 53, 178
  militarization of, 49
Politics and the American Language (O'Rourke), 9–10
"Politics and the English Language" (Orwell), 10–11, 213
populism, 183–184
Portrait of the Artist (Joyce), 58
poverty, "Making Poverty More Bearable" (O'Rourke), **207–217**
Powell, Lewis, 120, 209, 212
Powell Memo, 209, 212–213
presidential election (2000), 178
presidential election (2016). *See also* Clinton, Hillary; Trump, Donald
  "The Birther Business," **132–134**
  "Clinton Exhaustion," **128–129**
  Clinton's troubles, 141–142
  email hacks, 141–142
  "Hillary's Voice," **137–138**
  "It's the Voter Suppression, Stupid!" **139–140**
  "My Hillary Problem—and Yours," **115–116**
  non-voters, 139, 152, 154, 215
  "Pensive Pence," **135–136**
  popular vote, 96, 117, 138, 139–140, 142, 143, 148, 178
  Trump's win, 154
presidential politics
  divide in, 120
  vulgarity in, **117–118**
Presley, Elvis, 130
the primaries (2016)
  Clinton campaign, 128
  GOP process, 83
  "The Haunting of Hillary," **121–122**
  open, 131
  "Our Postsaterical Primaries," **94–95**
  "A Primary History Primer," **96–97**
  "Ted's Excellent Mansplaining," **123–125**
"A Primary History Primer" (O'Rourke), **96–97**
privatization, 211
The Program Era (McGurl), 28
prolife movement, 67, 101
protest
  economics of, 48, 109, 173, 208
  golden age of, 109, 191
  nonviolent, 171–172
  symbolic acts of, 109, 170–171
protest groups evolution (1960s–1970s), 172–178
pro-woman movement, 101
P-town Stories: or, The Meatrack (Skillings), 57, 194
publishing business, 15, 57, 201
Puerto Ricans, 47
Pulitzer Prize, 114
Pynchon, Thomas, 11, 114

Qaddafi, Muammar, 185
Quayle, Dan, 117, 136, 166–167, 177

race-baiting, 141
racism, 113, 132–133, 153–154, 181–183
radical underground, 46–49
Rahman, Omar Abdel, 185
Raines, Bonnie, 43
Raines, John, 43
The Rake's Progress (Stravinsky), 222
Rauner, Bruce, 214
"R. D. Skillings, Resolute Character" (O'Rourke), **192–194**
Read, Herbert, 10, 230
Read, Piers Paul, 230
The Reader (Schlink), 184
readers
  creating, 215–216

post–World War II, 103
test of authors for, 24
writers as, 26
reading, golden age of, 15, 55
Reagan, Ronald
celebrity candidate, 61, 126–127, 153
economics, 183
foreign involvement, 160
leadership qualities, 209
mentioned, 94
"Mourning Becomes Them," **77**
rise of, 176
"Similarities," **141–142**
vice president, 117
Reagan, Ronald, administration
economics, 48, 109
education policy, 119
illegal activities, 176
mentioned, 43
reverence for the rich, 209–210, 212
Reagan Democrats, 183
reality, words and, 75–76
"Reality-Based Shooter" (O'Rourke), **75–76**
refudiate, 73
Rehnquist Court, 106
Reilly, Charles, 70
Religious Freedom Restoration Act, 124
Republican Party (GOP)
2000 backlash, 178
bro culture, **165–168**
congresswomen, 151
language of progressives, appropriation of, 92
long game, 166–167, 214–215
obstructionism, 133
Planned Parenthood platform, 99
primary election process, 83–84
"A Primary History Primer," **96–97**
"Saving Social Security, Not," **85–86**
strategies, 166
supremacy, derailed, 177
Supreme Court nominees, 151–152, 165–168
tax dreams, 212
twenty-first century, 154
voter suppression, **135**, 139
The Resurrectionists (Collins), 201
"Revenge of the Sixties" (O'Rourke), **119–120**
A *Review of the FBI's Investigations of Certain Domestic Advocacy Groups* (Office of the Inspector General), 189
Revolutionary Road (Yates), 20, 24
revolutionary violence, age of, 46–49
Rice, Megan G., 107–108
"Richard and Roger" (O'Rourke), **54–64**
"Richie Rich, Baby Boomers, and, Look Out, 2018 Looming" (O'Rourke), **150–152**
right-wing, funding the, 177
The Rivals (Sheridan), 73
Rivington Street, 228, 233
Rockefeller, J. D., 211
Roe v. Wade, 101, 177, 179
Roger & Me (documentary), 210
role models, 22
Romero, Oscar, 180
Romney, George, 97
Romney, Mitt, 84, 88, 92–93, 95, 96–97, 99, 126–127, 140
Roof, Dylann, 49
Rosen, James, 42
Rosenberg trial, 175
Rosset, Barney, 103–104
Rowling, J. K., 205
Rubin, Robert, 118
Rumsfeld, Donald, 83
The Run of His Life (Toobin), 51
Rush, Bobby, 84
Ruskin, Ira, 243
Russo, Richard, 23
Ryan, Jack, 117
Ryan, Paul, 92, 135, 148
Ryan, William M., 219, 223–224, 225, 229, 231, 238

salary inflation, 119–120, 212
Sallie Mae legislation, 209
Samarasan, Preeta, 30
Samway, Patrick, 69–71
Sanders, Bernie
age of, 118
"Bye Bye Bernie," **130–131**
Cruz compared, 119
Hillary and, 115, 118, 121–122, 128–129, 130–131, 149, 154
mentioned, 123, 140
platform, 120, 215
possibility of, 152

Santa Fe Opera, 218, 220, 222, 228
Santorum, Rick, 88, 106
Sartre, John Paul, 104
satire, 74
"Saving Social Security, Not" (O'Rourke), **85–86**
The Scarlet Letter (Hawthorne), 18
Schlesinger, Arthur Jr., 10–11
Schlink, Bernhard, 184
Schulder, Diane, 240
Scoblick, Mary Cain, 186
Scoblick, Tony, 186
Scott, Eleanor Metcalf, 220
Scott, Susan, 220, 228
Scott, Winfield Townley, 220
second-wave feminism, 53, 67
The Secret Life of E. Robert Pendleton (Collins), 203
Seeger, Pete, 208
Segretti, Donald, 165
Seidman, Hugh, 222
Self-Portrait: Book People Picture Themselves (Britton), 19–20
self-publishing, 15, 201
September 11, 2001 terrorist attacks, 22, 110, 178, 189
"Seven Dirty Words" (Carlin), 105
sexual harassment, 81
Shahn, Alan, 197
Shahn, Ben, 196
Shahn, Judith, 195–197
Shakespeare, William, 73, 75, 103, 204
Shaw, Bernie, 52
Sheridan, Richard Brinsley, 73
Shields, Charles J., **14–25**
Shivani, Anis, 26–30
Shooters, Reality-Based, 75–76
Siegel, Lee, 54
Signs of the Literary Times: Essays, Reviews, Profiles 1970–1992 (O'Rourke), 9
Silber, Joan, 244
"Similarities" (O'Rourke), **141–142**
Simpson, O. J., 51, 177
Singer, Isaac Bashevis, 23
The Sirens of Titan (Vonnegut), 20
Sixties, Revenge of the, **119–120**
Skillings, Marissa, 193–194
Skillings, R. D., 56–57, 60–64
  Profile: R.D. Skillings, Resolute Character, **192–194**
Skillings, R. D., works
  Alternative Lives, 60
  How Many Die, 56, 194
  Memory for Marisa Rose, 56
  "Only Bones," 56
  pseudonym, 60
  P-town Stories: or, The Meatrack, 57, 194
  Summer's End, 60
  Taxi Driver, 58
  The Washashores, 194
  Where the Time Goes, 56–57
Slaughterhouse-Five (Vonnegut), 18
small presses, 15, 201
Smith, Patti, 61
Snow, C. P., 16, 198
Snow, John, 181–182
Snowden, Edward, 42–44
social change, 41–42, 47
socialism, military, 40
Social Security, **85–87**, 177
Sorrentino, Gilbert, 235–237, 239
Sorrows of Priapus (Dahlberg), 241
Souter, Justice, 106
Soviet Union, 180
space race, 172, 208
Spanidou, Irina, 11, 204, 244
Sperling, Gene, 76
spies, 44
Spock, Benjamin, 159, 185
Sputnik, 208
Starr, Ken, 166
State Secrets (Cowan), 32
Steelwork (Sorrentino), 235
Stein, Jill, 152
Steinem, Gloria, 41
Stendhal, 239
Stephen Hero (Joyce), 58
Stern, Carl, 35
Stewart, Jon, 74
Stewart, Martha, 90
Stockholm Syndrome, 52
Stone, I. F., 184
Stone, Roger, 149
Strand Bookstore, 19–21
Stravinsky, Igor, 222
Streep, Meryl, 94
student debt, 173
Student Nonviolent Coordinating

Committee (SNCC), 47
Students for Democratic Society (SDS), 191, 208
Stutzman, Marlin, 124
suffering, Dahlberg on, 223
The Sullivans, 180
Summer of Love, 173
Summer's End (Skillings), 60
Sumner, Gregory D., 18
Super Bowl, 98–99
Super Bowl Halftime (O'Rourke), **98–99**
"The Superfluity of Iowa" (O'Rourke), **88–89**
Supreme Court, 132, 143, 148, 151–152, **165–168**, 179, 215
Susan G. Komen for the Cure, 98
Suskind, Ron, 75
Swift Boat, 96, 166
Symbionese Liberation Army (SLA), 42, 50–53, 175, 178, 191

Talents and Technicians (Aldridge), 28
Tar Beach (Elman), 54–55
tax dreams, GOP, 212
Taxi Driver (Elman), 58
tax reform, 115, 211–212
Taylor, Elizabeth, 98
Tea Party, 108, **108,** 172–173
technology
  computer, 43–44
  culture and, 216
  reading vs., 55
"Ted's Excellent Mansplaining" (O'Rourke), **123–125**
teenager, 207
Teresa, Mother, 53, 68
terrorism, domestic, 178, 191
Terry, Randall, 101
Thatcher, Margaret, 94–95
Them (Gray), 188
The Theory of the Leisure Class (Veblen), 19
"The Things They Carried" (O'Brien), 160
Thomas, Clarence, 83, 168
Thompson, Hunter, 35, 54
Those Who Perish (Dahlberg), 58
Thurmond, Strom, 182–183
Todd, Chuck, 137
Tolson, Clyde, 94–95
Tolstoy, 103
Toobin, Jeffrey, 50–53
torture, 22, 111–112, 143
"Torture and Blubber" (Vonnegut), 22
"Torture? What Torture?" (O'Rourke), **111–112**
traditionalists, 27
A *Tragic Honesty: The Life and Work of Richard Yates* (Bailey), 21
"Transforming The Donald" (O'Rourke), **126–127**
trial reporting, 177
trials as entertainment, 177
The Tribes of America (Cowan), 45
Troubled Asset Relief Program (TARP), 97
Trump, Donald
  "Accidental Presidencies," **117–118**
  "The Birther Business," **132–134**
  "Brett Kavanaugh, a Suit, and the Bro Culture," **165–168**
  Cabinet of Deplorables, 154
  campaign, 119, **120**, 121–122, 123–125
  campaign model, 124
  discards, 149
  Dump Trump movement, 119
  executive orders, 143
  "It's the Voter Suppression, Stupid!" **139**
  mentioned, 130, 162
  party disruption, 215
  "Pensive Pence," **135–136**
  photos of, 126
  prolife position, 67
  the Russians and, 159
  "Transforming The Donald," **126–127**
  "Trump, Trumped, Trumpery," **143–144**
  "Trump Monkeys," **145–147**
  "Trump Rising," **148–149**
  tweets, 146–147
  vice-presidential pick, 135–136
  voters, 148, 151, 201
  "What a Dump!" the Presidency, That Is," **153–155**
Trump, Donald, characteristics
  boorishness, 139
  the buffoon, 148
  the capitalist, 157–158
  the distraction, 148
  the entitled, 150
  the humiliation, 12
  the nut, 146
  the overachiever, 131

Trump, Donald, characteristics, cont.
the racist, 153
signature, 143
the unhinged, 146
voice of, 137
women, treatment of, 145
Trump, Donald, compared
Cruz, Ted, 119
GWB, 142
Reagan, Ronald, 141–142
"Similarities," **141–142**
Trump, Ivanka, 149
Trump, Melania, 133–134, 145, 153
"Trump, Trumped, Trumpery" (O'Rourke), **143–144**
"Trump Monkeys" (O'Rourke), **145–147**
"Trump Rising" (O'Rourke), **148–149**
Tupamaros of Uruguay, 52
Turkey Hash (Nova), 195
"Two Young Poets Drunk" (Skillings), 63

Ulysses (Joyce), 58
underground movement, 46–49
union protests, 173, 183
University of Missouri at Kansas City, 218, 220, 223–224, 226, 230
Unstuck in Time (Sumner), 18
"Up Against the Workshop" (O'Rourke), **26–53**
Updike, John, 15, 63
U.S. Conference of Catholic Bishops, 100–101

Veblen, Thorstein, 19
Vietnam Veterans Against the War, 170
Vietnam War
end of the, 175–176
"Ken Burns, Boy Capitalist, and *The Vietnam War*," **156–161**
McCain's nomination and the, 96
Vietnam War protest movement
ambivalence in the, 184
baby boomers in the, 157
Catholic, 109
economics underlying, 48
ending the war and, 41
as history, 44–45
Hit & Stay (documentary), 66
individuals in the, 46
"Ken Burns, Boy Capitalist, and *The Vietnam War*," **156–161**
mainstreaming the, 40–41
movements replacing, 174
nonviolent, 107
participants, 15, 36–37, 40–41
social change and, 41–42
violence in the (*Days of Rage: America's Radical Underground, the FBI, and the Forgotten Age of Revolutionary Violence*), 46–49
Vietnam War veterans, 136, 156–157, 170
Virginia Tech shooting, 75–76
Voice, Hillary's (O'Rourke), **137–138**
Vonnegut, Jane, 18
Vonnegut, Kurt Jr., 14–25
vote, the popular, 96, 117, 138, 139–140, 142, 143, 148, 178
voters
Bush, George W., 148
Clinton, Hillary, 150
independent and swing, 73–74
non-voters, 139, 152, 154, 215
Obama, Barack, 150
Trump, Donald, 148
voter suppression, 139–140
voter-suppression laws, 214–215

Wallace, George, 138
Wallace, Lurleen, 138, 151
Wall Street salaries, 119, 212
war profiteer, 109
war profiteering, 213
The Washashores (Skillings), 194
Washington, Augustine, 133
Washington, George, 133
Wasserman Schultz, Deborah, 130–131
waterboarding, 111–112
Watergate, 33, 42, 165, 174
wealth gap, 29, 44, 81–82, 109, **119–120**, 146, 191
Weatherman, 35, 42, 47–48, 159, 175
Weather Underground, 46
Weather-woman persona, 48
Wenderoth, Joe, 186
West Barnstable, MA, 17
Whad'Ya Know (Feldman), 105
Whad'Ya Know (radio), 105
"'What a Dump!' the Presidency, That Is"

(O'Rourke), **153–155**
"When the Genial Spirits Fail" (Skillings), 63
Where the Time Goes (Skillings), 56–57
White Male Privilege, 168
Whitewater, 129
"Whither the New Catholic Left?" (O'Rourke), **170–191**
Whitman, Walt, 59
Wikileaks, 175
Wilkerson, Cathy, 47
Williams, Tennessee, 104
Williams, William Carlos, 59
Wills, Garry, 42, 101, 188
Wilson, Joe, 148
Winters, Ivor, 59
Wise Blood (O'Connor), 70–71
Wolfe, Tom, 35, 210–211
women
  abnegation to husbands' careers, 18
  Dahlberg on, 221–222, 225–227, 229
  Kavanaugh's treatment of, 167
  political wives, 132
  Trump's treatment of, 145
  underground movement and, 48
women's movements
  feminist movement, 32, 174
  second-wave feminism, 53, 67
  underlying the, 209
  women's liberation movement, 53, 177
Woodstock, 173
Woodward, Bob, 33, 165
Woolf, Virginia, 57, 201
words and reality, 75–76
Against the Workshop: Provocations, Polemics, Controversies (Shivani), **26–30**
World Trade Center bombing, 177–178
"Wrestling with Sharks" (Yates), 20
writers
  characteristics, 16
  of crime fiction, 11, 202, 204
  Dahlberg's test of an author, 24
  documenting specific, 57
  evolution of, 58–59
  experimental, 27
  fame and, 20–22
  Greatest Generation, 15
  income, 13, 15–16, 18–19, 34, 61, 72
  literary, noticed, 202
  noncommercial, 201–202
  older, fantasies of, 63
  older, helping, 58
  older, income of, 72
  older helping younger, 29
  outside, 203–204
  science fiction, 15–16
  talented, 204–205
  traditionalists, 27
  visiting, 16
  wives supporting, 18
writing
  Dahlberg on, 232
  to entertain, 22–23
  to formula, 113–114
  second books, 113–114
  teaching, 16, 23, 61–62, 225–227

Xavier, St. Francis, 52

Y-12 trespassers, 108
Yaddo, 69
Yates, Richard, 20–21, 23–24
Young, Todd, 124
youth culture, Summer of Love, 173
youth protest movement, 109, 173
yuppies, 207, 209, 213

Zak, Dan, 108
Zuckerberg, Mark, 82, 211
Zuckerman, Ed, 188
Zweig, Paul, 20